STUDENT STUDY GUIDE

to
Accompany

Exceptional Lives
Special Education in Today's Schools

Second Edition

by

Ann Turnbull
Rud Turnbull
Marilyn Shank
Dorothy Leal

Prepared by
Dorothy Leal
Ohio University
and
Marilyn Shank
University of Southern Alabama

Merrill,
an imprint of Prentice Hall
Upper Saddle River, New Jersey   Columbus, Ohio

©1999 by Prentice-Hall, Inc.
Upper Saddle River, New Jersey 07458

Printed in the United States of America

10 9 8 7 6 5 4

ISBN: 0-13-997701-5

Dear Student:

We always enjoyed working puzzles, but as general educators, we had some students in our classes who were puzzles we couldn't solve. Some of these students, no matter how hard they tried, didn't fit the curriculum we were required to teach. Others were bored with the standard curriculum and needed something different to challenge their curious minds. Because of these challenges, we became interested in helping students with exceptionalities learn.

Therefore, I (Marilyn) enrolled in my first special education class, which was probably similar to the one you are taking now. As I learned more about students with exceptionalities, I changed from viewing them as puzzles to having a vision of their potential. I also changed my career focus as a result. Little did I know that this one class would eventually lead me to attain a Ph.D. in Special Education, train college students to teach students with exceptionalities, and ultimately become a co-author for *Exceptional Lives: Special Education in Today's Schools*!

I (Dorothy) found the greatest obstacle to learning for most of the special students I encountered was their inability to understand and apply what they were required to read. Consequently, after over ten years in the classroom and five years developing literacy materials for a southeast Asian people whose language had never been written, I returned to graduate school to obtain a doctorate in the diagnosis and remediation of reading difficulties. I also found the tremendous potential and prior knowledge in my students as a key factor in learning. I have watched many students who had given up on learning come back to life as they discovered ways to become actively involved in their own reading and learning experiences.

Our experiences, as well as those of Rud and Ann Turnbull, who shared their background in a letter to you in the textbook, have allowed us to form a philosophy that emphasizes the contributions that people with exceptionalities make in our families, schools, and communities. We believe that the class you are currently taking is much more about attitude development than memorizing information.

Will this class change your vision for people with exceptionalities? That, in part, will depend on your openness to the people who enliven the pages of your textbook. You will read how six values—great expectations, positive contributions, inherent strengths, choices, relationships, and full citizenship—made a difference in their lives. Our great expectation for you is that you will capture a vision of how you can make a difference for your students by emphasizing those values in your classroom. If you become such a visionary, your life will be changed, and you will be instrumental in changing the lives of others.

Fourteen students in a pilot class openly examined their attitudes about individuals with exceptionalities as they read the textbook, participated in class activities, and completed projects. They caught the vision. On their class evaluations, one student commented: "This class changed my view of people with disabilities completely." Another wrote:

> I learned that exceptionalities are only skin deep. The use of the six values taught in this class will go a long way in helping the exceptional child as well as (other) children. Expect great things and great things will happen!

Our hope is that your learning experience will be just as meaningful.

Best wishes for your future journey!

TABLE OF CONTENTS

At the beginning of the *Student Study Guide*, you will find a number of resources: a listing of literature for and about children and adolescents, a blank "Collaborating for Success" chart, and a blank sample IEP form. These resources, as well as a listing of suggested videos by chapter, are also available on the *Companion Website* for this text at http://www.prenhall.com/turnbull. Also on the *Companion Website* are the sample quizzes contained in this *Student Study Guide,* with feedback covering the content of each chapter and links to special education resources on the Web.

The *Student Study Guide* is designed to provide you with a flexible, comprehensive review of the material presented in each chapter. The format for each chapter review is as follows:

Chapter Overview

Each chapter overview succinctly describes the chapter's highlights. It also provides a brief description of the exceptional life that is introduced in the chapter opening vignette and explains why the vignette subject was selected.

Chapter At-a-Glance

These charts provide you with an ordered preview of the chapter questions using the major four focus questions. After each focus question has been asked, the chapter outline is presented in the first column. In the second column is a summary of objectives. The third column lists key concepts related to the focus question and objectives. Following the chapter-at-a-glance chart, you will find a list of project options and key terms.

Guided Review

This review follows the chapter outline and asks you to respond to questions that relate to the major concepts. The chapter section head and subsection for each guided review question are also provided to help you locate answers. Boxes that provide clarification or enrichment will help you understand the content. Human interest stories will help you to appreciate how the six values relate to people with different types of exceptionalities. The boxes contain minicase studies, book reviews, quotations, anecdotes, or additional information about the student featured in the chapter.

Application Exercises

Each chapter includes two to three application exercises that take key information presented in the chapter and ask you to apply it in meaningful contexts. This activity is designed to help you apply and extend your understanding to everyday situations.

Answers to Chapter Margin Questions

Some of the margin notes in the textbook require specific answers. The answers to these are available at the end of chapters in the *Student Study Guide*.

Sample Quiz

A sample quiz is included to provide you with an opportunity to assess your ongoing knowledge. Questions in this quiz are similar but different to those provided in the *Test Bank* and include true-false and multiple-choice questions only. The sample quiz also provides a balance of lower-level and higher-level multiple choice questions.

The answers to the Application Exercises and Sample Quiz are located at the end of the *Student Study Guide*.

CHAPTER 1

Bode, J. (1989). *New kids in town: Oral histories of immigrant teens*. New York: Scholastic.

Byars, B. (1977). *The pinballs*. New York: Harper & Row.

Freedman, R. (1980). *Immigrant kids*. New York: E.P. Dutton.

Hunt, I. (1976). *The lottery rose*. New York: Berkley Books.

Levine, E. (1989). *I hate English*. New York: Scholastic.

Paterson, K. (1978). *The great Gilly Hopkins*. New York: Crowell. NEWBERY

Uchido, Yoshiko. (1991). *The invisible thread*. Englewood Cliffs, NJ: J. Messner.

CHAPTER 2

Avi. (1991). *Nothing but the truth: A documentary novel*. New York: Orchard Books.

Berger, L. & Lithwick, D. (1992). *I will sing life: Voices from the hole in the wall gang camp*. Boston: Little, Brown.

Cronin, Gay. (1995). *Two birthdays for Beth*. Indianapolis: Perspectives Press.

Dewitt, Hamilton. (1996). *Sad days, glad days: A story about depression*. Morton Grove, IL: Albert Whitman & Co.

Janover, C. (1993). *Josh: A boy with dyslexia*. Minneapolis, MN: Free Spirit Publishing Inc.

McCully, Emily. (1994). *My real family*. San Diego: Browndeer Press, Harcourt Brace Jovanovich.

Shreve, S. (1984). *The flunking of Joshua T. Bates*. New York: Knopf.

CHAPTER 3

Blank, J.P. (1976). *19 steps up the mountain: The story of the DeBolt family*. Philadelphia: Lippincott.

Cleary, B. (1983). *Dear Mr. Henshaw*. New York: Morrow.   NEWBERY

DeJong, M. (1954). *The wheel on the school*. New York: Harper. NEWBERY

Drimmer, F. (1988). *Born different: Amazing stories of very special people*. New York: A Bantam Skylark Book.

Lisle, J.T. (1990). *Afternoon of the elves*. New York: Orchard Books.

Voetberg. Julie. Photos by Taasha Owen. (1995). *I am a home schooler*. Morton Grove, IL: Albert Whitman & Co.

White, P. (1978). *Janet at school*. New York: Crowell.

CHAPTER 4

Gehret, Jeane. (1996). *The don't-give-up kid and learning differences*. Fairport, NY. Verbal Images Press.

Kennemore, T. (1983). *Wall of words*. London: Faber & Faber.

Levinson, M. (1985). *And don't bring Jeremy*. New York: Holt, Rinehart, & Winston.

Most, Bernard. (1990). *The cow that went oink*. New York: Harcourt Brace & Company.

Philbrick, W.R. (1993). *Freak the mighty*. New York: Scholastic.

Sachs, Marilyn. (1993). *Thirteen going on seven*. New York: Dutton Children's Books.

Schlieper, Anne. Illustrated by Mary Beth Schwark. (1995). *The Best Flight*. Morton Grove, IL: Albert Whitman & Co.

CHAPTER 5

Brooks, B. (1984). *The moves make the man*. New York: Harper & Row. NEWBERY

Hayden, Torey L. (1980). *One child*. New York: Avon Books.

Hayden, Torey L. (1981). *Somebody else's kids*. New York: Avon Books.

Hyde, M.O. (1983). *Is this kid crazy?* Philadelphia: The Westminster Press.

Klein, Norma. Illustrations by Kay Choroa. (1979). *Visiting Pamela*. New York: Dial Press.

Konigsburg, E. L. (1970). *George*. New York: Atheneum.

Nolan, Han. (1997). *Dancing on the edge*. New York: Harcourt Brace & Company. NATIONAL BOOK AWARD

Larsen, Hanne. (1978). *Don't forget Tom*. New York: Crowell.

CHAPTER 6

Cray, Elizabeth. (1992). *I'm frustrated*. Chicago: Parenting Press.

Duncan, Riana. (1989). *When Emily woke up angry*. Hauppauge, NY: Educational Series Inc.

Gehret, Jeanne. (1991). *Eagle eyes: A child's guide to paying attention.* Fairport, NY: Verbal Images Press.
Gehret, Jeanne. (1992). *I''m somebody too.* Fairport, NY: Verbal Images Press.
Janover, Caroline. Illustrated by Rick Powell. (1997). *Zipper, the kid with ADHD.* Bethesda, MD: Woodbine House.
Korman, Cliff and Esther Trevino. (1995). *Euke, the jumpy jumpy elephant.* New York: Specialty Press.
Moss, Deborah M. Illustrated by Carol Schwartz. (1996). *Shelley, the hyperactive turtle.* Bethesda, MD: Woodbine House.

CHAPTER 7

Fenner, C. (1997). *Yolanda's genius.* New York: Simon & Schuster. NEWBERY
Hamilton, V. (1971). *The planet of Jr. Brown.* New York: Macmillan.
Hayden, Torey L. (1995). *The tiger's child.* New York: Avon Books.
Hermes, P. (1990). *I hate being gifted.* New York: Putnam.
Keyes, D. (1983). "Flowers for Algernon." In *A book of short stories.* New York: Harcourt Brace Jovanovich.
Konigsburg, E. L. (1997). *A view from Saturday.* New York: Atheneum. NEWBERRY
L'Engle, M. (1962). *A wrinkle in time.* New York: Farrar, Strauss, & Giroux. NEWBERY
O'Brien, R. (1971). *Mrs. Frisby and the rats of NIMH.* New York: Atheneum. NEWBERY

CHAPTER 8

Byars, B. (1970). *The summer of the swans.* New York: Scholastic. NEWBERY
Christopher, Matt F. Illustrated by Foster Caddell. (1996). *Long shot for Paul.* Boston: Little, Brown.
Fleming, Virginia. Illustrated by Floyd Cooper. (1993). *Be good to Eddie Lee.* New York: Philomel Books.
Litchfield, Ada B. (1984). *Making room for Uncle Joe.* Morton Grove, IL: Albert Whitman & Co.
Rheingrover, Jean Sasso. Illustrated by Kay Life. (1996). *Veronica's first year.* Morton Grove, IL: Albert Whitman & Co.
Rylant, C. (1985*). Every living thing.* New York: Bradbury Press.
Testa, Maria. (1996). *Thumbs up, Rico!* Morton Grove, IL: Albert Whitman & Co.
Wright, Betty Ren. Illustrated by Helen Cogancherry. (1992). *My sister is different.* Austin, TX: Raintree Steck Vaughn.

CHAPTER 9

Blank, J.P. (1976). *19 steps up the mountain: The story of the DeBolt family.* Philadelphia: Lippincott.
Emmert, Michelle. (1996). *I'm the big sister now.* Morton Grove, IL: Albert Whitman & Co
Helfman, Elizabeth. (1995). *On being Sarah.* Morton Grove, IL: Albert Whitman & Co.
Metzger, Lois. (1997). *Ellen's case.* New York: Puffin Books.
Moran, George. (1994). *Imagine me on a sit-ski!* Morton Grove, IL: Albert Whitman & Co.
Sherkin-Langer, Ferne. (1995). *When Mommy is sick.* Morton Grove, IL: Albert Whitman & Co.

CHAPTER 10

Barrow, J. & Barrow, S. (1993). *There's a boy in here.* New York: Simon & Schuster.
Lane, H. & Pillard, R. (1978). *The wild boy of Burundi: A study of an outcast child.* New York: Random House.
Schulze, C. (1993). *When snow turns to rain.* Bethesda, MD: Woodbine House.
Stehli, A. (1991). *The sound of a miracle: A child's triumph over autism.* New York: Doubleday.
Thompson, Mary. (1996). *Andy and his yellow frisbee.* Bethesda, MD: Woodbine House.
Williams, D. (1992). *Nobody nowhere: The extraordinary autobiography of an autistic child.* New York: Times Books.
Yashima, T. (1965). *Crow boy.* New York: Scholastic.

CHAPTER 11

Althea. (1993). *I have diabetes.* Hong Kong: Dinosaur Publications.
Brown, Laurie Krasney and Marc Brown. (1996). *When dinosaurs die: A guide to understanding death.* Boston: Little, Brown.
Carter, Siri M. & Alden R. Photographs by Dan Young. (1996). *I'm tougher than asthma.* Morton Grove, IL: Albert Whitman & Co.
Gunther, J. (1949). *Death be not proud: A memoir.* New York: Harper Perennial.
Hanson, Regina. (1997). *The face at the window.* New York: Clarion Books.
McDaniel, Lurlene. (1991). *So much to live for.* New York: Bantam Books.

Rudner, Barry. Illustrated by Peggy Trabalka. (1992). *Will I still have to make my bed in the morning?* Louisville, KY: Art Print & Publishing Co.

White, R. & Cunningham, A.M. (1983). *Ryan White: My own story*. New York: Penguin.

CHAPTER 12

Fletcher, Jane Cowen. (1993). *Mama zooms*. New York: Scholastic.

Hesse, Karen (1997). *Out of the dust*. New York: Scholastic. NEWBERY

Imai, Miko. (1994). *Lilly's secret*. Cambridge, MA: Candlewick Press.

Killilea, M. (1952). *Karen*. New York: Dell Publishing.

Mayer, Gina and Mercer. (1992). *A very special critter*. New York: Golden Books.

Powers, M.E. (1986). *Our teacher's in a wheelchair*. Morton Grove, IL: Albert Whitman & Co.

Swells, Rosemary. (1990). *The little lame prince*. New York: Dial Books for Young Readers.

CHAPTER 13

Burke, M. (1984). *Reflections of a brother*. Washington, DC: National Head Injury Foundation.

Dickenson, M. (1987). *Thumbs up: The life and courageous comeback of White House Press Secretary Jim Brady*. Washington, DC: National Head Injury Foundation

Leaf, L.E. (1988). *Susan's dad: A child's story of head injury*. Washington, DC: National Head Injury Foundation.

Mahanes, F. (1985). *A child's courage, a doctor's devotion: Triumph over head trauma*. Washington, DC: National Head Injury Foundation

Warrington, J. (1981). *The Humpty Dumpty syndrome*. Washington, DC: National Head Injury Foundation

CHAPTER 14

Black, Irma Simonton. Illustrations by Seymour Fleischman. (1995). *The little old man who could not read*. Morton Grove, IL: Albert Whitman & Co.

Bourke, Linda. (1981). *Handmade ABC: A manual alphabet*. Reading, MA: Addison Wesley.

Kemp, G. (1980). *The turbulent term of Tyke Tiler*. Winchester, MA: Faber & Faber.

Schneider, M. (1978). *If only I could talk*. London: Heinemann.

Small, D. (1992). *Ruby Mae has something to say*. NY: Crown Publishers.

Stanek, Muriel. Illustrated by Judith Friedman. (1989). *I speak English for my Mom*. Morton Grove, IL: Albert Whitman & Co.

Thompson, M. (1992). *My brother, Matthew*. Bethesda, MD: Woodbine House.

CHAPTER 15

Booth, Barbara D. Illustrated by LaMarche, Jim. (1991). *Mandy*. New York: Lothrop, Lee, & Shepard Books.

Butts, Nancy. *Cheshire moon*. Arden, NC: Front Street Publications.

Lakin, Patricia. (1996). *Dad and me in the morning*. Morton Grove, IL: Albert Whitman & Co.

Litchfield, Ada B. Illustrated by Eleanor Mill. (1976). *A button in her ear*. Morton Grove, IL: Albert Whitman & Co.

Litchfield, Ada B. (1996). *Words in our hands*. Morton Grove, IL: Albert Whitman & Co.

McMahon, Patricia. Photos by John Godt. (1995). *Listen for the bus: David's story*. Mexico: Boyds Mill Press.

Rankin, L. (1991). *The handmade alphabet*. New York: Scholastic.

CHAPTER 16

Brown, Marc. (1979). *Arthur's eyes*. Boston: Little, Brown.

Davidson, M. (1965). *Helen Keller's teacher*. New York: Schoastic.

Freedman, Russell. (1997). *Out of darkness; The story of Louis Braille*. New York: Clarion Books.

Keller, H. (1954). *The story of my life*. Garden City, NY: Doubleday.

Kroll, Virginia L. Illustrated by Jill Kastner. (1995). *Naomi knows it's springtime*. Hong Kong: Boyds Mills Press.

Litchfield, Ada B. (1996). *A cane in her hand*. Morton Grove, IL: Albert Whitman & Co.

Wild, Margaret. (1993). *All the better to see you with!* Morton Grove, IL: Albert Whitman & Co.

Yolen, Jane. Illustrated by Remy Charelip and Demetra Marasles. (1977). *The seeing stick*. New York: Crowell.

Collaboration Goal: _____

Collaborators	Roles and Preparation	Possible Barriers	Solutions to Barriers	Modifications to Implementation	Ongoing Evaluation
Students with Disabilities					
Parents					
General Educator(s)					
Special Educator(s)					
Related Service Providers					
Administrative Personnel					
Students without Disabilities					
Others:					
ALL					

Shawnee Mission Public Schools
Special Education
Howard D. McEachen Administrative Center
7235 Antioch
Shawnee Mission, Kansas 66204-1798
Telephone 913 993-6200

Educating for Life

Individualized Education Program

Student #

TYPE
- ☐ Initial
- ☐ Interim
- ☐ Reevaluation
- ☐ Review

DATE

Current IEP

STATUS
- ☐ New Referral
- ☐ Continuing Student
- ☐ Entering with IEP
- ☐ Return to Spec. Ed.

STUDENT INFORMATION

Legal Name: Last	First	Initial	Birthdate	Age	Sex	Current Placement

School	Grade	Principal	Teacher/Counselor	Special Ed. Case Manager

Home Address	City, State	Zip	Home Phone	Lives With

Parent / Guardian of Home	Bus. Phone	Spouse of Home	Bus. Phone

Other Parent / Guardian	Address	City, State ZIP	Phone

PLANNING TEAM

The following people were involved in the development of this Individual Education Program.

Name	Title	Name	Title
	Parent		
	Student		
	Reg. Ed. Teacher		
	Spec. Ed. Teacher		
	Sch. Dist. Rep.		
	Eval. Interpreter		

PARENT

☐ Parent input and concerns were considered in formulating the IEP by:

☐ Parent did not respond. Attempts to obtain involvement:

Date: _____ Type: _____

STUDENT

☐ Student under age 14 for duration of this IEP
☐ Student input was considered in formulating the IEP by:

_____

☐ Student declined involvement.   Attempts to obtain involvement:

Date: _____ Type: _____

IEP DISTRIBUTION

Copies to:

Indicate your receipt of a copy of this IEP by initialling.

_____ _____ _____
Father   Mother   Student

Rev 12.1.97

CONSIDERATIONS

Health/Med. Considerations: VISION: _____ Adequate / Inadequate   HEARING: _____ Adequate / Inadequate
                                Date   Date

Diagnosis (if any):

- ☐ Academic / Cognitive strengths and needs considered
- ☐ Communication strengths and needs considered
  -     Student has limited English proficiency: **Yes / No**
- ☐ Prevocational / vocational strengths and needs considered
- ☐ Daily life strengths and needs considered
- ☐ Motor performance strengths and needs considered
- ☐ Social / Emotional strengths and needs considered (including behavioral)
  -     Behavior (to date) impedes student's learning or that of others: **Yes / No**
- ☐ Assistive Technology needs considered
- ☐ Special Considerations (Vision / Hearing Impaired):

> NOTE: Areas of identified educational need should be addressed through goals, services, and/or actions.

Relevant Strengths:

Parental Concerns:

Date of Most Recent Evaluation Considered: _____ Comments:

After making the above considerations, the following areas of unique need are judged by the IEP team to result from the student's exceptionality and require special education (specially designed instruction) to enable the student's involvement and progress in the general curriculum and/or to meet these unique needs (benefit from his/her education):

PRESENT LEVEL OF PERFORMANCE / GOAL / BENCHMARKS

Area requiring special education:

Present Level of Performance:

Impact upon involvement and progress in the general curriculum (ECSE - on participation in appropriate activities):

> **Goal 1:**

Criteria: Responsible:

Anticipated benchmarks between present level and goal:

How goal will enable the student to be involved in and progress in general curriculum and in meeting other educational needs:

How goal will be measured:

PRESENT LEVEL OF PERFORMANCE / GOAL / BENCHMARKS

Area requiring special education:

Present Level of Performance:

Impact upon involvement and progress in the general curriculum (ECSE - on participation in appropriate activities):

Goal ___ :

Criteria: Responsible:

Anticipated benchmarks between present level and goal:

How goal will enable the student to be involved in and progress in general curriculum and in meeting other educational needs:

How goal will be measured:

PRESENT LEVEL OF PERFORMANCE / GOAL / BENCHMARKS

Area requiring special education:

Present Level of Performance:

Impact upon involvement and progress in the general curriculum (ECSE - on participation in appropriate activities):

Goal ___ :

Criteria: Responsible:

Anticipated benchmarks between present level and goal:

How goal will enable the student to be involved in and progress in general curriculum and in meeting other educational needs:

How goal will be measured:

LEAST RESTRICTIVE ENVIRONMENT

LRE / Program Placement	Appropriate		Description of Program
	Y	**N**	More than one placement may be appropriate.
Regular classroom with or without supplementary aids / services			
Resource programs / support** _____ (program considered)			
Specialized Placements:** _____ (program considered)			

Appropriate Placement: ☐ Reg Class   ☐ Reg Class w/Resource Rm   ☐ Special Class

☐ Special School   ☐ Home   ☐ Residential Facility

**Rationale:

SPECIAL EDUCATION AND RELATED SERVICES

The following special education (specially designed instruction) and related services (services required to assist the student to benefit from special education) will be provided:

	Service	Anticipated Frequency	Anticipated Setting / Location	Responsible, Title	Anticipated Start Date	Anticipated Duration	Ant. End (or Review) Date
1							
2							
3							
4							
5							
6							
7							
8							

Person responsible for service on top line is case manager unless specified otherwise.

Comments:

9. Additional Recommendation:

10. Additional Recommendation (include any termination of previous services):

In light of regression and recoupment or other considerations -

Extended School Year: Eligible / Ineligible   For Goals:

Transportation Provided? Yes / No   Between: ☐ Home / School   ☐ Schools   ☐ School / Activities

Mode: **Reg / Lift**   Comments:

PROGRAM MODIFICATIONS / PERSONNEL SUPPORTS

Program modifications and/or supports for personnel (include anticipated frequency, location, and duration where appropriate):

SUPPLEMENTARY AIDS AND SERVICES

The following aids, services, and other supports are needed in regular education classes or other education-related settings to enable the student to be educated with other nonexceptional children to the maximum extent appropriate in accordance with the least restrictive environment for the student:

PROG. REPORT

Method of reporting progress to parents:

Frequency of reporting: At standard grading periods

PEER PARTIC.

Extent to which the student will not participate with nonexceptional peers in regular educ. programs (academic, non-academic, extracurric.):

STATE / DISTRICT ASSESSMENTS

State or Districtwide Assessments: ☐ Full Participation ☐ Modified Presentation ☐ Alternate Assessment
☐ Waive Participation

Modifications / Adaptations in administration of State / districtwide assessments:

Reason for Alternate Assessment or Waiver:

Alternate Assessment Method:

TRANSITION / GRADUATION PLAN (age 14 or older)

GRADUATION INFORMATION

Previous IEPs regarding graduation requirements have been reviewed. The student is scheduled to meet **standard / modified** graduation requirements. Notify counseling coordinator if requirements are modified. Once requirements have been modified they should remain that way.

Modifications:

Projected Graduation Date: _____ Upon completion of graduation requirements.

TRANSITION TARGET

Based on this student's interests and needs, the team has determined that he/she is in need of specialized transition services which **promote movement from school to following post-school activities:**

☐ Postsecond Educ/Training   ☐ Continuing/Adult Educ.   ☐ Community Participation

☐ Vocational Training   ☐ Adult Services   ☐ Other _____

☐ Integrated Employment   ☐ Independent Living   ☐ Other _____

TRANSITION SERVICES

Transition services are the following:

Instruction / Related Services (DO NOT LEAVE BLANK - state rationale if not needed):

Community Experiences (DO NOT LEAVE BLANK - state rationale if not needed):

Employment and/or Post-school Living (DO NOT LEAVE-BLANK - state rationale if not needed):

Daily Living Skills, including where appropriate, Functional Vocational Evaluation (OPTIONAL - No rationale necessary if no services needed.):

The student's preferences and interests were considered through the following involvement:

Other Agency Involvement - List representatives and type of involvement (e.g. Attended IEP, Phone call) :

☐ Notify KRS of Transition (16) -   ☐ Reevaluate in preparation for graduation. -

☐ Notify student and parent of rights / impending transfer of rights at reaching age of majority. (17) -

Educating for Life

Shawnee Mission Public Schools
Special Education
Howard D. McEachen Administrative Center
7235 Antioch
Shawnee Mission, Kansas 66204
Telephone 913 993-6200

Student #

Individual Education Program
Additional Notes

Name:

Date:

Rev 12.1.97

CHAPTER 1: PRELUDES, LAWS, STUDENTS, AND STAFF

CHAPTER OVERVIEW

Many factors influence students in today's world. This chapter examines the characteristics of today's students as well as important values that can influence their education for the better. This chapter lays a foundation for understanding the characteristics, strengths, and concerns of students with exceptionalities. These issues are then examined in light of judicial decisions that have impacted students' lives and the lives of those involved in their education. Special attention is given to highlighting the six principles of the Individuals with Disabilities Education Act (IDEA).

The life of fourteen-year-old Danny Ramirez vividly illustrates how one student, his committed family, and his teachers and peers have made—through persistence and with the law on their side—a significant difference for both Danny and many other students, too. We chose Danny Ramirez to highlight a student whose family has strongly advocated for inclusion and who have secured—sometimes only after a law suit and sometimes after other great efforts—what they wanted. In addition, Danny's story raises issues related to cultural and linguistic diversity that are critically important to consider in providing an appropriate education for all students.

CHAPTER AT-A-GLANCE

Chapter Outline	Instructional Goals	Key Concepts
WHAT IS THE VALUE-BASE OF THIS BOOK?		
What Is the Value Base for This Book?	• Recognize how values guide teaching techniques	• Six values define the foundation for this book: envisioning great expectations, enhancing positive contributions, building on strengths, acting on choices, expanding relationships, and ensuring full citizenship.
PROFILE OF SPECIAL EDUCATION STUDENTS AND PERSONNEL IN TODAY'S SCHOOLS		
Who Are the Students? • Total Number of Students • Age Groups of Students Served • Provision of Gifted Education • Disability Categories • Labels and Language • Socioeconomic, Racial, and Ethnic Profile Who Are Special Education Personnel?	• Identify the numbers, ages, categories of students identified with disabilities • Apply and understand the use of people-first language • Recognize the socioeconomic, racial, and ethnic profile • Explore the roles of different special education personnel	• Nearly 5.5 million students with disabilities were served in the 1994-1995 school year. Special education includes ten categories of disabilities as well as students who are gifted and talented. • People-first language is preferred because labels can be demeaning. • Culturally and linguistically diverse students with disabilities are overrepresented in special education. • Special education personnel include teachers, related service providers, administrators, paraprofessionals, and many others.
WHAT ARE THE RESULTS FOR STUDENTS WITH DISABILITIES?		
What Are Typical Results for Students with Disabilities? What Are Realistic Goals for Students with Disabilities?	• Examine actual results of special education • Describe realistic goals for students with disabilities	• The actual outcomes of special education are not encouraging. • Realistic goals include independence, productivity, and integration.
THREE LEADERS WHO CHANGED SPECIAL EDUCATION: A HISTORY OF REFORM		
Lloyd Dunn Evelyn Deno James Gallagher	• Recognize how special education has changed as a result of the efforts and contributions of key people	• Lloyd Dunn questioned the efficacy of special education. • Evelyn Deno proposed a cascade of services. • James Gallagher proposed individualized contracts between educators and students.

JUDICIAL PRELUDES TO FEDERAL SPECIAL EDUCATION LAW: A HISTORY OF DISCRIMINATION		
Two Types of Discrimination Two Revolutionary Judicial Decisions	• Identify types of discrimination practiced in schools • Understand how the judicial system has worked to establish students' rights	• Schools practiced both exclusion and misclassification. • In the early 1970s, federal courts ruled those practices unconstitutional and gave students a legal right to a free appropriate public education.

INDIVIDUALS WITH DISABILITIES EDUCATION ACT: INTRODUCTION AND ELIGIBILITY		
Introduction to IDEA: Progress but Problems Eligibility for Special Education: Need and Age Groups • Eligibility—Need • Eligibility for Special Education—Age Groups	• Identify the six principles that govern IDEA • Differentiate criteria for eligibility	• IDEA's six principles are zero reject, nondiscriminatory evaluation, appropriate education, least restrictive environment, procedural due process, and parent-student participation. • A student must have a disability and need special education and related services to be eligible for rights under IDEA, and age factors further determine those rights.

INDIVIDUALS WITH DISABILITIES EDUCATION ACT: SIX PRINCIPLES		
Zero Reject • Educability • Expulsion • Contagious Diseases	• Identify the purpose • Explain when students may not be rejected • Understand the value, context, and application of the zero reject principle	• Zero Reject prohibits the exclusion from school of any student who has a disability. It means that students may not be excluded because they are regarded as "ineducable," or have a behavior problem that is a manifestation of their disability, or have a contagious disease.
Nondiscriminatory Evaluation • Two Purposes • Evaluation to Eliminate Bias	• Identify the purposes • Understand the value, context, and application of a nondiscriminatory evaluation	• Nondiscriminatory evaluation determines whether a student has a disability and, if so, whether the student needs special education and what that education should be.
Appropriate Education • Planning for Individual Needs • Interpreting "Appropriate"—the Benefit Rule and the Process Rule	• Identify the purpose • Understand the value, context, and application for an appropriate education	• Appropriate education includes an Individualized Education Plan (IEP) and occurs when the schools follow IDEA's processes, when the student benefits, and when related services are made available.
Least Restrictive Environment (LRE) • Reasons for the Rule • The Rule: A Presumption in Favor of Inclusion • Setting Aside the Presumption • The Continuum of Services • Nonacademic Inclusion • Courts and LRE	• Identify the purpose • Understand the value, context, and application for the Least Restrictive Environment	• LRE requires students to be educated to the maximum extent appropriate with students who do not have disabilities. This means they must have access to the general curriculum.
Procedural Due Process • Due Process Hearing • Appeal to Court • Notice to Parents	• Identify the purpose • Understand the value, context, and application of procedural due process	• Procedural due process means parents and schools may use mediation or a due process hearing to resolve differences.

Parent-Student Participation	• Identify the purpose • Understand the value, context, and application of parent-student participation	• Parent and student participation works to encourage collaboration among parents, students, and educators and provide an appropriate education to a student with a disability.
FEDERAL FUNDING OF IDEA		
IDEA as Grant-in-Aid for States • Cost Pressures • Excess Costs Issues • Costs and Schools' Expanded Functions	• Describe characteristics of funding issues and procedures	• Rights run with revenues, so Congress grants money to states to help states pay for services if they agree to comply with the six IDEA principles. • As the number of students has increased, so has the cost increased. • Schools now perform many services formerly performed by agencies
OTHER FEDERAL LAWS: ENTITLEMENTS AND ANTIDISCRIMINATION		
Entitlements and Other Services Prohibition of Discrimination	• Analyze how entitlements serve students • Identify how the law has worked to prohibit discrimination	• Entitlements include vocational rehabilitation services and access to assistive technology based on qualification and eligibility standards. • Federal law prohibits discrimination based solely on a person's disability. • Section 504 of the Rehabilitation Act prohibits discrimination in regard to federal funds while the ADA prohibits it in nearly every other sector of American life.

PROJECT OPTIONS

1. Create a survey for local special and general educators to assess their understanding of how the "least restrictive environment principles" are being carried out in your school district. Include at least 10 questions and have a minimum of 10 special and 10 general educators fill out the survey. Then tally your answers and compare and contrast your findings. Chart your findings for the class.

2. Interview people from your local school board about how the procedural due process principle operates in your district. Present a written summary of how schools have been held accountable for complying with IDEA in your community.

3. Select an adolescent's or children's literature book dealing with the intersection of special education and low economic or multicultural themes. *Pinballs* by Betsy Byars is one good example. Construct a written, dramatic, or artistic project demonstrating how the six values to guide special education were or were not operative in the lives of the main characters. Or do this for a nonfiction book written by or about an individual with an exceptionality.

4. Conduct further research and prepare a class presentation on the different court cases that have affected the direction of special education throughout American history. Create compare/contrast diagrams to illustrate substantial differences and similarities among the different laws. See if you can interview a lawyer who specializes in legal issues surrounding special education. One good resource is the following book: Turnbull, H.R. and Turnbull, A. P. (1998). *Free Appropriate Public Education.* (5th Ed.) Denver, CO: Love Publishing Company.

KEY TERMS

Benefit standard

Job coach

Cross-categorical classes

Mediation

Due process hearing

National Council on Disability

Due process hearing officer

Process definition

Individualized Education Plan (IEP)

Supplementary aids and support services

Individualized Family Services Plan (IFSP)

Supported employment

GUIDED REVIEW

Schools and the Law

How far must public schools go to provide an appropriate education? As you will learn in this chapter, they must do whatever it takes to ensure that no student is excluded. For example, Jaime and Sherry Harrison have a rare and often fatal genetic condition that causes them to develop skin cancer if they are exposed even momentarily to bright lights. In their early years, they played in the moonlight and learned by candlelight. Their rural school in Meridian, California, adapted their facilities so the girls could attend school. Their mother Kim commented, "I'll never tell them they can't do things because of the sun. There has to be a way." As the girls' school demonstrates, there has to be a way for all children, regardless of exceptionality, to receive a public education.

See *People Weekly*, March 7–14, 1994, p. 178.

What Is the Value Base of This Book?

1. Identify the six values that guide special education practices as represented in your textbook. (See What Is the Value Base of This Book?)

    a. _____

    b. _____

    c. _____

    d. _____

    e. _____

    f. _____

Profile of Special Education Students and Personnel in Today's Schools

2. What percentage of all America's students were in special education during the school year 1994-1995? (See Who Are the Students?; Total Number of Students Served)

    _____

3. List the age groups of students served with special education and the percentage in each of the four categories. (See Who Are the Students?; Age Groups of Students Served)

Age Group	Percentage of Total Students Served

The School with No Name

When Stacey Bess was 26, she underwent surgery for thyroid cancer. Dana, one of her students, came to visit Stacey before she went in the hospital and brought her a teddy bear. Dana told her, "It helps to hold him tight when you tight when you are afraid. It really works. I promise."

Later Stacey found out how Dana had learned the secret of the bear's comfort. Dana had been locked in a basement for days without food or water. She was clutching tightly to the dirty bear that she offered to her teacher when the sheriff found her.

Stacey has written about Dana and other children she teaches in the School with No Name for homeless children in kindergarten through sixth grade. *Nobody Don't Love Nobody: Lessons on Love from the School with No Name* (Gold Leaf Press, 1994) reveals the difference that teachers like Stacey can make for children who are facing overwhelming challenges in today's society. Our hope is that one day you will have the experience of making a difference in a student's life.

See Plummer, W., & Free, C. (November 7, 1994). "Shelter in the heart." *People, 79.*

---

4. Which two categories of disabilities account for nearly three-fourths of all students with disabilities in the 1994-1995 school year? (See Who Are the Students?; Disability Categories)

   a. _____

   b. _____

5. List both advantages and disadvantages of labels for individuals with disabilities, noting which column is easiest to fill. (See Who Are the Students?; Labels and Language)

Advantages of Using Labels	Disadvantages of Using Labels

One way to examine how labels are used in society is by viewing films and reading books. In the resource section of this book, we have provided lists of videos and children's and young adult's literature that depict people with exceptionalities. If you would like to read other books or annotated descriptions of them, we recommend *Portraying Persons with Disabilities: Fiction* and *Portraying Persons with Disabilities: Nonfiction* (Friedberg, Mullins, & Sukiennik, 1992, Reed Publishing Company.)

6. Identify where special education students from low-income families live (See Who Are the Students?; Socioeconomic, Racial, and Ethnic Profile)

Residential Areas	Percentages Who Live in These Areas
Urban Areas	
Rural Areas	
Suburban Areas	

7. The fastest growing group of students in the country, taken without respect to race, is _____. This group of students primarily live in these three states:
a. _____, b. _____, and c. _____.
(See Who Are the Students?; Socioeconomic, Racial, and Ethnic Profile)

Neglected Parents?

In a study reported in *Exceptional Children* by Sontag and Schacht, Native American and Hispanic parents reported a greater need to receive information about how to get services as compared to white parents. When surveying all three groups of parents, only 37 percent reported that they had participated in a meeting with the educational agency concerning their child's educational program and signed papers that listed their child's goals and services. (Vol. 60, No. 5, pp. 422-433)

---

8. Based on teacher position vacancies, what three teaching areas are most greatly needed? (See Who Are Special Education Personnel?)
a. _____
b. _____
c. _____

What Are the Results for Students with Disabilities?

9. Identify at least four recent trends in employment for individuals with disabilities. (See What Are the Results for Students with Disabilities?)
a. _____
b. _____
c. _____
d. _____

10. Match the term established by Congress to indicate the outcomes or results for individuals with disabilities with their definition. (See What Are the Results for Students with Disabilities?)

a. _____ Independence	1. Persons with disabilities will have income-producing work, or their work will contribute to a household or community.
b. _____ Productivity	2. Persons with disabilities will use the same community resources and participate in the same community activities as persons who do not have disabilities.
c. _____ Integration	3. Persons with disabilities will assert control and choice over their own lives.

Three Leaders Who Changed Special Education: A History of Reform

11. What characterized the three individuals who have changed special education practices? (See Three Leaders Who Changed Special Education: A History of Reform)

_____

12. Match major accomplishments with the special education leaders who accomplished them. (See Three Leaders Who Changed Special Education: A History of Reform)

a. _____ Lloyd Dunn	1. Proposed the concept of a cascade of services, favoring individualized, student-centered education.
b. _____ Evelyn Deno	2. Advocated for a special education contract to safeguard against incorrect and permanent placements. This focus led the way for IEPs and a due process hearing.
c. _____ James Gallagher	3. Advocated for students with mild disabilities to have general class placements; recommended that labels describe the nature of the education the students would receive; focused the need for nondiscriminatory assessment.

Judicial Preludes to Federal Special Education Law: A History of Discrimination

13. Historically, name two ways schools discriminated against students with disabilities. (See Judicial Preludes to Federal Special Education Law: A History of Discrimination; Two Types of Discrimination)

   _____

   _____

14. What important outcome for special education sprang from the 1954 school race-desegregation case *Brown v. Board of Education*? (See Judicial Preludes to Federal Special Education Law: A History of Discrimination; Two Types of Discrimination)

   _____

   _____

15. What are the names of the two 1972 court cases that resulted in two jurisdictions: (a) creating free appropriate public education to all students with disabilities, (b) educating students with disabilities in the same schools as students without disabilities, and (c) putting into place certain procedural safeguards so that students with disabilities can challenge schools that do not live up to the courts' orders? (See Judicial Preludes to Federal Special Education Law: A History of Discrimination; Two Revolutionary Judicial Decisions)

   _____

   _____

Looking Back at *Brown v. Board of Education*

In 1994, the fortieth anniversary of *Brown v. Board of Education*, researchers reevaluated the issue of segregation (see *U.S. News and World Report*, May 23, 1994, pp. 33-36 and *Newsweek*, May 16, 1994, pp. 26-32; 53 for more information). They found that many African Americans still feel segregated in integrated public schools. Joanne Hayman, a grandmother, commented that she had "high hopes" when schools were integrated. But now she has changed her mind because she has seen her grandchildren struggle in integrated schools. "They all had such promise. . . . (In segregated schools) people pushed you because they believed in you. I can't say that is happening now" (Johnson, *U.S. News and World Report*, p. 35). Others, though, point to the value of integration. Edgar Epps, a professor, stated that people who want to go back to segregation "either have bad memories or weren't alive during segregation" (Johnson, *U.S. News and World Report*, p. 35).

   The low self-esteem that many African-American students experience in public schools suggests that public policy can force schools to change their structure, but may have little effect on attitudes. The attitudes that you have as a teacher about the value of all your students, regardless of race, gender, religion, or exceptionality can make a significant difference in their self-esteem.

Individuals with Disabilities Education Act: Introduction and Eligibility

16. What is the 1975 "Education of All Handicapped Students Act" now known as? (See Individuals with Disabilities Education Act: Introduction and Eligibility; Introduction to IDEA: Progress but Problems)

   _____

17. What does "IDEA" stand for? (See Individuals with Disabilities Education Act: Introduction and Eligibility; Introduction to IDEA: Progress but Problems)

   _____

18. IDEA's implementation has been impeded by (a)_____and
    (b) _____. (See Individuals with
    Disabilities Education Act: Introduction and Eligibility; Introduction to IDEA: Progress but Problems)

19. Match the components of IDEA's three parts: (See Individuals with Disabilities Education Act: Introduction and Eligibility; Introduction to IDEA: Progress but Problems)

a. _____ Part A	1. Benefits students who are between the ages of 3 and 21.
b. _____ Part B	2. Benefits infants and toddlers.
c. _____ Part C	3. Sets out the findings of fact on which Congress justifies the rest of IDEA along with the purposes and policies that Congress intends to implement by enacting IDEA.

20. According to IDEA, what qualifies a student to be eligible for special education services? (See Individuals with Disabilities Education Act: Introduction and Eligibility; Eligibility for Special Education: Need and Age Groups)

    a. _____

    b. _____

21. According to the IDEA categories in Part C, what additional categories are included for children aged three to nine? (See Individuals with Disabilities Education Act: Introduction and Eligibility; Eligibility for Special Education: Need and Age Groups)

    _____

IDEA: Six Principles

22. In the first column, list the names of each of the six principles governing the education of students with disabilities. In the second column, briefly identify the major characteristic of the principle. In the third column, write out any questions you still want to know about IDEA. (See IDEA: Six Principles)

Name of Principle	Major Characteristic	Questions About This Principle
a.		
b.		
c.		
d.		
e.		
f.		

23. The written plan for serving students aged three through twenty-one is called a(n)
    _____ _____ _____. The written plan
    for serving infants and toddler from birth through two (also called "zero to three") is called
    a(n) _____ _____ _____ _____.
    (See IDEA: Six Principles; Appropriate Education)

24. Identify some other terms used to indicate the least restrictive environment. (See IDEA: Six Principles; Least Restrictive Environment)

    _____

    _____

    _____

Federal Funding of IDEA

25. Congress grants federal money to state and local educational agencies (school districts) to assist them in educating students ages _____ to _____. (See Federal Funding of IDEA)

26. What is meant by referring to IDEA as a typical "grant-in-aid" law? (See Federal Funding of IDEA)

_____

_____

Other Federal Laws: Entitlements and Antidiscrimination

Covert Discrimination
ADA and Section 504 prohibit discrimination. But discrimination can be subtle. David Ruebain, as a teenager with a disability wrote that it's not so much those with disabilities, but the rest of the world that needs rehabilitation. "Don't pat on the head, offer help, talk to [people with disabilities] out of pity," he says. Talk to them because you like them. Otherwise, don't bother."
See Helen Exley, ed. (1984). *What It's Like to Be Me* (New York: Friendship Press).

27. List two other federal laws that affect special education and students in these programs. (See Other Federal Laws: Entitlements and Antidiscrimination)

_____

_____

28. Who is entitled to the assistance of a job coach? (See Other Federal Laws: Entitlements and Other Services)

_____

29. How is "supported employment" defined in your textbook and how is this an entitlement? (See Other Federal Laws: Entitlements and Other Services)

_____

_____

30. For legal purposes, Section 504 of the Rehabilitation Act and ADA defines a person with a disability as one who has the following three characteristics. (See Other Federal Laws: Entitlements and Antidiscrimination)

_____

_____

_____

Barrier Free Education
In this chapter, you learned about how the law demands appropriate accommodations to prohibit discrimination against people with disabilities. The law focuses on eliminating barriers.
The Internet is famous for leveling the playing field for people with disabilities. One web site is expanding the field into education. *Barrier Free Education* (http://atlanta.arch.gatech.edu/BFE) promotes the philosophy that "Access to education is a universal right." The site, which is maintained by the College of Architecture at Georgia Tech, emphasizes that educators need to take a leadership role in providing appropriate accommodations. The site contains numerous links concerning generic disability, vision, mobility, speech, and cognitive issues to assist teachers, parents, and students.
As you read through your textbook, be sure to check out the other web sites listed at the end of each chapter in Resources.
See Vanessa Ira. (1998). "Barrier Free Education." *Exceptional Parent, 28*(2), 30.

APPLICATION EXERCISES FOR CHAPTER 1

Application Exercise 1a. Dignifying Labels

See how many alternate words with dignity that you can generate for each word to avoid. Try thinking of other words to avoid to add to this list. Then generate a list of guidelines that helped you determine which words to use and which ones to eliminate.

Words to Avoid	Words with Greater Dignity
Cripple/ Invalid	
Handicapped	
Birth defect	
Victim	
Normal (referring to persons without disabilities as "normal" infers that those with disabilities are abnormal)	
Deaf mute/deaf and dumb	
Crazy/ Insane	
Slow	
Confined to a wheelchair	

Application Exercise 1b. IDEA's Six Principles

Reread the section on IDEA's six principles. Using what you have read, determine which principle is being described.

Principle	Descriptors
a. Zero reject	_____ 1. Seeks to make the schools and parents accountable to each other for carrying out the student's IDEA rights
b. Nondiscriminatory evaluation	_____ 2. Defines what kind of special education and related services the student will receive
c. Appropriate education	_____ 3. Related services are not available to a student unless the student requires them in order to benefit from special education
d. Least restrictive environment	_____ 4. A mechanism for shared decision making
e. Procedural due process	_____ 5. The value of relationships is reflected in this principle
f. Parental and student participation	_____ 6. Distinguishes between an appropriate education and the best education possible
	_____ 7. Provides an opportunity for mediation and/or a due process hearing
	_____ 8. Determines whether a student has a disability
	_____ 9. Students may not be excluded based on educability, disability related behavior or contagious diseases.

_____ 10. Plans for individual needs and follows the IDEA process

_____ 11. Requires notification concerning the school's decisions about their children

_____ 12. IDEA creates a presumption in favor of educating students with disabilities with those who do not have disabilities unless the student cannot benefit from being educated with students who do not have disabilities.

_____ 13. Includes another, less adversarial accountability technique: the parent-student participation principle

_____ 14. Evaluation to eliminate bias, including test bias

_____ 15. Schools must offer a continuum or range of services from more to less typical and inclusive.

Application Exercise 1c: Assessing What You've Learned

To summarize the major concepts in this chapter, identify how the six values* are important to the concepts for each major chapter section**.

* <u>Six Values</u>: envisioning great expectations, enhancing positive contributions, building on strengths, acting on choices, expanding relationships, and ensuring full citizenship.

** <u>Major Sections</u>: What Is the Value Base of This Book?; Profile of Special Education Students and Personnel in Today's Schools; What Are the Results for Students with Disabilities? Three Leaders Who Changed Special Education: A History of Reform; Judicial Preludes to Federal Special Education Law: A History of Discrimination; Individuals with Disabilities Education Act: Introduction and Eligibility; Individuals with Disabilities Education Act: Six Principles; Federal Funding of IDEA; Other Federal Laws: Entitlements and Antidiscrimination.

ANSWERS TO MARGIN QUESTIONS

This chapter included only a few reflective questions, asking for personal perspectives.

Circle the correct answer.

TRUE OR FALSE

T or F   1.   Over five million children in the U.S. are now receiving some form of special education.

T or F   2.   According to the NLTS, students with disabilities face dismal prospects after leaving school.

T or F   3.   Evelyn Deno proposed the concept of a cascade of services.

T or F   4.   The zero reject principle ensures that each person with a disability receives free public academic, vocational, and physical education.

T or F   5.   A student confined to an institution due to severe disabilities must still receive the best education possible at public expense.

MULTIPLE CHOICE

6.   Which of the following is <u>not</u> mentioned as a contributing factor to the likelihood that a child will receive special education?

    a.   Family income

    b.   Parental education level

    c.   Race

    d.   Birth weight

7.   For what is James Gallagher known, according to the authors?

    a.   Advocating for a special education contract safeguarding against incorrect and permanent placements

    b.   Suggesting new roles for special educators

    c.   Rejecting the term "mentally retarded"

    d.   Urging system sorting to tailor treatment for each child

8.   What had a major impact on some Congressional sponsors of antidiscrimination bills affecting persons with disabilities?

    a.   PAC money from the NEA

    b.   Family members with disabilities

    c.   Testimony from AIDS patients who suffered discrimination

    d.   Civil rights groups and progressive educators

9.   Which is true concerning at-risk infants and toddlers?

    a.   States are required to provide services to those at risk of experiencing a substantial developmental delay if they did not receive early intervention services.

    b.   States are required to provide services to an infant starting immediately after birth if notified by a physician that the child is at risk.

    c.   States have the option of providing services to at-risk infants and toddlers to age three.

    d.   States are required by IDEA to identify all at-risk infants but do not have to provide services to them until age three.

10.   To what does the zero reject principle refer?

    a.   A rule against excluding any student with a disability from a free, appropriate education

    b.   A law that no child can be rejected from attending his or her local public school

    c.   A law that all children must receive the best education possible

    d.   Prohibition against exclusion from general education classes for any student with a disability

11.   Nathan's parents want him to have a full time aide in his general education class because of his multiple disabilities. Must the school district provide such an aide?

    a.   Yes, because he is in the category of multiple disabilities.

    b.   Only if his parents also volunteer their help in his class.

    c.   No, because it would cost too much money.

    d.   Only if he requires an aide in order to benefit from his special education.

12. Hyung has active tuberculosis. Who will decide if he can attend public school?
     a. His parents
     b. The school
     c. A panel of medical experts
     d. The state disability determination board

13. What is the purpose of nondiscriminatory evaluation?
     a. To make sure minority students with disabilities can benefit from affirmative action in schools
     b. To determine whether a student has a disability and if so, what special education and services are needed
     c. To ensure diversity is practiced in the public schools and its testing centers
     d. To make sure standardized tests are not biased against African Americans

14. You are a third grade teacher in a general education class. A new student has come into your class whom you feel does not belong there because of a disability, but her parents do not want her placed in an "MR" class and stigmatized. What is the IDEA rule?
     a. Your opinion as the lead teacher must be respected.
     b. The school district should avoid an expensive court case and thus adhere to the parents' wishes.
     c. The student must remain in a general education class unless, even with the help of aids and support services, she cannot benefit from it.
     d. At the principal's discretion, the student can be moved to a special education class if she is taking up too much of your time.

15. What does IDEA provide when parents and state or local educational agencies disagree?
     a. A neutral judge determines who should prevail
     b. Covered expenses for students' individual needs
     c. A mediator meets weekly with parents to counsel them about the family's personal needs.
     d. A court-appointed lawyer will present the family's case and they usually receive a monetary settlement.

SHORT ANSWER

16. How does IDEA define special education?

   _____

   _____

17. What is the two-part standard for eligibility for special education?

   _____ and _____

18. What disabilities account for 75% of all special education services?

   _____

ESSAY

19. Discuss and rank the six values of this book from the point of view of (a) a special educator, (b) a general educator, (c) a parent, (d) a school administrator, and (e) a community member.

20. Compare and contrast and explain the purpose for each of the six principles of the Individuals with Disabilities Education Act.

CHAPTER 2: IMPLEMENTING IDEA'S PRINCIPLES

CHAPTER OVERVIEW

In this chapter you will learn how parents and schools jointly conduct nondiscriminatory evaluations and develop appropriate education with individualized approaches to teaching students with disabilities. A special focus in this chapter is on cooperative learning.

This chapter continues to look at the life of fourteen-year-old Danny Ramirez to provide a context for understanding how the six principles are implemented in one student's life. It also demonstrates how Danny can look forward to the future because school practices have changed.

CHAPTER AT-A-GLANCE

Chapter Outline	Instructional Goals	Key Concepts
NONDISCRIMINATORY EVALUATION: SCREENING, PREREFERRAL, AND REFERRAL		
Screening	• Recognize the two purposes of nondiscriminatory evaluation • Become familiar with purposes and types of screening tests	• The purposes are (a) to determine whether a student has a disability and (b) to decide the nature of the special education and related services the student needs. • Screening involves routine tests to help determine which students qualify for special education.
Prereferral	• Identify the purposes and context for prereferral	• Prereferral occurs to provide help to teachers experiencing challenges in teaching students and to guard against misidentifying students as having disabilities. • Prereferral occurs when a student's general education teacher asks others to identify instructional strategies to address learning and behavioral challenges.
Referral	• Explain the deciding factors for a referral	• A referral occurs when an educator or a parent submits a formal request for the student to be considered for a full and formal nondiscriminatory evaluation.
NONDISCRIMINATORY EVALUATION PROCEDURES AND STANDARDS		
Nondiscriminatory Evaluation Procedures and Standards	• Identify why a nondiscriminatory evaluation is given • Explore the characteristics of a nondiscriminatory evaluation	• A nondiscriminatory evaluation is given to determine whether the student has a disability and, if so, what the student's special education and related services needs are. • IDEA contains detailed procedural safeguards to ensure that evaluation is free of cultural and linguistic bias. • Procedural safeguards relate to the breadth and timing of the assessment, administration of the assessment procedures, parent notice and consent, and interpretation of assessment information.
Assessment Instruments • Norm-referenced Tests • Criterion-referenced Tests	• Recognize the difference between norm-referenced and criterion-referenced tests	• Norm-referenced tests are standardized and compare a student with his or her age- or grade-level peers. • Criterion-referenced tests determine whether a student has mastered a particular skill and compares the student to a standard of mastery.

Administration of Nondiscriminatory Assessments • Cultural and Linguistic Bias • Parental Input on the Evaluation Team Compiling Assessment Data and Making Evaluation Decisions	• Describe which aspects of a nondiscriminatory evaluation can highly influence the resulting treatment and outcome	• Cultural and linguistic bias can result in differential treatment. • Parents provide invaluable information. • All assessment data and evaluations should be seen by all team members.
APPROPRIATE EDUCATION		
Developing the IFSP/IEP • IDEA Requirements • Age-Specific Provisions • Participants • Contents • Timelines • IFSP/IEP Conferences	• Become familiar with IDEA requirements • Describe characteristics of IFSP/IEP conferences	• IDEA provides rights for infants through age twenty-one and participants must include the same people from the evaluation team. • The IFSP must include the present levels of development, family's resources, priorities, and concerns, and major outcomes. It describes the services that the child and family will receive and provides for a family-directed assessment and supports and services. It must be reviewed at six-month intervals. • The IEP must contain the student's present levels of educational performance, goals, and special education and services. It must be in effect at the beginning of each school year and be reviewed at least once a year. • IDEA requires that parents be members of the educational team; it expects school and family collaboration.
Implementing the IFSP/IEP Instructional Methods: • Cooperative Learning • Evaluation of Student Progress	• Explain the characteristics and benefits of cooperative learning • Describe how to evaluate student progress	• Cooperative learning consists of positive interdependence, face-to-face interaction, individual accountability/ personal responsibility, interpersonal and small-group skills, and group processing. • A few benefits include higher achievement, more advanced reasoning, enhanced creativity, and greater ability to take another's perspective. • Monitoring student progress typically includes grading modifications.

PROJECT OPTIONS

1. With several other students, write a script for a multidisciplinary team conference that demonstrates the value of collaboration. This may be either a referral conference or an IEP conference. Present this as a skit to the class, having each person take a different team member role. Be sure to include a parent and the student and to consider all aspects discussed in this chapter.
2. In a local school, get permission to examine IEPs for three different students. Discuss, compare, and contrast the stated objectives on the basis of clarity and practicality. Evaluate the related services as they relate to the objectives. Then, take what you have learned and prepare overhead transparencies to demonstrate your findings about the practical usefulness of IEPs.
3. Design either an educational card or board game for your future classroom that requires collaboration among the team members for an IEP. Describe the game in detail, drawing pictures to illustrate what it will look like and listing needed materials. Better yet, actually make the game!

4. Conduct further research and prepare a class presentation on assessment instruments. Create compare/contrast diagrams to illustrate substantial differences and similarities among the different tests. Prepare a lesson plan and test for your peers. Make the test based on the best characteristics that you've learned about assessment instruments.

KEY TERMS

Adaptive behavior	Portfolio assessment
Assessment	Prereferral
Bell-shaped curve	Referral
Cooperative learning	Reliability
Criterion-referenced tests	Screening
Evaluation	Self-advocates
Evaluation team	Validity
Norm-referenced tests	

CHAPTER 2 GUIDED REVIEW

An Alaskan Pioneer

High-school teacher David Langford, dissatisfied with the bleak results on assessment measures of his primarily indigenous Alaskan students, decided to search for a new way to instruct them. While on sabbatical at Arizona State University, he attended a continuous improvement seminar hosted by McDonnell Douglas Helicopter Corporation. Inspired, David read everything he could find on the quality movement in management. When he failed to get administration to make schoolwide changes based on his findings, he decided "the way to get others to change was to change myself." He trained his students in quality measurement methods. Their first project was to monitor student's most asked questions. The three questions were: What are we going to do today? Why do we have to do this? and What's my grade?

David concluded that his students were not involved in the purpose of their education, but only short-term results. He determined to get them to know and believe in the long-term purpose of their efforts. In addition, he started giving students responsibility for their own work and assessment of their progress. They graded their own papers and analyzed their results, plotted areas where they needed additional study, and worked in teams to share information. He also included a week-long ropes course into his curriculum to encourage team-building. All his students read Stephen Covey's *Seven Habits of Highly Effective People*, a book that emphasizes goal setting and collaboration. After seeing dramatic changes in the commitment and progress of David's students, the administration decided to implement his methods schoolwide.

See Martha Peak, (1995). "Alaskan Pioneer." *Management Review, 84*(9), p. 15.

Framework for Implementing IDEA

1. In your own words, summarize the six IDEA principles and their purpose and the key components for each one. (See Framework for Implementing IDEA)

IDEA Principle	Purpose	Key Components
1.		
2.		
3.		
4.		
5.		
6.		

Nondiscriminatory Evaluation: Screening, Prereferral, and Referral

2. What are the two purposes of nondiscriminatory evaluation? (See Nondiscriminatory Evaluation; Screening, Prereferral, and Referral)

    a. _____

    b. _____

3. List the four steps of a nondiscriminatory evaluation and circle the ones NOT required by IDEA but are a matter of good practice. (See Nondiscriminatory Evaluation; Screening, Prereferral, and Referral)

    a. _____

    b. _____

    c. _____

    d. _____

4. Match the definitions for a nondiscriminatory evaluation. (See Nondiscriminatory Evaluation; Screening, Prereferral, and Referral)

1. Prereferral	(a) _____ A routine test that helps school staff identify which students might need further testing to determine whether they qualify for special education.
2. Screening	(b) _____ Occurs when an educator or a parent submits a formal request for the student to be considered for a full and formal nondiscriminatory evaluation.
3. Referral	(c) _____ Occurs when a student's general education teacher asks others (educators and families) to help problem-solve in order to identify instructional strategies to adequately address learning and behavioral challenges.

5. List some examples of screening tests. (See Nondiscriminatory Evaluation; Screening, Prereferral, and Referral; Screening)

    a. _____

    b. _____

    c. _____

6. What students do not undergo the screening process in order to have disabilities identified? (See Nondiscriminatory Evaluation; Screening, Prereferral, and Referral; Screening)

   _____

7. What are the two purposes for prereferral? (See Nondiscriminatory Evaluation; Screening, Prereferral, and Referral; Prereferral)

   a. _____

   b. _____

8. Identify some of the consequences and dangers of classification and explain the danger. (See Nondiscriminatory Evaluation; Screening, Prereferral, and Referral; Prereferral)

   a. _____

   b. _____

   c. _____

9. IDEA prohibits schools from classifying into special education any students who have

   a. _____ or

   b. _____ . (See Nondiscriminatory Evaluation; Screening, Prereferral, and Referral; Prereferral)

10. What types of information is a typical part of the referral form? (See Nondiscriminatory Evaluation; Screening, Prereferral, and Referral; Referral)

    a. _____

    b. _____

    c. _____

    d. _____

Nondiscriminatory Evaluation Procedures and Standards

When you review test instruments, we encourage you to pay attention to the sample of students or families for whom the standardization was done. Pay particular attention to the racial, ethnic, and exceptionality characteristics of the people represented in the standardization sample. Do these characteristics reflect a cross-section of students? What is the likelihood of the test being used to assess only those students who were represented in the standardization sample? What difference do you think it makes if some racial, ethnic, and exceptionality groups are left out of standardization?

11. What two questions does a nondiscriminatory evaluation answer? (See Nondiscriminatory Evaluation Procedures and Standards)

    a. _____

    b. _____

The Assessment/Instruction Relationship

Does your local news media discuss the results of your district's yearly standardized assessment? One of the major concerns about classwide standardized assessment is that teachers feel pressured to teach to the test: they find out the content of the test and develop their instruction around it. Instead, appropriate instruction starts with goals and objectives from the curriculum's scope and sequence charts and individual IEPs. Assessment measures are constructed to measure the student's progress toward those goals and objectives. If a student fairs poorly on a test, the teacher uses this information to improve instruction for that student. Assessment becomes meaningless without the goal/instruction/assessment link.

12. Under the 1997 amendments to IDEA, who must be included on the evaluation team? (See Nondiscriminatory Evaluation Procedures and Standards)

    a. _____

    b. _____

    c. _____

    d. _____

e. _____

f. _____

13. Explain the difference between assessment and evaluation: (See Nondiscriminatory Evaluation Procedures and Standards; Assessment Instruments)

	Refers to	*Examples of*
Assessment		
Evaluation		

14. Norm-referenced tests compare a student with _____ , while criterion-referenced tests compare a student to _____. (See Nondiscriminatory Evaluation Procedures and Standards; Assessment Instruments)

15. A test is said to be _____ if it yields similar results across time and among raters. It is said to be _____ if it measures what it says it measures. (See Nondiscriminatory Evaluation Procedures and Standards; Assessment Instruments)

IQ and Culture

The book *The Bell Curve* (The Free Press, 1994) by social scientist Charles Murray includes a controversial chapter about IQ differences between races and the degree to which intelligence is inherited. Murray concluded that heredity plays a larger role than environment and that early intervention programs such as Head Start are doomed to failure. He has many critics, however, who say that IQ can be improved and that current IQ tests are inadequate measures of intelligence. Allman (*U.S. News and World Report*, October 24, 1994, p. 73) pointed out that the book misses many of "the mind's wondrous talents" such as insight and creativity. You can read more about Murray's book and his critics' viewpoints in the following articles:

Newsweek, October 24, 1994, pp. 53-62

Time, October 24, 1994, pp. 66-67

U.S. News and World Report, October 24, 1994, pp. 73-80

---

16. A nineteen-year-old student took an IQ test and found he had a mental age of 17. Based on the IQ formula given in your textbook, what would be his IQ?_____

    (See Nondiscriminatory Evaluation Procedures and Standards; Assessment Instruments)

17. Identify at least five problems that may arise when administering norm-referenced intelligence tests to students with exceptionalities. (See Assessment Instruments; Norm-referenced tests; Intelligence Tests)

    a. _____
    b. _____
    c. _____
    d. _____
    e. _____

18. List four benefits of criterion-referenced tests over norm-referenced tests for students with exceptionalities. (See Assessment Instruments; Criterion-referenced Tests; Intelligence Tests)

    a. _____
    b. _____
    c. _____
    d. _____

19. Identify the three aspects of a nondiscriminatory evaluation that are involved in the administration of tests, typical expectations, and alternatives that meet the need. (See Nondiscriminatory Evaluation Procedures and Standards; Administration of Nondiscriminatory Assessments)

Aspect of Nondiscriminatory Assessment	Typical Expectations	Alternative Possibilities
a.		
b.		
c.		

20. Explain why portfolio assessment is so effective in assessing student learning. (See Administration of Nondiscriminatory Assessments; Cultural and Linguistic Bias)

_____

_____

21. One of the most challenging times for many families is the _____
_____. (See Administration of Nondiscriminatory Assessments; Compiling Assessment Data and Making Evaluation Decisions)

Performance Assessment: Making It Work

Performance or authentic assessment, which includes a variety of assessment measures such as portfolios, exhibitions, open-ended questions, and projects, can be "little more than a work folder" if teachers and students do not understand its purpose. Four practices guide California's use of performance assessment. First, teachers articulate performance standards and assessment design. Collaboratively, they determine (a) the meaningfulness of tasks, (b) a menu of assessments to include, (c) criteria and processes for interpretation. Second, they make sure the measures are useful for improving instruction. This step requires teacher training to ensure that teachers have the ability to analyze student work. Third, students are taught to use the assessment to improve their learning. They have opportunities to practice self-assessment by revisiting past performances. Fourth, the consequences of using performance assessment are monitored to learn their impact on teaching and learning.

See "Making Sure That Assessment Improves Performance" (1994), *Educational Leadership, 51*(6), 55-58.

Appropriate Education

22. How are the rules for students ages 14 to 21 different than for students age three to twenty-one? (See Developing the IFSP/IEP; IDEA Requirements)

_____

_____

23. What individuals must be part of the IFSP/IEP team? (See Developing the IFSP/IEP; IDEA Requirements)

_____

24. Examine Figures 2-7 and 2-8 and identify unique characteristics of the content of the IFSP and the IEP. (See Developing the IFSP/IEP; IDEA Requirements; Contents of the IFSP/IEP)

Unique to IFSP	Unique to IEP

25. If a parent does not want to participate in the IEP meeting, what happens next? (See Developing the IFSP/IEP; IDEA Requirements; Contents of the IFSP/IEP)

_____

_____

26. By what point in the school year must the IEP be developed? (See Developing the IFSP/IEP; IDEA Requirements; Contents of the IFSP/IEP)

_____

27. What is the one principal reason for a mandatory review conference? (See Developing the IFSP/IEP; IFSP/IEP Conferences)

_____

28. List the two goals for implementing an IFSP/ IEP. (See Implementing the IFSP/IEP)
    a. _____
    b. _____

29. Give the five basic components of cooperative learning and explain how each one works. (See Implementing the IFSP/IEP; Instructional Methods; Cooperative Learning)

Characteristic	How It Works
1.	
2.	
3.	
4.	
5.	

30. The IFSP/IEP must contain a statement concerning how _____

_____

    (See Implementing the IFSP/IEP; Evaluation of Student Progress)

31. When given a choice, general education teachers typically prefer _____ type grades as more helpful than _____

    grades. (See Implementing the IFSP/IEP; Evaluation of Student Progress)

General-Education Friendly IEPs

Michael Giangreco and Ruth Dennis researched ways to make IEPs for students with multiple disabilities general-education friendly. Their research revealed several factors that inhibited the friendliness of IEPs for general education: writing in a vague or inconsistent manner; including sweeping statements; identifying goals and objectives that (a) seemed functional but lacked substance, (b) required change from teachers or other adults rather than the student, or (c) were based on discipline-specific values and practices; and stating promises that are hard to keep. General-education friendly IEPs, by contrast, included generalized learning outcomes, set family-centered priorities based on valued life outcomes, emphasized usefulness, distinguished staff from student goals, and identified goal responsibilities that could be shared across disciplines.

See "Dressing your IEPs for the general education climate." *Remedial and Special Education*, October, 1994.

APPLICATION EXERCISES FOR CHAPTER 2

Application Exercise 2a. Identifying Stages of a Nondiscriminatory Evaluation

After reading the "Nondiscriminatory Evaluation: Screening, Prereferral, and Referral" section of the text, select which of the three stages of evaluation (screening, prereferral, referral) is taking place in each of the following situations:

1. Jami has been bringing home poor work for months now. Jami's parents have asked for a full and formal nondiscriminatory evaluation.

   Stage: _____

2. Jill has not been paying attention in class and not completing her work. Jill's teachers have been examining her records to see how she performed on both intelligence and achievement tests. They also asked the school nurse to administer a vision and hearing test.

   Stage: _____

3. George has been having learning difficulties. He can't seem to grasp the math concepts presented in class and has been steadily falling behind with his classwork. Mr. McCutcheon, his teacher, has asked the guidance counselor and school nurse to help assist him. Ms. Safran, the guidance counselor, sat in one day when Mr. McCutcheon was teaching and later gave him some suggestions for how to deliver the instruction more effectively for that student. Together they brainstormed ways to help George.

   Stage: _____

4. Chanpen has only been in the U.S. a few months. Her English is limited and she doesn't seem to be making any effort to communicate. Ms. McMath, her third grade teacher, has expressed concern that she may have a serious disability. Several other school personnel have been asked to assist to determine if Chanpen's difficulties arise from a disability or from the cultural and linguistic differences she is experiencing.

   Stage: _____

5. Mr. Martin has tried everything he knows to help Sam learn science. Sam appears not only disinterested, but hostile. He becomes angry when Mr. Martin tries to help him. Ms. Sexton has observed Mr. Martin teaching and trying to help Sam. Together they brainstormed some new ideas and Mr. Martin tried them, but without success.

   Stage: _____

Application Exercise 2b. IQ Scores in the Classroom

Reread Box 2-3, "Into Practice: Best Practices for IFSP/IEP Conferences." Then match the practice with the place in the process where this practice belongs.

a. Preconference Preparation	_____ 1. Determine the amount of time participants have available for the conference.
b. Initial Conference Proceedings	_____ 2. Identify objectives to expand the positive contributions the student can make to family, friends, and community.
c. Review of Formal Evaluation and Current Levels of Performance	_____ 3. Avoid educational jargon as much as possible and clarify diagnostic terminology.
d. Development of Annual Goals and Objectives	_____ 4. Solicit information from the family about their preferences and needs regarding the conference.
e. Determination of Placement and Related Services	_____ 5. Ask if the family members desire clarification of their legal rights.
f. Concluding the Conference	_____ 6. Discuss the benefits and drawbacks of viable placement options.
	_____ 7. Share with family members and advocates the names and qualifications of all personnel who will provide services.
	_____ 8. Summarize the findings, including strengths, gifts, abilities, and needs.
	_____ 9. Encourage all participants to share their expectations for the student" participation in the home, school, and community.
	_____10. Identify strategies for ongoing communication among participants.
	_____11. Assign follow-up responsibility for any tasks requiring attention.
	_____12. Prepare an agenda to cover the remaining components of the IEP conference.

Application Exercise 2c: Assessing What You've Learned

Based upon the major sections* in this chapter, construct a twenty-question criterion-referenced test to summarize the major concepts covered in this chapter.

*Major Sections: Framework for Implementing IDEA; Nondiscriminatory Evaluation: Screening, Prereferral, and Referral; Nondiscrimination Evaluation; and Appropriate Education.

ANSWERS TO CHAPTER 2 MARGIN QUESTIONS

This chapter included only a few reflective questions, asking for personal perspectives.

SAMPLE QUIZ FOR CHAPTER 2

Circle the correct answer.

TRUE OR FALSE

T or F   1.   IDEA specifies who will be on the referral team for a student with disabilities.

T or F   2.   All public school students must be tested to determine whether they qualify for special education.

T or F   3.   Parents must be informed and provide written consent before each evaluation of their child.

T or F   4.   Intelligence tests generally measure a sample of a student's performance on tasks related to learning, memory, reasoning, and comprehension.

T or F   5.   The most current assessment procedures are specific, highly detailed, and appropriate for a specific exceptionality.

MULTIPLE CHOICE

6.   Which of the following is <u>not</u> an aspect of an appropriate education for Danny Ramirez?
   a.   Acknowledging his preferences
   b.   Building on his strengths
   c.   Providing an education that helps him to achieve his preferred outcomes
   d.   Encouraging student control of an IEP

7.   What are the purposes of prereferral?
   a.   Safeguarding against misidentification and helping teachers with challenging students
   b.   Screening for learning difficulties and exploring cultural differences that might exist
   c.   Assessing strategies for evaluation and interpreting test results
   d.   Determining classification and assisting students to accommodate to general education

8.   What is a norm group?
   a.   Students randomly chosen to represent the entire population
   b.   The normal distribution of a characteristic in the general population
   c.   The students with IQs in the normal range of 90-110
   d.   The students in a general education class who do not require special education

9.   Nine-year-old Linda is undergoing an assessment of her adaptive behavior. What will be considered during this process?
   a.   How she behaves compared to peers her age who do not have disabilities
   b.   How she performs on the Wechsler Test
   c.   Whether she is ready for the transition process
   d.   Whether her outcome-oriented rights have been put in place

10.   Her nondiscriminatory evaluation team has determined that Shawnine has a disability. What is the next step for the team?
   a.   Place her in the least restrictive educational environment.
   b.   Develop an IEP.
   c.   Identify the closest Parent to Parent program for her family.
   d.   Determine the special instruction that she needs.

11.   What is the typical IQ classification range for identifying students with mental retardation and giftedness?
   a.   Below 60 for retardation and above 140 for giftedness
   b.   Below 65 for retardation and above 140 for giftedness
   c.   Below 70 for retardation and above 130 for giftedness
   d.   Below 70 for retardation and above 125 for giftedness

12. For what ages does IDEA provide federal money to guarantee students with disabilities a free appropriate public education?
    a. Birth to eighteen
    b. Birth to twenty-one
    c. Three to eighteen
    d. Preschool through high school

13. What is the formula for calculating IQ?
    a. Chronological age divided by mental age
    b. Mental age × 100 × chronological age
    c. Mental age ÷ chronological age × 100
    d. Chronological age × mental age ÷ Wechsler score

14. In implementing the IFSP/IEP, what are two issues that need to be addressed?
    a. Conducting annual assessments and selecting an appropriate placement
    b. Assuring parent participation and fostering cooperative learning
    c. Training the parents in supplementing instruction and emphasizing great expectations
    d. Selecting appropriate instructional methods and determining evaluation strategies

15. Which of the following is not considered a basic component of cooperative learning?
    a. Personal responsibility
    b. Face-to-face interaction
    c. Positive interdependence
    d. Individual competition

SHORT ANSWER

16. What are the four steps typically followed in accomplishing the purposes of nondiscriminatory evaluation?

    a. _____
    b. _____
    c. _____
    d. _____

17. What are the two types of frequently used tests?

    a. _____
    b. _____

18. Define reliability and validity in tests.

    _____
    _____
    _____

ESSAY

19. Describe the nondiscriminatory evaluation procedures and standards. (Fig 2-4, p. 50)

20. Explain how the IFSP and IEP serve as tools to help students succeed in their education. Integrate important points about the contents, timelines, and implementation for the IFSP and IEP.

CHAPTER 3: SPECIAL EDUCATION TODAY: INCLUSION AND COLLABORATION

CHAPTER OVERVIEW

Students with exceptionalities can benefit greatly from inclusion and collaboration. A background of the various reforms in general and special education provides the framework for understanding how inclusion builds on and draws together the strengths offered by each reform. Each stage of the evolution of inclusion is closely examined, including the new 1997 amendments to IDEA. Collaboration is explored through an explanation of the roles of various potential collaborators.

This chapter examines the role of inclusion and collaboration in the life of fourteen-year-old Danny Ramirez. Danny's experience of being part of other students' lives and being part of the school has meant being in the same programs as the students who do not have disabilities. His experiences mirror some of the major issues surrounding both inclusion and collaboration today.

CHAPTER AT-A-GLANCE

Chapter Outline	Instructional Goals	Key Concepts
SCHOOL REFORM		
School Reform via Goals 2000.	• Describe how the Goals 2000 law serves as a vehicle for making the promise of IDEA a reality for all students • Identify the two themes permeating special education reform	• Goals 2000 provides foundations for all students (a) to start school ready to learn, (b) to have at least a 90% graduation rate, (c) to demonstrate competency in basic content areas, (d) to be the first in the world in math and science, (e) to be literate adults, (f) to have safe, disciplined, and drug-free schools, (g) to increase teachers' skills, and (h) to build on school partnerships with increased parental involvement. • Inclusion and collaboration permeate all of special education reform.
School Reform via the Individuals with Disabilities Education Act	• Describe how the 1997 changes in IDEA have sought to improve services to students	• IDEA now uses an outcome-based approach to special education and also connects state and local educational agencies to school reform.
INCLUSION		
Mainstreaming	• Recognize characteristics of mainstreaming	• Mainstreaming integrates students with disabilities only in nonacademic portions of the general education program.
The Regular Education Initiative • Madeleine Will and special education reform • Controversy over Regular Education Initiative	• Explain Will's role in the Regular Education Initiative • Analyze the issues involved in the controversy	• Madeleine Will brought to focus the issues and deficits involved in special education programs. • At the core, the issues focused on the way students are taught as well as the structure and organization of special education.
FIRST-GENERATION INCLUSION		
The Evolution Toward Inclusion	• Understand influences on the evolution of inclusion	• Opposition to the REI, both financial and logistical in nature, moved ahead the challenge to the very nature of schools.
"Caught in the Continuum"	• Explain how students were "caught in the continuum"	• Students "caught in the continuum" were not considered for general education classrooms

42

Revising the Concept of the Continuum	• Identify the goal that joined the inclusive school movement with the Regular Education Initiative	• The goal was a new partnership between special and general education.
Extent of Implementation	• Compare inclusive placements for students of different ages	• A larger percentage of elementary than high school students are in general education; almost half of preschoolers are served in general education classrooms.
Three Key Components • Home-School Placement • Age- and Grade-Appropriate Placements • Special Education Supports Exist Within General Education Classes	• Identify options for achieving the home-school principle • Explain key issues at the heart of the inclusion debate • Define how supports for inclusion differ	• Three options include the neighborhood school, a transportation school, and a school of choice. • Issues include eliminating the continuum of services, increasing the amount of time students spend in the general education classroom, and defining "all students." • First-generation models <u>add</u> teaching procedures and resources while second-generation models are characterized by <u>systemic</u> change.
Challenges Encountered in First-Generation Inclusion	• List specific obstacles to inclusion	• Obstacles include time, class size, and severity of disabilities.
SECOND-GENERATION INCLUSION		
Crossroads: From First to Second Generation Inclusion	• Summarize the major difference between first- and second-generation inclusion	• Second generation requires that change must be systemic and the education enterprise needs to be redesigned at the systems level.
Key Issues for Second Generation Inclusion	• Explain the expectations for second-generation inclusion	• Second-generation inclusion expects schoolwide reform, teacher renewal, intensive support for students, and a retreat from education based on labels.
THE INCLUSION REQUIREMENTS OF IDEA: THE LEAST RESTRICTIVE ENVIRONMENT		
The Basic Rule: Rebuttable Presumption	• Describe the rebuttable presumption	• IDEA creates a presumption in favor of inclusion requiring nondiscriminatory evaluation and appropriate education (IEP) that are linked to including a student in the general curriculum.
Provisions Advancing Inclusion	• Explain how new provisions work to the student's advantage	• The student begins in the general curriculum and is gradually removed from it only when supplementary aids and services make it impossible for the student to benefit from being educated there.
COLLABORATION AS A PREREQUISITE FOR INCLUSION		
Definition	• Define the key components of collaboration	• Collaboration is an interactive process that builds on the expertise, interests, and strengths of everyone involved in the educational process.
Rationale for Collaboration	• Explain how collaboration can be justified	• Collaboration is justified on the basis of the schools' need to become "adhocracies" and on the basis of research on student outcomes, professional outcomes, and systemwide outcomes.

Roles of Potential Collaborators • Students • Parents • Teachers • Related-Service Providers • Paraprofessionals • Language Translators and Interpreters • Administrators	• Identify the roles of potential collaborators	• For students, self-determination is an important part of their curriculum and leads to them being effective collaborators in their own education. • For parents, collaboration is best done through power-sharing; teacher's power over parents discourages collaboration. • For teachers, collaboration requires them to reconceptualize their roles. • For related-service providers, language translators and interpreters, paraprofessionals, and administrators, it includes being essential parts of a collaboration team.

PROJECT OPTIONS

1. Create a survey for local special and general educators to assess their understanding of how the "least restrictive environment principle" is being carried out in your school districts. Include at least 10 questions and have a minimum of 10 special and 10 general educators fill out the survey. Then tally your answers and compare and contrast differences. Chart your findings for the class.

2. Obtain a copy of IDEA. Make a time line, comparing and contrasting beliefs about inclusion during the last five decades in educational history.

3. Compose a poem or short story illustrating both the positive and negative stances on inclusion. Then illustrate the beliefs with either original pictures or pictures from magazines.

4. Based on a thorough search of websites on inclusion, construct a chart demonstrating the most recent implementations of inclusion for the four different age levels discussed in this text: preschool, elementary, middle and secondary, and postsecondary. Then create a presentation to the class that requires group discussion and collaboration to solve specific problems uncovered.

KEY TERMS

Continuum

Facilitative role

Information-giving role

Paraprofessional

Self-determination

CHAPTER 3 GUIDED REVIEW

Perspectives on Inclusion

A parent of a young child with autism expressed the following perspective on the value of inclusion:

"Young people with disabilities only aspire to what is expected of them. You put them in special education they learn to wash dishes. You mainstream they can learn to live in a normal society. We will not allow Jason to use his handicap as an excuse to achieve less than his full potential."

However, another parent expressed her concern about the social isolation that can occur for students with exceptionalities who are placed in but do not participate in general classrooms:

"My son sits at the same table as general education kids, but there is no interaction . . . Some of his classes contain joint activities, but 'togetherness' is not being facilitated."

In this chapter, you read about the second-generation inclusion movement, which emphasizes making sure that justification is written in IEPs for not including students. Furthermore, when students are included, they are expected to be active participants in general education.

School Reform

1. For Goals 2000 to be effective, what three areas must schools redesign to accommodate students with disabilities? (See School Reform via Goals 2000)

    a. _____

    b. _____

    c. _____

2. The provisions of the 1997 IDEA reauthorization seek to improve services to students in five important ways. Identify the goals or outcomes and then define what is involved in these improved services. (See School Reform via IDEA)

Goal/Outcome	Identifying Characteristics
a.	
b.	
c.	
d.	
e.	

You can read about a principal who personally reformed her school in inner-city Philadelphia in the book *For the Children* (Madeline Cartwright, 1993, Doubleday Books). She considered the filthy, vermin-ridden school, which housed a discouraged staff and troubled children, "a challenge made to order."

3. In school reform, both inclusion and collaboration build on different principles of IDEA. Identify which principles work for both inclusion and collaboration. (See School Reform via IDEA)

    a. Inclusion: _____

    _____

    b. Collaboration: _____

    _____

Alternative Schools

Can you imagine attending a school that was run by the Walt Disney Co.? Disney has built the Celebration School and Teaching Academy outside of Orlando, FL. The school houses 1,400 students in prekindergarten through twelfth grade. This is only one example of private enterprise taking over schools in hopes of improving education and making a profit at the same time. Impatient with school reforms, many parents are demanding change and welcoming businesses into their schools. Jane Carroll, a parent in Hartford, CT, explained her reasons for doing so: "Nothing has changed over the years, nothing has happened. Now, I want something to happen" (Gibbs, *Time*, p. 48). That something was Education Alternatives, Inc., a company that agrees to pay the bills, train the teachers, and develop the curriculum in exchange for one-half of every dollar it saves the school system.

Inclusion

4. What are the four consecutive phases of special education reform for inclusion? (See Inclusion)

    a. _____

    b. _____

    c. _____

    d. _____

5. In the early days of mainstreaming, students normally participated in what portions of the program? (See Inclusion; Mainstreaming)

_____

Inclusion Resources

Do you want to learn more about inclusion? *Toward Inclusive Classrooms* (National Education Association) has many practical, helpful ideas on promoting inclusion by curricular activities. It emphasizes inclusion at all levels from elementary to secondary schools and includes a helpful resource list. The book moves beyond philosophy to answer some of the real hard "how-to" questions.

Exceptional Children (1994, Vol. 60, No. 6) contains articles that address the relationship of inclusion to the development of positive self-identity, a policy study on implementing the IDEA least restrictive environment principles, and the current status of inclusion for students with learning disabilities.

In addition, *Expectations Unlimited, Inc.* (P.O. Box 655, Niwot, CO 80544, 303-652-2727) has a free catalog that lists videotapes, audiotapes, and books on inclusion and related issues.

---

6. Match the stage of inclusion with its characteristics. (See Inclusion)

1. Mainstreaming	a. _____ Madeleine Will criticized special education services for its lack in several key areas.
2. The Regular Education Initiative	b. _____ Special educators called on general educators to assume more responsibility and general educators viewed this as outsiders' attempt to direct them into undesired roles.
	c. _____ Placed students with disabilities in general education classes with their peers who do not have disabilities to the maximum extent appropriate.
	d. _____ Most of the students with disabilities participated in the nonacademic portions of the program only.

First-Generation Inclusion

7. What were some of the key influencing factors in the evolution toward inclusion? (See First-Generation Inclusion; The Evolution Toward Inclusion)

_____

_____

8. What was the basic goal of the inclusive school movement? (See First-Generation Inclusion; Revising the Concept of the Continuum)

_____

9. Identify strengths and weaknesses for each of the following stages of inclusion. (See First-Generation Inclusion; Revising the Concept of the Continuum)
   a. Mainstreaming: _____

   _____

   b. The Regular Education Initiative: _____

   _____

   c. The Initial Inclusion Concept: _____

   _____

10. Match the percentages for educational placements of students with disabilities. (See First-Generation Inclusion; Extent of Implementation)

Placement Location	Percentage
1. _____ Separate school	a. 43.9%
2. _____ Separate class	b. 27.5%
3. _____ Residential facility	c. 23.5%
4. _____ General education class	d. 3.7%
5. _____ Homebound/ hospital	e. 0.7%
6. _____ Resource room	

11. Identify the three components of first-generation inclusion. (See First-Generation Inclusion; Three Key Components)
    a. _____
    b. _____
    c. _____

Judith Heumann, Assistant Secretary for Special Education and Rehabilitative Services, U.S. Department of Education, states her perspective on the current inclusion debate: "Historically, we have had two educational systems: one for students with disabilities and one for everyone else. We are working to create an educational system that values all students." Heumann goes on to say that the general education classroom in the neighborhood school ought to be the first option for students with disabilities. She also emphasizes that teachers and administrators will need special training for that option to work.
See *Exceptional Parent*, September 1994, p. 37.

12. Home-school placement means that students should attend their _____.
    This means that they should attend the same school that they would attend if _____
    _____. (See Three Key Components; Home-School Placement)

13. What are three options to achieve the home-school principle? (See Three Key Components; Home-School Placement)
    a. _____
    b. _____
    c. _____

14. Describe the pros and cons for each of the major issues at the heart of the inclusion debate. (See Three Key Components; Age- and Grade-Appropriate Placements)
    a. Eliminating the continuum of services:

    _____

    b. Increasing the amount of time students spend in general education classrooms:

    _____

    c. Defining "all students":

    _____

15. Explain the difference between being "based-in" and "confined to" general education classrooms. (See Three Key Components; Age- and Grade-Appropriate Placements)

    _____

16. The core issue of the debate over inclusion is whether the dominant theme in education decision making for students with exceptionalities is and should be _____ or should be _____ (See Three Key Components; The Meaning of "All")

17. Which factor most distinguishes first- and second-generation inclusion? (See Three Key Components; Special Education Supports Exist Within General Education)

   _____

Inclusion and Racism

Students of color are often overrepresented in special education. However, in their article "The Color of Inclusion," Terry Meier and Cheryl Render Brown emphasize that students of color can be "labeled, marginalized, even rendered invisible, without ever leaving the general classroom." The authors contend that even if these students are taken out of special education classes, a dual educational system will continue to exist, unless we are "willing to examine honestly the role that racism plays in meting out educational opportunities in our schools."

See *The Journal of Emotional and Behavioral Problems* (1994), *3*(3), pp. 15-18.

---

18. The focus of general education practice is on the _____ while the special educator's focus has always been on the _____. (See First-Generation Inclusion; Challenges Encountered in First-Generation Inclusion)

19. List the six major themes of successful inclusion. (See First-Generation Inclusion; Challenges Encountered in First-Generation Inclusion)

   a. _____

   b. _____

   c. _____

   d. _____

   e. _____

   f. _____

Second-Generation Inclusion

20. First-generation inclusion focuses on how to make _____ and _____ rather than the second-generation inclusion focus on _____ change. (See Second-Generation Inclusion; Crossroads: From First- to Second-Generation Inclusion)

21. Identify expectations for second-generation inclusion along with the required change. (See Second-Generation Inclusion; Key Issues for Second-Generation Inclusion)

	Expectation	*Change Needed*
Expectation 1		
Expectation 2		
Expectation 3		
Expectation 4		

The Inclusion Requirements of IDEA: The Least Restrictive Environment

22. When may separate classes, separate schooling, or other removal from the general educational environment occur? (See The Inclusion Requirements of IDEA: The Least Restrictive Environment; The Basic Rule: Rebuttable Presumption)

_____

_____

23. List and describe three provisions advancing inclusion set out by IDEA. (See The Inclusion Requirements of IDEA; Provisions Advancing Inclusion)

_____

_____

_____

Collaboration as a Prerequisite for Inclusion

24. Define *collaboration*. (See Collaboration as a Prerequisite for Inclusion; Definition)

_____

25. Name the four roles you will play as a professional educator. (See Collaboration as a Prerequisite for Inclusion; Definition)

_____

_____

_____

_____

Community Education

Community members are not the only ones who can experience awkwardness when they encounter a child with a disability. Sometimes parents experience awkwardness with knowing how to speak to others about their child. Lisa Abelow Hedley describes this dilemma. Her daughter, who has dwarfism, contrasts dramatically with her mother's six-foot stature.

At first, Lisa found herself accosting strangers who were little people, trying to make a connection This was an overreaction, she says, especially when she found herself providing one of these strangers with a ride in her car. She discovered that stature is "a relatively superficial bond." Lisa had to contend with the insensitivity of a friend who suggested that she have her daughter put up for adoption, for the good of the community. And then she also experienced the openness of a child who asked if her daughter was really a dwarf. When she answered yes, the child said, "That's okay. It doesn't matter how tall you are if your heart's in the right place." Lisa believes that people's reaction often reveals more about themselves than others want them to know. Her suggestions for other parents? "Speak out of respect [about your child] and from the heart."

See Hedley, L. A. "A Child of Difference." *The New York Times Magazine* (October 12, 1997), pp. 94-98.

---

26. Identify the roles of future potential collaborators by listing the benefits and outcomes of collaboration for each collaborator. Use the IEP form provided in this Student Study Guide to be sure you cover the breadth of collaboration required for the success of students with exceptionalities. (See Collaboration as a Prerequisite for Inclusion; Roles of Potential Collaborators, as well as the "Collaborating for Success" at the beginning of this Student Study Guide)

Collaborator	Role of Collaborator	Outcomes for Student
a. Student		
b. Parents		
c. Teachers		
d. Related-Service Providers		
e. Paraprofessionals		
f. Language Translators and Interpreters		
g. Administrators		

27. Define "power-relationships" and describe some of the benefits of "power-sharing." (See Collaboration as a Prerequisite for Inclusion; Roles of Potential Collaborators)

_____
_____
_____
_____

Cooperative Learning

Cooperative learning is one technique that allows students to help each other to learn curricular content. There are several different types of cooperative learning formats, and we suggest that you read more about this valuable instructional tool. Two good sources are the *Cooperative Learning Center* (202 Pattee Hall, University of Minnesota, Minneapolis, MN 55455, 612-624-7031) and the *Team Learning Project* (Center for Research on Elementary and Middle Schools, The Johns Hopkins University, 3505 N. Charles Street, Baltimore, MD 21218, 301-338-8248). Norma Dyke (1990) suggests that when you are using cooperative learning in your classes, you will want to teach your students the following guidelines:

1. Make sure everyone knows the material.
2. No one is finished until everyone knows the answers.
3. Ask all teammates for help before asking the teacher.
4. Talk with a soft voice.
5. Tell your teammates HOW to get the answer.
6. Be sure everyone agrees on the answer before checking the answer sheet.

APPLICATION EXERCISES FOR CHAPTER 3

Application Exercise 3a. Identifying Placements for Students with Disabilities

See if you can identify which educational placement is most typical as represented in the following scenarios. Also tell what percentage of students have placements in this setting.

1. Josephina has multiple physical disabilities and requires many paraprofessionals helping her everyday. She enjoys other children, but requires full time on-site supervision.
    Setting: _____
    Percentage: _____

2. Rolando benefits from daily interactions with peers, even though his hearing loss is moderate. He enjoys the many hours he spends in the general education class, but also receives additional help from the speech language pathologist four afternoons a week.
    Setting: _____
    Percentage: _____

3. Abdul's learning disabilities have not prevented him from being one of the most popular kids in the class. His sense of humor and ability to make his teachers smile make the school day more pleasant for all of his peers. He has several peer buddies who help him with difficult assignments. A special tutor for reading comes to his class and works with him there.
    Setting: _____
    Percentage: _____

4. Jenny's swimming accident resulted in a traumatic brain injury. She has required extensive rehabilitation following hospitalization and has received special education services during this time. With continued collaboration on the part of her teachers and rehabilitation personnel, her parents expect her to one day be back in a regular class.
    Setting: _____
    Percentage: _____

5. Gopal was born blind, but his parents soon recognized how bright he was. Since he was a preschooler he has benefited from excellent instruction from teachers who were visually impaired as well as enjoyed interactions with peers who were blind. His school participates in collaborative sports and extracurricular activities with the local elementary school.
    Setting: _____
    Percentage: _____

6. Erin's speech difficulties require extensive teaching from the speech language pathologist. However, for math, art, and physical education, she often participates with other children at her own grade level.
    Setting: _____
    Percentage: _____

Application Exercise 3b. Matching Collaborators with Professional Roles

Collaboration is been defined as "an interactive process that enables people with diverse expertise to generate creative solutions to mutually defined problems." First define the professional role, and then match the collaborator with the most typical professional roles.

Collaborator	Professional Role and Definition
1. _____Students	a. Supportive role:
2. _____Parents	
3. _____Special educators	b. Facilitative role:
4. _____General educators	
5. _____Related-service providers	c. Information-giving role:
6. _____Paraprofessionals	
7. _____Language translators and interpreters	d. Prescriptive role:
8. _____Administrators	

Application Exercise 3c. Collaborating for Success

Working collaboratively with two partners, construct a written summary of the six major concepts in this chapter.* In addition to the written summary, turn in a list of activities that you did together collaboratively. Then evaluate which aspects of collaboration worked most effectively for an assignment like this.

* Six Major Chapter Topics: School Reform, Inclusion, First-Generation Inclusion, Second-Generation Inclusion, The Inclusion Requirements of IDEA: The Least Restrictive Environment, and Collaboration as a Prerequisite for Inclusion

ANSWERS TO CHAPTER 3 MARGIN QUESTIONS	
Page 85	Danny's parents strongly concur with the supporters of the Regular Education Initiative. They report that Danny has derived significant benefits from being in general education classrooms and being challenged by his curriculum. Danny's general education language arts teacher agrees that Danny has made tremendous gains while being in his classroom. In fact, his teacher reported that one of the best things that had happened was when he gave an assignment and Danny exclaimed, "This is easy!"
Page 101	Danny would strongly benefit from the individualized instruction within his general education classroom. It could aid him in learning difficult concepts and have the advantage of a variety of instructional approaches. It would also likely enhance his self-esteem to not experience the need to be singled out for special instruction and to recognize that all students could benefit from this specialized assistance.
Page 110	Many parents feel intimidated by all of the legal regulations, jargon, and educational approaches. Since conferences often are comprised of four to six professionals and usually just one parent (mother), it is very difficult for many parents to speak up and to be an equal participant. One of the roles that you can assume in educational conferences is to help conduct them in a way so that parents are "on an equal playing field."

SAMPLE QUIZ FOR CHAPTER 3

Circle the correct answer.

TRUE OR FALSE

T or F   1.   Although people have different perspectives about the issue of inclusion, it is agreed that the primary objective for students with disabilities is to provide them with an appropriate education.

T or F   2.   The technique of collaboration developed from the Regular Education Initiative.

T or F   3.   About half of the infants, toddlers, and preschoolers with disabilities are in general education or early intervention programs.

T or F   4.   The inclusion movement opposes IDEA's continuum concept.

T or F   5.   If Sarah is based in a general education classroom she must spend 100% of her time in class there but can still receive assistance from special service providers in the room throughout the day.

MULTIPLE CHOICE

6.   Which of the following was not mentioned as a means of making Danny's inclusion possible?

    a. Organizing a circle of friends

    b. Using techniques such as cooperative learning

    c. Modifying the general education curriculum

    d. Providing a bilingual aide

7.   What was the emphasis of the Regular Education Initiative?

    a. Enhancing social relationships

    b. Preparing students with severe and multiple disabilities for adult living

    c. Celebrating diversity and reorganizing the delivery of special education services and supports

    d. Improving the academic performance of students with mild and moderate disabilities

8.   Approximately what percentage of students with disabilities are assigned to resource rooms?

    a. 43%

    b. 27%

    c. 15%

    d. 6%

9.   What is a difference between charter schools and magnet schools?

    a. Magnet schools are free; charter schools charge tuition.

    b. Charter schools cannot discriminate while magnet schools can have competitive admission.

    c. Charter schools are created by parents and teachers to reflect their educational philosophy and values.

    d. Magnet schools focus on math, science, and technology and often use a lottery system for admission.

10.   What is one way in which paraprofessionals and special education teachers are identified in first-generation inclusion?

    a. They spend too much time with students and don't allow students enough independence.

    b. Students call them by their first names.

    c. They carry clipboards and use pushcarts from classroom to classroom.

    d. They are paid less and receive less respect than in second-generation inclusion models.

11.   Who are the primary advocates for inclusive education?

    a. Leaders in the field of severe and multiple disabilities

    b. Parents of children with mild to moderate disabilities

    c. Researchers, political appointees in Washington, D. C., and university professors

    d. Special education teachers and The American Association of Paraprofessionals

12. What is necessary for successful second-generation inclusion?
   a. Increased number of special education teachers and paraprofessionals to meet the individual needs of students with disabilities
   b. Curriculum adaptation
   c. Increased federal funding to fulfill IDEA mandates
   d. A redesign of the educational system

13. What is mentioned as a key challenge in implementing collaboration?
   a. Finding bilingual teachers
   b. Arranging schedules
   c. Ensuring parental cooperation
   d. Promoting student participation

14. Zac is a student with special needs in your class. He has an apparently poor attitude toward other students. What is an appropriate way the authors suggest to include him?
   a. Collaborate with the school counselor to set up a reward system for completing class assignments.
   b. Assign an aide to distract him when he exhibits poor behavior.
   c. Ask Zac which peers he would like to work with and have this small group practice verbal responses with him.
   d. Carefully choose activities that allow him to work alone.

15. You are the principal of Hawthorne Elementary and have a total of nine paraprofessionals. If you follow the national average, how many of them will you assign to special education and related services?
   a. Eight
   b. Six
   c. Four
   d. One

SHORT ANSWER

16. Identify four of the eight goals for Goals 2000.
   a. _____
   b. _____
   c. _____
   d. _____

17. What are the two related themes of school reform in special education?
   a. _____   b. _____

18. Identify the four roles you as a professional will be able to play in schoolwide collaboration.
   a. _____
   b. _____
   c. _____
   d. _____

ESSAY

19. Describe obstacles to inclusion reported by teachers and possible appropriate solutions
20. Describe the major themes of successful inclusion.

CHAPTER 4: LEARNING DISABILITIES

CHAPTER OVERVIEW

A specific learning disability is the most commonly identified disability in today's schools. This chapter examines the changes and controversies occurring in the field and how these impact students, families, and communities today. In chapter 4, you will learn to (a) recognize students who have learning disabilities, (b) become sensitive to their needs, and (c) provide appropriate learning opportunities for them, whether they are in general education or special education settings. You will study the difficult concept of *discrepancy* as it relates to specific examples. You will learn how individual states identify students with learning disabilities because the criteria vary so much across states. Curriculum-based assessment measures as well as the importance of standardized intelligence and achievement tests for establishing discrepancy will be discussed. You will discover how to use academic clubs, phonological awareness, graphic organizers, computers, learning strategies, and other approaches to improve instruction for students with learning disabilities.

The life of fifth grader Raquel (pronounced Rachel) Osorto provides an illustration of a typical student with learning disabilities. Raquel has a significant discrepancy between her ability and achievement in several academic areas. Her evaluation presented special challenges, however, because she is bilingual. The team needed to determine whether her reading and written expression discrepancies were actually due to specific learning disabilities or her use of English as a second language. Raquel has made tremendous strides in reading as a result of participating in a program called *Language!* that emphasizes phonological awareness.

CHAPTER AT-A-GLANCE

Chapter Outline	Instructional Goals	Key Concepts
WHAT ARE LEARNING DISABILITIES?		
Defining Learning Disabilities • Classification Criteria	• Grasp the complexity in defining learning disabilities	• The definition of learning disabilities has been much debated, but the IDEA and NJCLD definitions are commonly used.
Describing the Characteristics • Learning Characteristics • Reading • Written Language • Mathematics • Memory • Metacognition • Behavioral and Social Characteristics	• Describe key characteristics of learning disabilities • Recognize the diversity of characteristics experienced by students with learning disabilities	• Each state has criteria for identifying students with learning disabilities which typically includes three parts: a severe discrepancy between demonstrated ability and actual achievement, exclusion of other factors, and substantiated need for special services. • Students with learning disabilities are a heterogeneous population with varied learning, behavioral, and social characteristics.
Identifying the Causes of Learning Disabilities • Neurological Causes • Genetic Causes	• Identify potential causes of learning disabilities	• Research suggests that learning disabilities may be caused by central nervous system dysfunction that results in deficits in visual-spatial processing and phonological awareness.
Identifying the Prevalence of Learning Disabilities	• Recognize prevalence rates and recent trends	• Approximately 50% of all students with disabilities have learning disabilities. In 1995, 5.8% of all public-school students had learning disabilities.

WHAT ARE EVALUATION PROCEDURES?		
Determining the Presence of a Learning Disability	• Explain the characteristics of different types of assessments used to determine the presence of learning disabilities	• Nondiscriminatory evaluation includes the use of standardized intelligence and achievement tests to determine discrepancy. • Curriculum-based assessment can be norm-referenced or criterion-referenced.
Determining the Nature and Extent of Special Education and Related Services • Curriculum-based Assessment • Developing the IEP	• Recognize the importance of careful planning and explanations in developing the IEP plan for students with learning disabilities	• The IEP process should include careful explanation of the term *learning disabilities* to the student and family.
WHAT AND HOW DO PROFESSIONALS TEACH?		
Curriculum • Reading • Written Language • Mathematics • Academic Clubs	• Differentiate among curriculum options available for use with students with learning disabilities	• Specific curricular approaches in reading (phonological awareness), written expression (process approach), and mathematics (creating active learners) benefit students with learning disabilities. • Academic clubs can encourage motivation, generalization, and age-appropriate content skills in general education classrooms.
Methods • Learning Strategies • Graphic Organizers • Overcoming Learned Helplessness • Computer Technology	• Evaluate different methods that are effective for varied student needs	• Effective methods such as specific learning strategies, graphic organizers, overcoming learned helplessness, and computer technology help students to compensate for learning disabilities.
HOW IS PARTICIPATION ENCOURAGED?		
Inclusion	• Examine how students are best served in an enabling environment	• The Least Restrictive Environment must focus on the student rather than the place in order to be the most enabling environment.
Collaboration • Collaboration with Professionals • Collaboration with Peers • Collaboration with Family	• Explore ways to collaborate on behalf of students with learning disabilities	• Effective collaboration methods include CLASP for general and special educators and peer tutoring for students. • Making homework meaningful and ability appropriate helps improve relationships with families.
Careers: Who Are the Professionals?	• Examine the role of the resource teacher for students with learning disabilities	• Resource teachers provide assessment, development of IEPs, collaborate with general classroom teachers, meet with parents, and sometimes co-teach.
WHAT ARE PROGRAM OPTIONS?		
Early Intervention and Preschool Years	• Describe characteristics of effective preschool programs	• Programs such as the Language Acquisition Preschool address the language processing deficits of young children at risk for learning disabilities.
Elementary Years	• Describe characteristics of effective elementary programs for students with learning disabilities	• *Language!* is a structured curriculum that teaches phonological awareness along with reading comprehension, grammar, writing, and spelling.

Middle and Secondary Years	• Describe characteristics of effective programs for middle and secondary students	• Service learning can increase motivation and self-esteem for students with learning disabilities.
Transitional and Postsecondary Years	• Describe characteristics of effective program options for adults with learning disabilities	• Landmark College teaches learning strategies, organizational skills, and self-advocacy to students with learning disabilities.

PROJECT OPTIONS

1. Investigate recent research about one type of academic learning disability (reading, math, written language). Include a web search. Summarize the newest and best of what you find by presenting the new information according to the section headings of this chapter. Discuss how the new research changes expectations for students with learning disabilities. Include a list of your sources.

2. Get permission to work with the learning disabilities specialists in two local schools. Find out about a particular student's program. With parental permission, ask the specialists to identify (1) the severe discrepancy, (2) the diagnostic assessment used, and (3) the interventions used. Observe at least three different students receiving intervention and evaluate the strengths and weaknesses of the interventions.

3. Write a dramatic presentation demonstrating best/worst practices when working with students with learning disabilities. For example, you might choose a parent/student, teacher/student, or administrator/student interaction. Include demonstrations of effective methods, interventions, or programs contrasted with ineffective ones.

4. Write a narrative poem about a student with learning disabilities who has been helped by some type of cooperative learning, peer tutoring, or other collaborative intervention.

KEY TERMS

Basic psychological processes

Central nervous system dysfunction

Concomitance

Curriculum-based assessment

Dysgraphia

Dyslexia

Generalization

Metacognition

Mnemonic

Peer tutoring

Phonological awareness

Scope and sequence chart

Severe discrepancy

Subtyping

CHAPTER 4 GUIDED REVIEW

> **"I'm going to do what I promised. I'm going to save your life."**
>
> Dr. Fred Epstein whispered these lines to a young patient immediately before surgery. Dr. Epstein, who is coauthor with Elaine Shimberg of *Gifts of Time* (1993, William Morrow & Co.), is a pediatric neurosurgeon. Many of his colleagues refer to him as a miracle worker. He has been willing to perform surgeries that others considered impossible and, as a result, has saved many young lives.
>
> Dr. Epstein also has learning disabilities. His grades in college were only average, and his chemistry grades were "abysmal." He applied to four medical schools and was rejected by all of them. His father, a psychiatrist, intervened and Dr. Epstein was finally accepted by New York Medical College.
>
> Perhaps his struggles with learning disabilities have helped him to develop the patience and tenacity that resulted in his success. He emphasizes, "I don't accept children dying."
>
> See *Reader's Digest,* February 1993, pp. 192-228.

What Are Learning Disabilities?

1. When a student reaches the point of _____ _____, they refuse to risk failure in order to safeguard their fragile self-esteem. (See What Are Learning Disabilities?)
2. The definition adopted by the National Joint Committee on Learning Disabilities (NJCLD) differs from IDEA's definition. Fill in the blanks in the chart to compare and contrast the IDEA and NJCLD definitions. (See What Are Learning Disabilities?; Defining Learning Disabilities)

Definition	*IDEA*	*NJCLD*
Perceived cause		
Areas affected		
Inclusionary criterion		
Exclusionary criterion		
Need criterion		

3. Most states and local school districts require that students with learning disabilities be identified by a severe discrepancy between _____ and _____. (See What Are Learning Disabilities?; Defining Learning Disabilities; Classification Criteria)
4. Name and describe the three criteria required to receive the learning disabilities classification. (See What Are Learning Disabilities?; Defining Learning Disabilities; Classification Criteria)
    a. Criterion: _____
       Description:_____
    b. Criterion: _____
       Description:_____
    c. Criterion: _____
       Description:_____

5. No matter what characteristics manifest, students with learning disabilities often face challenges related to _____, _____, and _____ _____. (See What Are Learning Disabilities? Describing the Characteristics)

Collective Perspectives on Issues Affecting Learning Disabilities (Pro-Ed, 8700 Shoal Creek Boulevard, Austin, TX 78757, 512-451-3246) contains brief position statements on a variety of topics by the National Joint Committee on Learning Disabilities (NJCLD). This relatively inexpensive book would be an excellent addition to your library.

---

6. Describe identifying characteristics for each of the five categories of learning disabilities. (See What Are Learning Disabilities?; Describing the Characteristics)

Category of Learning Disability	Identifying Characteristics
Reading	
Written language	
Mathematics	
Memory	
Metacognition	

7. Dyslexic characteristics are a subgroup of reading disability characteristics that represent a developmental _____ _____.
   Recent research suggests that dyslexia may stem from difficulty in _____ _____. (See What Are Learning Disabilities?; Describing the Characteristics; Reading)

8. Students with learning disabilities in mathematics may also have difficulties with _____. (See What Are Learning Disabilities?; Describing the Characteristics; Mathematics)

9. Rank order five different types of learning styles according to how you personally learn. Put a number one next to your strongest learning style. (See What Are Learning Disabilities?; Identifying the Causes of Learning Disabilities; Neurological Causes)
   a. _____
   b. _____
   c. _____
   d. _____
   e. _____

You may have heard of controversial treatments or methods for assisting students with learning disabilities, such as vision training, megavitamin therapy, the Feingold diet, Irlen (colored) lenses (also referred to as scotopic lenses), or chiropractic manipulation. The research on these approaches is inconclusive, at best. It is important to note that megavitamin therapy can actually be dangerous to a student's health.

---

10. As a result of research involving brain-mapping, three types of problems in how language is processed have been identified. List these three types of problems. (See What Are Learning Disabilities?; Identifying the Causes of Learning Disabilities; Neurological Causes)

    a. _____

    b. _____

    c. _____

11. Research studies, especially those involving twins, indicates that almost _____% of reading disabilities are caused by genetic factors. (See What Are Learning Disabilities?; Identifying the Causes of Learning Disabilities; Genetic Causes)

12. Students with learning disabilities represent close to _____% of all students served in special education. Between 1977 and 1995, the percentage of students identified as having learning disabilities increased from 1.8% to _____ of total public K-12 enrollment. Based on those figures, it is probable that at least _____students in every class of 30 students will be identified as having a learning disability. (See What Are Learning Disabilities?; Identifying the Prevalence of Learning Disabilities)

What Are Evaluation Procedures?

13. In the field of learning disabilities, what is the most common intelligence test used to identify learning disabilities? _____. This test is often used concurrently with the _____ Test which measures student _____. (What Are Evaluation Procedures?; Determining the Presence of a Learning Disability)

14. What are three types of discrepancies that are used in various states to identify learning disabilities? Name and describe each one. (What Are Evaluation Procedures?; Determining the Presence of a Learning Disability)

    a. _____

    b. _____

    c. _____

15. What three things must be taken into account when developing curriculum-based assessment? (What Are Evaluation Procedures?; Determining the Nature and Extent of Special Education and Related Services; Curriculum-Based Assessment)

    a. _____

    b. _____

    c. _____

16. What is one of the most important components of the IEP process for students with learning disabilities? (What Are Evaluation Procedures?; Determining the Nature and Extent of Special Education and Related Services; Developing the IEP)

    _____

Making Sense of What's in Print

You can find many articles about learning disabilities in the popular press and on the Internet. How do you decide whether these articles accurately portray learning disabilities? Joan Rankin and Susan Phillips, in their article "Learning Disabilities in the Popular Press: Suggestions for Educators," emphasize that there are several questions you should ask while you read: What is the major focus or intent of the article? What is the author's perspective (e.g., medical/neurological, educational/instructive, telling a story about a real or fictitious person with learning disabilities, trying to get you to buy a product)? What are the author's qualifications? Is the information supported by research or expert opinion? How are *learning disability* and other terms defined by the author? Are parental rights addressed? Does the article provide advice? If so, what are the recommendations? You can ask these questions as you read about other exceptionalities besides learning disabilities.

See *Teaching Exceptional Children,* Spring 1995, pp. 35-39.

What and How Do Professionals Teach?

17. Many approaches to curriculum and methods for students with learning disabilities have been tried over time. Describe two approaches no longer in use and then name and describe the style of teaching used in many curricula today. (See What and How Do Professionals Teach?; Historical Approaches)

    a. _____

    b. _____

    c. _____

    _____

18. Describe one way to help students achieve phonological awareness. (See What and How Do Professionals Teach?; Curriculum; Reading)

    _____

    _____

    _____

19. Describe methods for teaching students with learning disabilities more effectively in reading, written language, mathematics, and academic clubs. (See What and How Do Professionals Teach?; Curriculum)

Curricular Area	Effective Teaching Approaches
Reading	
Written Language	
Mathematics	
Academic Clubs (general content areas)	

20. Name and describe examples of three academic tasks for instruction in learning strategies. (See What and How Do Professionals Teach?; Methods; Learning Strategies)

    a. Strategy: _____

       Examples:_____

    b. Strategy:_____

       Examples:_____

    c. Strategy:_____

       Examples:_____

21. Describe some classroom adaptations useful in an inclusionary setting for students with learning disabilities. (See What and How Do Professionals Teach?; Methods; Overcoming Learned Helplessness)

    _____

    _____

    _____

22. What are some advantages of using computers for students with learning disabilities? (See What and How Do Professionals Teach?; Methods; Computer Technology)

    _____

    _____

    _____

How Is Participation Encouraged?

23. What is the most common placement for students with learning disabilities? (See How Is Participation Encouraged?; Inclusion)

    _____

24. Describe the major components of the successful collaboration Project CLASP. (See How Is Participation Encouraged?; Collaboration; Collaboration with Professionals)

    a. _____

    b. _____

    c. _____

    d. _____

    e. _____

25. Two factors that ensure continuous improvement in general/special educator teams are

_____ and

_____.

(See How Is Participation Encouraged?; Collaboration; Collaboration with Professionals)

26. Describe components and benefits for classwide peer tutoring. (See How Is Participation Encouraged?; Collaboration; Collaboration with Peers)

    a. Components: _____

_____

    b. Benefits: _____

_____

27. Collaboration with family can be especially effective for homework. What are four ways to make homework easier for students with learning disabilities and their families? (See How Is Participation Encouraged?; Collaboration; Collaboration with Peers)

    a. _____

    b. _____

    c. _____

    d. _____

28. What career works to provide instruction and encouragement for students with learning disabilities? (See How Is Participation Encouraged?; Careers)

_____

What Are Program Options?

Freebies

The HEALTH Resource Center, a national clearinghouse on postsecondary education for individuals with disabilities, offers free booklets on numerous topics. A few of their many titles include "Focus on College Admissions Tests," "Young Adlts with Learning Disabilities an d Other Special Needs: Guide for Selecting Postsecondary Transition Programs," "Technology and Learning Disabilities," and "National Resources for Adults with Learning Disabilities." Their address is One Dupont Circle, Suite 800, Washington, DC 20036. Their phone number is 800/544-3284.

---

29. Over _____% of students with learning disabilities do not complete high school compared to _____% of the general school population. (See What Are Program Options?)

30. List key features for each of the following programs for students with learning disabilities. (See What Are Program Options?)

Program	Key Features
The Language Acquisition Preschool	
Language! Program: J.F. Greene	
Service Learning	
Landmark College, Putney, Vermont	

Don't Waste Your Time

When Janice Anderson Connolly entered her Period 7 class on her first day of teaching, she knew she was in for a challenge. One of the students commented, "Lady, don't waste your time. We're the retards."

She later learned that most of the students were children of migrant workers. Their attendance and motivation were poor, and no one expected them to graduate from high school. Janice decided that she wouldn't give up on them as others had. She went to the board the next day and wrote "ECINAJ" and told them that was her first name. After a few comments about her weird name, she wrote "JANICE" on the board. She explained to them that she had a learning disability and couldn't write her own name when she began school. Janice also told them that she couldn't spell words or do math. "That's right. I was a 'retard'. I can still hear those awful voices and feel the shame."

Her understanding of their dilemma reached the kids. She maintained high expectations for them and helped them to discover that they could learn and learn well. Two years later, all 14 of her Period 7 students graduated, and six received college scholarships.

See "The First Year of Teaching: Real World Stories from America's Teachers," 1992, *Mentor*, pp. 26-31.

APPLICATION EXERCISES FOR CHAPTER 4

Application Exercise 4a. Identifying Characteristics of Learning Disabilities

See if you can tell by the description provided which characteristic of learning disabilities each of the following students demonstrates.

1. Shayla thinks that when Andrew says "Yeah, right" in a sarcastic manner, he means that he agrees with what she is saying.
   _____

2. Nigel refuses to try whenever his teacher tries to show him how to add with regrouping.
   _____

3. Mina often forgets her homework.
   _____

4. Miguel doesn't know how to study for a test.
   _____

5. Ingrid doesn't seem to be able to concentrate on her work.
   _____

6. Tobias interrupts when others are talking.
   _____

7. Pei-lin is good in math but performs below grade level in reading.
   _____

Application Exercise 4b. Determining Eligibility Based on Severe Discrepancy

You have read that when schools determine a severe discrepancy, they typically compare the discrepancy between a student's IQ and achievement scores. A particular state uses a one-and-one-half standard deviation discrepancy between full-scale IQ and achievement to determine learning disabilities (23 points). In which subject areas does each student qualify for services in that state?

	Full-scale IQ	Reading	Mathematics	Written Language
Jose	116	92	99	101
Chanpen	103	100	86	81
Julie	123	100	96	89

Application Exercise 4c. Metacognitive Learning Strategies

Based upon the five major questions* addressed in this chapter, use a different metacognitive strategy to summarize the major concepts concerning learning difficulties. For each major chapter question, describe the strategy you used to learn the concepts of this section.

*Five Major Questions: What Are Learning Disabilities? What Are Evaluation Procedures? What and How Do Professionals Teach? How Is Participation Encouraged? What Are Program Options?

ANSWERS TO CHAPTER 4 MARGIN QUESTIONS

Page 124   If students could qualify on the basis of problems with social skills, many students without an achievement/academic discrepancy could qualify. Thus, many students who did not meet the federal definition would be eligible, and the prevalence would mushroom.

Page 155   Classwide peer tutoring could be used on a daily basis to help students learn terminology and review key concepts. Students could also be paired for research projects.

SAMPLE QUIZ FOR CHAPTER 4

Circle the correct answer.

TRUE OR FALSE

T or F   1.   A student must meet at least two out of three criteria to receive the learning disabilities classification.

T or F   2.   Students with learning disabilities share typical profiles.

T or F   3.   The percentage of students identified as having learning disabilities is about 6% of total public K-12 enrollment.

T or F   4.   Brain-mapping research indicates that a relationship exists between learning disabilities and abnormalities in the language-processing parts of the brain.

T or F   5.   According to the Council for Learning Disabilities, the use of discrepancy formulae in comparing IQ and achievement tests should be discontinued.

MULTIPLE CHOICE

6.   What kind of challenges do students with learning disabilities often face?

    a. Learning, social skills, and behavior

    b. Learning, physical disabilities, and limited language proficiency

    c. Learning, attitude, and aggression

    d. Learning, aggression, and poverty

7.   Jaime has dyslexia. In school, what difficulties will he most likely face?

    a. Poor concentration during story time

    b. Difficulties in word recognition, reading comprehension, and spelling

    c. Difficulties in motor skills and metacognition

    d. Poor handwriting and memory

8.   Among the students served in special education, what is the percentage of those with learning disabilities?

    a. 15%

    b. 30%

    c. 50%

    d. 65%

9.   Whose work with central nervous system dysfunction laid the foundation for the field of learning disabilities?

    a. Samuel Kirk

    b. Evelyn Deno

    c. Lloyd Dunn

    d. James Hinshelwood

10.   What is a benefit of concurrently using the Wechsler tests for intelligence and achievement?

    a. Both tests had the same original norm group, thus simplifying the comparison of a student's IQ and achievement scores.

    b. When ordered together, a purchase discount is available.

    c. All states use these basic tests, thus facilitating student transfers to other districts.

    d. Severe discrepancies tend to be lessened in scores, which clarifies the criteria for standard deviations.

11. Which of the following is <u>not</u> typically reviewed by the evaluation team during a reevaluation of a student with learning disabilities?
    a. Portfolio assessment
    b. Ecological assessment
    c. Behavior rating scale
    d. Neurological causes

12. Meg is developing a criterion-referenced curriculum-based assessment instrument. Which of the following will <u>not</u> be necessary for her to consider?
    a. The time limit and level of mastery are reasonable.
    b. The test items directly reflect the objectives emphasized in the curriculum.
    c. The norm group is composed of a representative group of students from the district.
    d. The items are clearly stated.

13. What did research show about students who received perceptual motor training?
    a. They did not improve their ability to deal with academic material.
    b. They did not improve their skills on processing tests.
    c. They minimized their dyslexia and generally improved their grades.
    d. They showed fewer signs of mixed dominance.

14. What causes the downward spiral once students experience learned helplessness?
    a. Lack of instruction or misidentification of disabilities
    b. Peer ostracism
    c. Lowered self-esteem and achievement
    d. Parental neglect and/or scolding

15. Which of the following is <u>not</u> mentioned as a benefit of peer tutoring?
    a. Mastering skills
    b. Gaining confidence
    c. Lessening teacher workload
    d. Increasing socialization

SHORT ANSWER

16. How does a learning disability differ from mental retardation?
    _____
    _____

17. What are the three criteria most states use to identify students as having learning disabilities?
    a. _____
    b. _____
    c. _____

18. List some of the areas of difficulty a student with dyscalculia might have.
    _____
    _____

ESSAY

19. What are four types of reading difficulties mentioned in the chapter, and state appropriate interventions for each one?

20. Give suggestions for encouraging a discouraged student in mathematics.

CHAPTER 5: EMOTIONAL OR BEHAVIORAL DISORDERS

CHAPTER OVERVIEW

This chapter examines two of the many and varied definitions associated with emotional and behavioral disorders. It also examines both emotional and behavioral characteristics of students, with a discussion of how to distinguish between externalizing and internalizing behavior patterns. Both biological and environmental causes are examined and explored. Evaluation procedures focus on direct observations with applied behavior analysis and contingency contracts. Concentration in this chapter is on restoring hope, setting limits, and encouraging a productive self-concept and personal wellness. Productive ways to include and collaborate on behalf of students with emotional or behavioral disorders are discussed, with a particular focus on peer mediation. Four program options that successfully help students with emotional or behavioral disorders to overcome difficulties and lead productive lives are presented.

The life of thirteen-year-old Jennifer Shulman demonstrates the challenges and joys of working with students with emotional or behavioral disorders. Since early childhood, Jen has experienced many of the externalizing and internalizing behaviors that characterize students with emotional or behavioral disorders. After she took an overdose of a prescribed medication, she and her family began to receive intensive services from her wraparound team in Chicago. The chapter emphasizes the importance of this type of collaborative approach to meet the needs of students with emotional or behavioral disorders.

CHAPTER AT-A-GLANCE

Chapter Outline	Instructional Goals	Key Concepts
WHAT ARE EMOTIONAL OR BEHAVIORAL DISORDERS?		
Defining Emotional or Behavioral Disorders	• Identify key components among models for defining emotional or behavioral disorders	• Students with emotional or behavioral disorders are those whose behavior and adjustment problems are chronic, severe, and adversely affect their lives. • Numerous definitions of emotional or behavioral disorders have been proposed over the years, but no single definition is universally embraced.
Describing the Characteristics • Emotional Characteristics • Behavioral Characteristics • Academic Characteristics	• Describe key characteristics of emotional or behavioral disorders	• Students may exhibit emotional disorders, including, but not limited to, anxiety disorder, major depression, bipolar disorder, oppositional-defiant disorder, conduct disorder, eating disorders, or schizophrenia. • There are two broad categories of behavioral disorders: externalizing (aggressive, acting-out, antisocial behaviors) and internalizing (withdrawn, fearful, anxious, depressed, or lacking in social competence). • Most students with emotional or behavioral disorders have academic problems.
Identifying the Causes of Emotional or Behavioral Disorders • Biological • Environmental	• Explain differences between biological and environmental causes of emotional or behavioral disorders	• Biological causes include genetics and biological insults. • Environmental causes include living conditions and child abuse. • There is rarely one determining factor.
Identifying the Prevalence of Emotional or Behavioral Disorders	• Examine prevalence rates overall as well as within special education	• Prevalence estimates vary considerably from 3% to 5%. However, only about 1% are identified. • Emotional or behavioral disorders is the fourth largest category in special education.

WHAT ARE EVALUATION PROCEDURES?		
Determining the Presence of Emotional or Behavioral Disorders	• Identify specific tools useful for determining emotional and behavioral disorders	• A checklist of internalizing and externalizing behaviors can be useful for teachers.
Determining the Nature and Extent of Special Education and Related Services	• Understand how to use direct observations and applied behavior analysis to help educate students with emotional or behavioral disorders	• Direct observations of student behavior along with applied behavior analysis and contingency contracts allow professionals to monitor student performance toward achieving specific objectives.
WHAT AND HOW DO PROFESSIONALS TEACH?		
Curriculum	• Analyze key components of curriculum that lead to success for students with emotional or behavioral disorders	• Curriculum needs to reflect the interests of students and guarantee success initially. • The PATH curriculum teaches students respect and responsibility through three phases: emotional recognition and communication, self-control, and social problem solving.
Methods • Restoring Hope • Setting Limits • Encouraging a Productive Self-Concept • Personal Wellness	• Recognize important characteristics of methods that help students change	• Restoring hope, encouraging a productive self-concept, setting limits, listening, and taking care of oneself are important methods for helping students change.
HOW IS PARTICIPATION ENCOURAGED?		
Inclusion	• Summarize issues affecting the inclusion of students with emotional or behavioral disorders	• There are differing perspectives on the most appropriate place to educate these students. • Once identified as having emotional or behavioral disorders, most students are educated in self-contained classes.
Collaboration • Professional Collaboration • Family Collaboration • Community Collaboration • Peer Collaboration	• Examine ways to collaborate on behalf of students with emotional or behavioral disorders	• Many students with emotional or behavioral disorders require multiple services that involve several disciplines, including education, mental health, public welfare, and the juvenile justice system. • Peer mediation involves the voluntary resolution of differences between peers in the presence of trained peer mediators.
Careers	• Identify careers available that work with students with emotional or behavioral disorders	• Career options include classroom teachers, counselor, therapist, behavior specialist, social worker, psychologist, or psychiatrist.
WHAT ARE PROGRAM OPTIONS?		
Early Intervention and Preschool Years	• Describe characteristics of effective preschool programs	• The Parents as Teachers program helps the parents use the skills they already have by providing support and helping them uncover answers to their questions.
Elementary Years • Parent Partners • The Buddy Program	• Describe characteristics of effective elementary school programs	• LASDE's WRAP project is an innovative inclusion program whose goal is to keep students in their community schools and keep their families together by "wrapping" needed services around them.

Middle and Secondary Years	• Describe characteristics of effective programs for middle and secondary students	• The creative and flexible use of available personnel has been effective in meeting the needs of students with serious behavior problems in inclusive secondary settings.
Transitional and Postsecondary Years	• Describe characteristics of effective program options for adults	• Jobs Design helps young adults through a systematic action approach to meeting individual needs.

PROJECT OPTIONS

1. Interview a school counselor to ascertain (a) how many students with emotional or behavioral problems have a record of juvenile delinquency, (b) how delinquency has been handled in the school, and (c) what the philosophy of the school counselor is for these students. Based on observation after permission is obtained from the school and parents, select two students and classify the type of behavior problems they have experienced. Then, based on what you have learned in this chapter, plan additional ways to help these students.

2. Find a cooperating teacher who will allow you to observe that class and do direct observations on a student. Then develop a contingency contract for the student and teacher to use.

3. Research discipline methods that have been proven effective in all classrooms. Evaluate these methods and prioritize them for students with emotional and behavioral disorders.

4. Write a short drama about a student with an emotional or behavioral disorder. Create three different endings based on different methods to help students overcome their difficulties.

KEY TERMS

Anxiety disorder

Attachment disorder

Behavioral earthquakes

Bipolar disorder

Conduct disorder

Contingency contract

Direct observation

Eating disorders

Emotional or behavioral disorder

Externalizing behavior

Internalizing behavior

Major depression

Natural or logical consequence

Oppositional-defiant disorder

Projective test

Schizophrenia

Social maladjustment

CHAPTER 5 GUIDED REVIEW

Animals Teach Kids to Care

At Green Chimneys, students with severe emotional and behavioral disorders who have been referred by psychiatric hospitals treat injured and orphaned wildlife and care for farm animals. The students relate to the fact that most of the animals have been abused and feel unwanted. Dr. Samuel Ross, founder and director of Green Chimneys, explains that if a child who has been poorly nurtured himself can learn to nurture an animal, it becomes easier for him to relate to peers and adults. "Trust is established, and the child risks the human connection. The goodness of the child is unleashed."

See *People Weekly*, October 31, 1994, pp. 121-123.

What Are Emotional or Behavioral Disorders?

1. IDEA defines "emotionally disturbed" in two ways. Fill in the missing information that helps clarify the many facets of this disorder. (See Defining Emotional or Behavioral Disorders)

    a. The term means a condition exhibiting one or more of the following characteristics over a long time and to a marked degree that adversely affects a student's educational performance:

    _____

    _____

    _____

    _____

    _____

    b. The term includes schizophrenia. The term does not apply to students who are

    _____   _____, unless it is

    determined that they have an emotional disturbance.

2. IDEA limits what schools may do by way of disciplining students with disabilities. Summarize the two major rules concerning discipline procedures. (See Defining Emotional or Behavioral Disorders)

    a. _____

    _____

    b. _____

    _____

Socially Maladjusted

Are we making a serious error by not providing special education and related services for students who are socially maladjusted? One evening in the fall of 1993 in Indianapolis, the Ghetto Boys, a drug-trafficking gang, opened fire outside the Blackburn Terrace housing project. The intended target was uninjured. Instead, a 16-year-old girl was killed and a 7-year-old boy who was watching Monday night football was critically wounded. In another gang-related incident, a 14-year-old girl was shot by an 11-year-old boy. His fellow gang members later killed him to prevent the possibility that he might implicate them to the police.

Children are dying at the hands of other children for not giving "props" (proper respect). According to one reporter, many children are living in "an ecology of terror."

You can read more about gang-related violence in the following articles: *Time*, September 12, 1994, p. 44; *Time*, September 19, 1994, pp. 55-63; *U.S. News & World Report*, January 17, 1994, pp. 22-33.

---

3. Identify the main points of the definition for emotional or behavioral disorders that is preferred by the Mental Health and Special Education Coalition (MHSEC). (See Defining Emotional or Behavioral Disorders)

    a. _____

    _____

    _____

b. _____
_____

c. _____
_____

4. The primary difference between IDEA's and MHSEC's definitions is that IDEA's definition does not include students with _____ _____; while the MHSEC definition does include them. (See Defining Emotional or Behavioral Disorders)

5. Describe emotional characteristics that lead to students being identified as having emotional or behavioral disorders. (See Describing the Characteristics; Emotional Characteristics)

	Key Word Descriptors	*Indicators/ Symptoms*
Anxiety disorder		
Major depression		
Bipolar disorder		
Oppositional-defiant disorder		
Conduct disorder		
Eating disorders		
Schizophrenia		

6. What percentage of young people are affected by anxiety disorders, the most common childhood disorder? (See Describing the Characteristics; Emotional Characteristics)
_____% to _____%

Helping Students Who Are Depressed

We highly recommend that you get a copy of the paperback book *Understanding Your Teenager's Depression* by Kathleen McCoy (Perigee, 1994). The book will show you how to recognize troubled teenagers and provides guidelines for helping them. One of the facts about teenagers who are depressed that McCoy emphasizes is that they often act out and exhibit risk-taking behaviors rather than demonstrating the typical internalizing behaviors so commonly associated with depression. Furthermore, if a student demonstrates any kind of change in behavior from what is typical for her, you will want to watch her closely for other signs of depression or possible suicidal behaviors.

Remember, if you suspect a student might be suicidal, ask him directly. If he is not thinking about suicide, he will tell you no. However, if he is considering suicide, he will probably be relieved that you cared enough to ask. Also ask if he has a plan. If he does, then it is important to get him therapeutic help immediately.

---

7. Externalizing and internalizing behaviors are two broad categories of behavioral disorders. Externalizing behaviors are characterized by _____

_____

Internalizing behaviors are characterized by _____

_____

(See Describing the Characteristics; Behavioral Characteristics)

8. Would you describe each of these students as demonstrating internalizing or externalizing behaviors? If they are externalizing, are they overt or covert? (See Describing the Characteristics; Behavioral Characteristics)

Behavior	Internalizing/Externalizing	Overt/Covert
a. Sondra pouts when she is asked to do her work.		
b. Janika shoves students as she changes classes.		
c. Matilda daydreams a lot and seems to be lost in another world.		
d. Habb isolates himself in the back of the room during group activities.		
e. Eric tells you to "shove it" whenever you give him an assignment.		

9. Fire setting, sleep disturbances, self-abuse, and depression are examples of behavioral _____. (See Describing the Characteristics; Behavioral Characteristics)

10. What type of academic performance would you expect from a student identified as having emotional or behavioral disorders? Why? _____
_____ (See Describing the Characteristics; Academic Characteristics)

11. The graduation rate for students with emotional or behavioral disorders is _____%, while the rate for students without disabilities is _____% and students with disabilities is _____% (See Describing the Characteristics; Academic Characteristics)

12. Some examples of biological causes include _____
_____. (See Identifying the Causes of Emotional or Behavioral Disorders; Biological Causes)

13. As an educator, you will want to be familiar with medications students with emotional or behavioral disorders take. List five things you should find out from parents about the student's medication. (See Identifying the Causes of Emotional or Behavioral Disorders; Biological Causes)

a. _____

b. _____

c. _____

d. _____

e. _____

A Child Called "It"

David Peltzer has written powerful books about the horrible physical and emotional abuse he suffered as a child. A caring substitute teacher recognized his pain and initiated procedures to have Dave removed from his home. Although he developed emotional and behavioral disorders from the abuse, he eventually overcame them. Dave has received commendations from Presidents Reagan, Bush, and Clinton. He was also the only American who received the prestigious Outstanding Young Person of the World award in 1994. If you have not read his books, we recommend that you do so. The titles are *A Child Called "It": An Abused Child's Journey from Victim to Victor* (Health Communications, 1995) and *The Lost Boy: A Foster Child's Search for the Love of a Family* (Health Communications, 1997). The third book in the series, *A Man Called Dave*, might be published by the time you read this.

---

14. Name and describe three factors that can trigger emotional or behavioral disorders. (See Identifying the Causes of Emotional or Behavioral Disorders; Environmental Factors)

    a. _____

    b. _____

    c. _____

15. Prevalence estimates vary considerably for this population, varying from _____% to _____% of all children. However, only _____ % of all school-age students receive services, even though this is the _____-largest category of students receiving special education services. (See Identifying the Prevalence of Emotional or Behavioral Disorders)

What Are Evaluation Procedures?

16. What are some tools used to determine the presence of emotional or behavioral disorders? (See Determining the Presence of Emotional or Behavioral Disorders)

    a. During prereferral or referral:_____

    b. During the nondiscriminatory evaluation process:

       _____

       _____

17. Direct observation involves _____ and _____ , the specific behaviors of a student for a specified time while students are engaged in a specific activity. Name and describe the five observable and measurable dimensions of behavior recorded during direct observations. (See Determining the Nature and Extent of Special Education and Related Services; Direct Observation)

    a. _____

    b. _____

    c. _____

    d. _____

    e. _____

18. Explain how applied behavior analysis works, including the role of a contingency contract. (See Determining the Nature and Extent of Special Education and Related Services; Direct Observation)

    _____

    _____

    _____

    _____

What and How Do Professionals Teach?

19. List benefits resulting from incorporating students' personal interests into curriculum assignments. (See What and How Do Professionals Teach?; Curriculum)

    a. _____

    b. _____

    c. _____

20. Name the focus and then describe the three successful phases of the PATHS curriculum for helping students with inappropriate behaviors and social skills. (See What and How Do Professionals Teach?; Curriculum)

	Focus	Description
Phase 1		
Phase 2		
Phase 3		

21. Identify the most important characteristics of the four methods discussed in this chapter for working with students who have emotional or behavioral disorders. (See What and How Do Professionals Teach?; Curriculum)

Method/ Strategy	Characteristics
Restoring Hope	
Setting Limits	
Encouraging a Productive Self-Concept	
Personal Wellness	

22. Empowerment helps students _____
    _____. (See What and How Do Professionals Teach?; Methods; Setting Limits)

23. Provide 5 ways to make your classroom rules more meaningful. (See What and How Do Professionals Teach?; Methods; Setting Limits)
    a. _____
    b. _____
    c. _____
    d. _____
    e. _____

24. Explain how to use natural or logical consequences to help students learn from experiences rather than receiving detention or losing points. (See What and How Do Professionals Teach?; Methods; Encouraging a Productive Self-Concept)
    _____
    _____

How Is Participation Encouraged?

25. Why doesn't the CCBD support inclusion for students with emotional or behavioral disorders? (See How Is Participation Encouraged?; Inclusion)
    _____
    _____

26. Rank order the educational placements of students with serious emotional disturbances, from (a) largest to (e) smallest percentages: Resource room, separate school, residential facility, homebound/hospital, regular class. (See How Is Participation Encouraged?; Inclusion)

a. _____ d. _____

b. _____ e. _____

c. _____

27. Using the chapter's text, figures, and boxes, identify ways different people are collaborating on behalf of students with emotional or behavioral disorders. (See How Is Participation Encouraged?; Collaboration)

_____

_____

The Compassionate School
How can schools work with students and families when abuse is involved? In her book *The Compassionate School: A Practical Guide to Educating Abused and Traumatized Children*, Gertrude Morrow offers some effective practices. She includes tested procedures for detecting and reporting child abuse, along with suggestions for helping students in the classroom. The book also discusses how to help depressed or suicidal students.

Collaborator	Strategies, Guidelines, and Approaches
Professional	
Family	
Community	
Peer	

28. Peer mediation reduces _____ _____, _____, and _____ _____. (See How Is Participation Encouraged?; Collaboration; Peer Collaboration)

29. Name six career options for working with students who have emotional or behavioral disorders. (See How Is Participation Encouraged?; Careers)

a. _____ d. _____

b. _____ e. _____

c. _____ f. _____

What Are Program Options?

30. Describe important characteristics of how the wraparound process works in schools. (See What Are Program Options?; Elementary Years)

_____

_____

31. More students with emotional disabilities _____,
_____, and _____ than students
with other disabilities. (See What Are Program Options?; Transitional and Postsecondary Years)

32. Summarize key features for each of the following programs. (See What Are Program Options?)

Program	*Key Features*
Parents as Teachers	
LASDE's WRAP project	
Inclusive Secondary Settings	
Jobs Design	

Therapeutic Teachers

What makes a therapeutic teacher? According to Brian Abrams and Amiel Segal (1998), such a teacher has several identifiable characteristics. The first is good mental health. Therapeutic teachers also communicate caring, respect, and confidence in themselves and others. They exhibit and model self-control and stress-coping skills, with an ability to de-escalate tension in a classroom. By establishing trust and rapport with students, therapeutic teachers can tell when students are frustrated or experiencing anxiety. They also identify and respect student's needs, values, interests, and talents. Therapeutic teachers protect their students' dignity and do not resort to threats or confrontations. Instead, they create a positive classroom climate and display enthusiasm and positive expectations. How do you measure up?

See "How to Prevent Aggressive Behavior" in *Teaching Exceptional Children, 30*(4), 10-15.

APPLICATION EXERCISES FOR CHAPTER 5

Application Exercise 5a. Identifying Emotional Characteristics

Match the name of the disorder with the student's symptoms.

1. Anxiety disorder	a. _____ Jonee seems like a content child on some days, always talking with anyone who will listen. On others she withdraws and appears unhappy and morose.
2. Major depression	b. _____ Sita can't go to sleep at night unless she says the alphabet forward and backward. She also holds her breath for ten seconds between each bite of food she eats.
3. Bipolar disorder	c. _____ Jaime can never admit someone else is right. His insistence on being right often leads to violent outbursts of swearing and angry accusations.
4. Oppositional-defiant disorder	d. _____ Rochelle binges on large amounts of chocolate and sweets and then later vomits the food. She denies taking or eating the food and tries to cover for her cravings.
5. Conduct disorder	e. _____ Tomas experiences a rapid heartbeat and dizziness associated with unpleasant situations.
6. Eating disorders	f. _____ Jonathan sleeps whenever he has a chance. When he's awake, he's convinced he's ugly and worthless. He often cries for long periods.

7. Schizophrenia	g. _____ Anita feels as though she does not receive the attention she needs. Recently, when others weren't looking, she started small fires in trash cans. She also steals food from other's lunches.
	h. _____ Lois feels hopeless no matter what she does. She has once attempted suicide, but was unsuccessful.
	i. _____ Ragy is unable to experience pleasure and spends large amounts of time daydreaming. During this time, hallucinations are common.

Application Exercise 5b. Identifying Types of Observations

Identify which of the five types of observations is being demonstrated in the following examples. Types include: frequency, magnitude, duration, latency, and topography.

1. Mr. Singh measures how long it takes Diane to begin her work after he asks her to do so.

    Type of Observation: _____

2. Ms. Mitias measures how many times Maria talks during a class period.

    Type of Observation: _____

3. Mrs. Norris uses a rating scale to determine the severity of Garland's acting out behaviors.

    Type of Observation: _____

4. Mr. Martin measures how long Jill is out of her seat.

    Type of Observation: _____

5. Miss Eaglesfly records specific responses that Amelia gives when students greet her and then decides whether they were appropriate or inappropriate.

    Type of Observation: _____

Application Exercise 5c. A Collaborator's View of Emotional or Behavioral Disorders

Explain how a specific collaborator might answer each of the five major questions* addressed in this chapter. Summarize each of the major concepts through the eyes of your selected collaborator.

*Five Major Questions: What are emotional or behavioral disorders? What are evaluation procedures? What and how do professionals teach? How is participation encouraged? What are program options?

ANSWERS TO MARGIN QUESTIONS

All margin notes provided information or asked reflective questions rather than asking questions needing answers.

SAMPLE QUIZ FOR CHAPTER 5

Circle the correct answer.

TRUE OR FALSE

T or F　1.　The IDEA definition of emotionally disturbed excludes students with social maladjustment, while the MHSEC definition includes it.

T or F　2.　Female teenagers are more likely than males to commit suicide.

T or F　3.　Students with externalizing behaviors are generally rated unfavorably on both peer-related and teacher-related adjustments.

T or F　4.　The Children's Defense Fund claims that two-thirds of the students who need services for emotional and behavioral disorders are not receiving help.

T or F　5.　The ultimate goal of a point system is to help students achieve appropriate behavior in order to win a reward or privilege.

MULTIPLE CHOICE

6.　To what does DSM-IV refer?

    a.　Diagnostic and Statistical Manual of Mental Disorders

    b.　Direct Supervisory Measures for Mental Health, Major Behavior Disorders, and Maladjustment

    c.　Disorders related to Schizophrenia and Mental Health (four major categories)

    d.　Handbook on Defiance, Suicide and Major Depression

7.　Which of the following is <u>not</u> considered an anxiety disorder?

    a.　Phobia

    b.　Obsessive-compulsive disorder

    c.　Post-traumatic stress disorder

    d.　Schizophrenia

8.　What percentage of young people are affected by anxiety disorder?

    a.　5-6%

    b.　8-10%

    c.　12-15%

    d.　17-20%

9.　Jenna, one of your high school students, seems increasingly unhappy and withdrawn. She has just told you "My parents would be better off without me." What do the authors suggest?

    a.　Promise her that she can confide in you and that you will keep everything she says confidential.

    b.　Act as her therapist, since she has no money and no one to help.

    c.　Tell her that you care and that she should not consider suicide an option, since it is selfish and would make everyone feel sad.

    d.　Remind her that she will probably feel better next week and that you are available to listen.

10.　What is the graduation rate for students with emotional or behavioral disorders?

    a.　About 20%

    b.　About 35%

    c.　About 55%

    d.　About 70%

11.　Which of the following children is most likely to be overlooked in prereferral for services?

    a.　Paige, a girl who has a history of substance abuse

    b.　Caitlin, who is anorectic

    c.　Masud, an African-American boy

    d.　Ramiro, who causes no problems but is withdrawn

12. What does research indicate will improve the conduct and engagement of students with emotional or behavioral disorders?
    a. Incorporating personal interests into curriculum assignments
    b. Substituting community-wide activities on campus instead of school dances and other dating events
    c. Bringing sports heroes to school assemblies for motivational talks
    d. Mandating community work assignments for students who have been suspended

13. Danielle, one of your students who has an emotional disorder, is trying to hurt you by spreading a false rumor about you. What does Dreikurs suggest that you do?
    a. Tell Danielle that you care about her no matter what she says or does, but you will enforce consequences for her actions.
    b. Ignore the rumor and concentrate on making your class such an enjoyable place that the students will defend you.
    c. Discuss the situation with Danielle's IEP team and request her reassignment to another class.
    d. Advise the principal that the rumor is false and avoid the subject with Danielle so she can see that you cannot be hurt by her.

14. Which of the following has been shown to reduce drop-out rates, suspensions, and student assaults?
    a. Intensive counseling
    b. Community support
    c. Peer mediation
    d. Hospitalization followed by controlled medication

15. What does Alan Amtzis cite as an underlying root of substance abuse?
    a. The absence of a strong connection between self and environment
    b. Desire for money
    c. Poverty
    d. Inability to communicate effectively

SHORT ANSWER

16. Name the two major eating disorders and their characteristics.

    _____

    _____

17. Define *child abuse* and state what you should do if you suspect one of your students is being abused.

    _____

    _____

    _____

18. Identify three academic characteristics you may frequently see in students with emotional or behavioral disorders.
    a. _____
    b. _____
    c. _____

ESSAY

19. Discuss the difficulties associated with externalizing and internalizing behavior patterns and identify ways to handle these patterns in a classroom.

20. Explain the relationship between causes of emotional and behavioral disorders and specific characteristics.

CHAPTER 6: ATTENTION-DEFICIT/HYPERACTIVITY DISORDER

CHAPTER OVERVIEW

Attention-deficit/Hyperactivity disorder (AD/HD) has become a prominent disability in American education. This chapter examines the controversy over AD/HD and clarifies the different types and characteristics. An in-depth look at the causes is reported, with recent research findings that shed light on ways to best serve students with AD/HD. Several relevant evaluation procedures are presented and discussed. The importance of effective curriculum and methods is highlighted with successful examples. The role of inclusion and collaboration are explained with more examples of ways to seek the success of students with AD/HD. Key components of successful programs at four levels are presented as a means to further understand and apply ways to build on students' inherent strengths and abilities.

The life of fifth grader Taylor Wiggand, who has the combined type of AD/HD, which manifests characteristics of inattention and hyperactivity-impulsivity, helps demonstrate and clarify issues revolving around students who daily experience the challenges associated with AD/HD. Taylor comes from a large, supportive family, including foster children. As with many other students with AD/HD, he receives accommodations for his AD/HD in the general classroom and does not need special education or related services.

CHAPTER AT-A-GLANCE

Chapter Outline	Instructional Goals	Key Concepts
WHAT IS ATTENTION-DEFICIT/ HYPERACTIVITY DISORDER?		
Defining AD/HD Types of Attention-Deficit/Hyperactivity Disorder	• Examine different ways to define and identify students with AD/HD	• Students with AD/HD are served under the other health impairments category. • There are three types of AD/HD: Inattentive type, hyperactive-impulsive type, and the combined type.
Describing the Characteristics • Separating Facts from Feelings • Having a Sense of Past and Future • Using Self-Directed Speech • Breaking Apart and Recombining Information • Positive Traits Associated with AD/HD	• Describe key characteristics of students with AD/HD • Identify positive characteristics of students with AD/HD	• Students with AD/HD appear to experience a developmental delay of inhibition, which affects their ability to separate facts from feeling, use self-directed speech, and break apart and recombine information. • Students with AD/HD often demonstrate creativity and a sense of humor.
Identifying Causes of AD/HD • Environmental • Biological	• Compare and contrast environmental and biological causes of AD/HD	• Probable causes are more likely biological than environmental, and it is likely that more than one cause is responsible.
Identifying the Prevalence of AD/HD	• Provide prevalence figures for AD/HD today	• Prevalence estimates of AD/HD are 3% to 5% of the general population.
WHAT ARE EVALUATION PROCEDURES?		
Determining the Presence of AD/HD • Assessment Instruments for AD/HD • Cultural Issues in Diagnosis	• Compare different ways to determine the presence of AD/HD	• Diagnosis of AD/HD is often by a psychologist, psychiatrist, or physician. • Behavior rating scales designed for AD/HD and continuous performance tests are often used. • Some may falsely appear to have AD/HD to evaluators outside their culture.

Determining the Nature and Extent of Special Education and Related Services	• Recognize the ways students with AD/HD may receive appropriate services	• Students may receive an IEP, if needed, or they may receive a 504/ADA plan. Appropriate accommodations for skill deficits are included in each plan.
WHAT AND HOW DO PROFESSIONALS TEACH?		
Curriculum	• Identify characteristics of curriculum options that benefit students with AD/HD	• Students benefit from curriculum that incorporates relevance, novelty, variety, choices, and activity.
Methods • Medical Management • Education • Coaching • Counseling • Organizational Training • Behavior Management	• Evaluate how different methods are most effective for varied student needs	• A multimodal approach to intervention, which may include medication, behavior management, coaching, education, counseling, and/or organization training, is essential for students with AD/HD.
HOW IS PARTICIPATION ENCOURAGED?		
Inclusion	• Examine placement options where students with AD/HD are best served	• The general classroom is the appropriate placement for most students with AD/HD.
Collaboration • Collaboration with Other Professionals • Collaboration with Family • Collaboration with Peers	• Explore ways to collaborate on behalf of students with AD/HD	• Professional collaboration provides students with consistency to monitor the effects of medication. • Families need to learn positive and negative strategies to use to survive the Big Struggle. • Sometimes having only one close friend can make a positive difference for a student with AD/HD.
Careers	• Examine careers available that work with students with AD/HD	• General educators have an opportunity to make a positive contribution for students with AD/HD. • School psychologists or therapists also work with students who have AD/HD.
WHAT ARE PROGRAM OPTIONS?		
Early Intervention and Preschool Years	• Describe characteristics of effective preschool programs	• Early intervention needs to concentrate on family involvement.
Elementary Years	• Describe characteristics of effective elementary school programs	• Elementary students benefit from a multisensory, motivational program such as KanDoo.
Middle and Secondary Years	• Describe characteristics of effective programs for middle and secondary students	• Effective programs such as those at LeHigh concentrate on coordination of efforts for students across all teachers involved.
Transitional and Postsecondary Years	• Describe characteristics of effective program options for adults with AD/HD	• Adults also need a multimodal approach to intervention. • Coaches benefit this population as well.

PROJECT OPTIONS

1. Read a book written for children or adolescents about an individual with AD/HD. Choose one of the following options:
   a. Write a report or do an art project that demonstrates how the six values were or were not met in the life of the individual with AD/HD.
   b. Write a skit for one of the critical scenes in the book that could be reenacted by students.
   c. Describe how you would use this book in a classroom to develop sensitivity and respect toward individuals with AD/HD.

2. Volunteer at least three hours of your time to tutor a student with AD/HD. Write a report of what you learned from your experience. (You may need to have this approved through the Department of Special Education at least two weeks in advance.)

3. Develop a friendship with an individual with AD/HD. Write a report near the end of the quarter telling what that friendship has meant to you.

4. Keep a journal for one week. For each entry, speculate how your day would have been different if you had AD/HD.

KEY TERMS

Combined type of attention-deficit/hyperactivity disorder

Predominantly inattentive type of attention-deficit/hyperactivity disorder

Continuous performance tests

Pseudo-ADD

Developmental delay of inhibition

Psychotropic medication

Multimodal treatment

Stress-induced agitation syndrome

Predominantly hyperactive-impulsive type of attention-deficit/hyperactivity disorder

Teratogens

CHAPTER 6 GUIDED REVIEW

"If a man does not keep pace with his companions, perhaps it is because he hears a different drummer. Let him step to the music which he hears, however measured or far away."—Henry David Thoreau

What Is Attention-Deficit/Hyperactivity Disorder?

1. In the controversy over AD/HD, what are two identified concerns? (See What Is Attention-Deficit/Hyperactivity Disorder?)
   a._____
   b. _____

2. Who is often considered the father of AD/HD? (See What Is Attention-Deficit/Hyperactivity Disorder?)
   _____

3. Under what category does IDEA offer services for students with AD/HD? Why is it considered under this category? (See Defining Attention-Deficit/Hyperactivity Disorder)

     Category: _____

     Explanation: _____

4. Between _____% and _____% of children with AD/HD also have a learning disability. (See Defining Attention-Deficit/Hyperactivity Disorder)

5. To be eligible to receive a diagnosis of AD/HD as an additional diagnosis, students must have symptoms that are excessive for his or her _____age rather than _____age. (See Defining Attention-Deficit/Hyperactivity Disorder)

6. List the four criteria that the American Psychiatric Association uses to define AD/HD. (See Defining Attention-Deficit/Hyperactivity Disorder).

	Criterion Characteristics
Criterion A	
Criterion B	
Criterion C	
Criterion D	

Calvin and Hobbes

Calvin, from the "Calvin and Hobbes" comic strip by Bill Watterson, exemplifies the combined type of AD/HD. One minute Calvin is staring into space, oblivious to everything around him and daydreaming that he is fleeing awful bug beings from Zartron-9. The next, he has to face the principal for a comment he impulsively blurted out in class. He explains to the principal that the comment was "not an attitude, it's a fact!" You can learn a great deal about AD/HD from reading "Calvin and Hobbes."

7. What is "pseudo-ADD" and how do you distinguish it from AD/HD? (See Defining Attention-Deficit/Hyperactivity Disorder)

     _____

     _____

8. Match the type of AD/HD with the identifying descriptions. (See Defining Attention-Deficit/Hyperactivity Disorder)

1. Inattentive Type	a. _____ Usually an underachiever
2. Hyperactive-Impulsive Type	b. _____ Students who are inattentive and hyperactive
3. Combined Type	c. _____ Students who can't sit still and talk excessively
	d. _____ Students who are forgetful and easily distracted
	e. _____ Students who may be accident-prone
	f. _____ Students who daydream, lose things, and do not follow through
	g. _____ Students with hyperactive thinking but bodies in slow motion
	h. _____ Students who may become workaholics

Guess Who Might Have AD/HD

Did Ben Franklin, Winston Churchill, and Albert Einstein have AD/HD? How about Bill Clinton? Neurologist Bruce Roseman says yes to all of these. In his opinion, President Clinton may be "a pill away from greatness."

See *Time,* July 18, 1994, pp. 43-50.

---

9. Name and briefly describe the four characteristics of a developmental delay of inhibition. (See Describing the Characteristics of AD/HD)

   a. _____

   b. _____
   _____

   c. _____
   _____

   d. _____
   _____

10. Explain the process of reconstitution that students with AD/HD find so difficult. (See Describing the Characteristics; Breaking Apart and Recombining Information)

    _____
    _____

11. List some positive traits associated with AD/HD. (See Describing the Characteristics; Positive Traits Associated with AD/HD)

    a. _____   c. _____
    b. _____   d. _____

A Triumph Over Human Suffering

Ned Hallowell, a psychiatrist who also has AD/HD, says that the diagnosis and treatment of AD/HD represent a triumph of "science over human suffering." AD/HD is only one of the many brain syndromes society is learning to address, he says, "without scorn or hidden moral judgment. As we begin to bring mental suffering out of the stigmatized darkness it has inhabited… we all have reason to rejoice."

See "What I Learned from ADD." (1997, June/July) *Psychology Today, 30*(3), pp. 40-45.

---

12. Describe the three biological explanations for AD/HD that have moved to the forefront. (See Identifying the Causes of AD/HD; Biological Explanations)

Biological Explanation	What It Means	What It Suggests
Genetics		
Pre-, peri-, and postnatal trauma		
Brain differences		

13. Name some teratogens that may increase the likelihood that a child will develop AD/HD. (See Identifying the Causes of AD/HD; Biological Explanations; Pre-, Peri-, and Postnatal Trauma)

    _____   _____
    _____   _____
    _____   _____

14. What have position emission therapy scans on adults and children with and without AD/HD shown about causes of AD/HD? (See Identifying the Causes of AD/HD; Biological Explanations; Brain Differences)

    _____
    _____

15. What is the effect of neurochemical imbalances in AD/HD? (See Identifying the Causes of AD/HD; Biological Explanations; Brain Differences) _____

    _____
    _____

16. How many students in a typical general education classroom would you expect to find with AD/HD?_____ to _____ children. What is the current reported ratio of boys to girls? _____ boys to _____ girls. (See Identifying the Prevalence of AD/HD)

17. What are some possible reasons why AD/HD seems to occur more often in the United States than other countries? _____
    _____ (See Identifying the

    Prevalence of AD/HD)

What Are Evaluation Procedures?

I Write from Experience
After I helped write the first edition of this textbook, I was diagnosed with the inattentive type of AD/HD by a psychologist. The diagnosis was later confirmed by a neuropsychologist. Why did I ask to be tested? *DSM IV* had just been published, and as I researched the inattentive type for the first edition, I started thinking about my own history. Years of disorganization, daydreaming, missed deadlines, and forgotten important events and tasks rushed into my awareness. I thought about the time I was called down to the nurse in high school for a hearing test, probably because a teacher was concerned about my inattentiveness. I received the nickname "Lightning" from one person, a sarcastic response to my tendency to move in slow motion.
Despite having the typical AD/HD abilities to hyperfocus and be creative, which allowed me to complete a doctorate and write chapters for *Exceptional Lives*, the condition had severely impacted my adulthood. No matter how much I accomplished, I always had a sense that I would be able to do so much more if I could just get myself together.
Receiving the diagnosis gave me permission to stop beating myself up for my symptoms and ask for support. I take medication for the condition; the result has been that I feel like part of a cloud has lifted from my brain. I still face challenges in managing my everyday life. I am a client of Lee Donald, the professional organizer who shared suggestions for you in the textbook. Her assistance has been invaluable.
I share this with you to help you realize that people who seem successful can struggle with AD/HD. Many adults have never been diagnosed, and the result can be a life of frustration and low self-esteem.
—Marilyn Shank

18. What should you do if you suspect a child may have AD/HD? (See Determining the Presence of Attention-Deficit/Hyperactivity Disorder) _____

    _____

19. Name, give the purpose for, and describe three assessment instruments for determining the presence of attention-deficit/hyperactivity disorder. (See Determining the Presence of Attention-Deficit/Hyperactivity Disorder)

Name	*Purpose*	*Description*

20. Explain how stress-induced agitation syndrome is both similar to and different from AD/HD. (See Determining the Presence of Attention-Deficit/Hyperactivity Disorder; Cultural Issues in Diagnosis)

Similarities: _____

_____

Differences: _____

_____

21. In addition to IDEA, two other laws provide protection against discrimination for students with disabilities such as AD/HD. Explain how each of these laws function in determining the nature and extent of special education and related services. (See Determining the Nature and Extent of Special Education and Related Services)

Law	Function
Section 504 of the Rehabilitation Act	
The Americans with Disabilities Act (ADA)	

An Awakening

Gary Roy worked 13 years for a college degree he never attained and held 128 jobs. Finally, a psychologist informed him that he had not "outgrown" the AD/HD he had as a child, as he and his family had been told. Once Roy started taking Ritalin again as part of multimodal treatment, his life began to change. He obtained his ham-radio license and became a Civil Defense radio supervisor. Roy says, "Right after I started the treatment, I saw *Awakenings*. I cried and cried because that was how I felt, like I had awakened."

See "The Not So Young and Restless" by G. Cowley and J.C. Ramo. (1993, July 26). *Newsweek*, pp. 48-49.

22. What four behavior issues are generally addressed in identifying specific skill deficits? (See Determining the Nature and Extent of Special Education and Related Services)

a. _____

b. _____

c. _____

d. _____

What and How Do Professionals Teach?

23. The primary difference in curriculum for students with AD/HD and those without AD/HD is
_____. (See Curriculum)

24. Five key words that are important to successful curriculum presentation for students with AD/HD are
_____, _____, _____,
_____, and _____. (See Curriculum)

Now or Not Now?

When you are given an assignment at the beginning of the semester, how do you plan for completing it? According to Dave deBronkart, the tendency for people with AD/HD is to think of tasks in only two ways: now or not now. With an extraordinary ability to finish things "all at once," they can unexpectedly and creatively complete tasks in "a mad flurry of activity." Others, seeing these remarkable results, chide the person with comments such as "See what you can do when you apply yourself?" It's not a matter of willpower or laziness, Bronkart contends. Instead, the problem is a lack of depth perception for the passage of time, resulting in an inability to perceive that task deadlines are getting closer. Your students with AD/HD will need to understand their misperception of time and how to work around it.

See "The ADD Sense of Time" at http://www.ruralnet.net/~bobseay/debr.htm

25. The use of concurrent treatment approaches is called _____ treatment. Match the type of intervention method with its characteristics. (See Methods)

1. Medical Management	a. ____ Doesn't usually result in identifiable changes in student behavior
2. Education	b. ____ Helps students to structure developmental tasks
3. Coaching	c. ____ As many as 60% to 80% of students with hyperactivity/impulsivity respond favorably to use of stimulants.
4. Counseling	d. ____ Rewards a student for completion of each task and subtask
5. Organizational Training	e. ____ Includes teaching students to respond to comments from others
6. Behavior Management	f. ____ Encourages and helps students gain perspective

26. Medication doesn't force kids to do their homework or teach them social skills. It just makes them
_____. (See Methods; Medical Management)

How Is Participation Encouraged?

27. Inclusion of students with AD/HD is more successful when _____ and creativity are applied. (See Inclusion)

28. Identify the benefits for all involved in a student's success when different collaborators participate. (See Collaboration)

Collaborator	Benefits
Professional Collaborator	
Family Collaborator	
Peer Collaborator	

29. What is the "Big Struggle" and how can it be lessened? (See Collaboration; Collaboration with Family)_____
_____

30. List four careers that work directly with students with AD/HD. (See Careeers)
_____, _____,
_____, _____,

What Are Program Options?

31. Identify the needs of students with AD/HD and name some proven ways to meet those needs at each of the following age levels. Use ideas discussed in each of the program options discussed in this chapter. (See What Are Program Options?)

Age Level	Student Needs	Effective Ways to Meet Student Needs
Early Intervention and Preschool Years		
Elementary Years		
Middle and Secondary Years		
Transitional and Postsecondary Years		

AD/HD-Friendly Jobs

Making the transition from school to work is often challenging for people with AD/HD. In school, they had clear assignments and deadlines. Many times, in the workplace, workers must set their own deadlines and perform with minimal direction. According to Kathleen Nadeau, an editor of *ADDvance*, AD/HD-friendly jobs minimize paperwork, allow immediate response to short-term tasks, provide support and structure, emphasize the worker's interest, allow variety and stimulation, have a comfortable stress level, and are supervised by an organized, supportive individual.

See http://www.addvance.com/article2.html

APPLICATION EXERCISES FOR CHAPTER 6

Application Exercise 6a. Identifying Types of AD/HD

Match the type of AD/HD experienced with the characteristics. Choose from Inattentive, Hyperactive-Impulsive, and the Combined types.

1. Jaime can't seem to sit still. He has trouble controlling his body as well as what he says.

   Type: _____

2. Gopal always forgets his homework, even when his teacher calls the night before. He often appears to be daydreaming when the teacher is giving whole group instruction.

   Type: _____

3. Hannah talks all the time. She loves to explain everything to everyone. Her peers call her "motor-mouth" while others make fun of her. She often blurts out answers before the teacher has finished the question. Her talking tends to annoy her neighbors.

   Type: _____

4. When the teacher needs help organizing things in the classroom, he knows not to enlist the aid of Matilda. Matilda can't keep track of papers and loses things every day. On field trips she has been known to get lost.

   Type: _____

5. Nadia spends a lot of time doodling. Even when she's supposed to be taking notes, her pages are cluttered with pictures. She never seems to be paying attention and can't seem to sit still in class. She leaves her seat to show her pictures to peers and has a hard time connecting to the teacher's lessons.

   Type: _____

6. Otis tries hard to do well on tests, but he makes careless mistakes. He doesn't seem to listen to directions and then invents his own.

   Type: _____

Application Exercise 6b. Accommodations for Students with AD/HD

Match the teaching accommodation for the specific AD/HD need.

1. Inattention	a. ____ Set up and practice appropriate ways for Linda to relate to her peers.
2. Impulsiveness	b. ____ Develop a self-monitoring system for Jose for his talking during class.
3. Motor Activity	c. ____ Make sure Kissan writes down his homework assignments and then ask him to tape record his homework.
4. Academic Skills	d. ____ Help Marcy set short-term goals for the term project due in one month.
5. Organization and Planning	e. ____ Give Samena specific times when she can get up and take notes to peers during class.
6. Compliance	f. ____ Set up a contract with Benjamin to reward him for each five times he raises his hand before speaking out.
7. Socialization	g. ____ Encourage Maeghan to use a word processor and/ or tape recorder for written assignments to compensate for difficulty in writing ability.

Application Exercise 6c. Coaching the Concepts

Based upon the five major questions* addressed in this chapter, write out or tape record a short play detailing the interactions between a student with AD/HD and his/her coach summarizing the major concepts dealing with AD/HD. Include cueing behavior by the coach.

*Five Major Questions: What is attention-deficit/hyperactivity disorder? What are evaluation procedures? What and how do professionals teach? How is participation encouraged? What are program options?

ANSWERS TO MARGIN QUESTIONS

Page 231 — The vignette suggests that Taylor has the following characteristics:

Inattention: has difficulty in giving close attention to details, sustaining attention on tasks, listening, following through, and organizing; also is distracted, forgetful.

Hyperactivity-impulsivity: has difficulty in playing or engaging in leisure activities, runs about or climbs excessively; acts as if "driven by a motor"; has difficulty waiting.

Page 233 — The use of process writing, as described in Chapter 4, provides a good way to break down assignments. Assign different due dates for prewriting; checking databases; gathering resources; outlining; finishing note cards; drafting; peer-, self-, and teacher-editing, and completing the final draft.

Page 256 — There are many ways to create special times with individual students. You can create a special time by asking the student to help you in the classroom before or after school or during breaks, as long as the two of you participate in the activity together. Have each student pick a special day. Sit with that student at lunch on the special day and give the other students opportunities to share what they like about that student on that day. Attend a special event the student is participating in and make sure to speak to the student before or after. As the student enters or exits the class, ask about his day. Invite the student to share a snack during a break.

SAMPLE QUIZ FOR CHAPTER 6

Circle the correct answer.

TRUE OR FALSE

T or F   1.   AD/HD is the most commonly diagnosed childhood psychiatric disorder.

T or F   2.   AD/HD is considered a chronic health problem that causes limitations in vitality.

T or F   3.   About half the children with AD/HD are never identified as such.

T or F   4.   Factors other than heredity explain only 1% to 10% of hyperactive-impulsive behavior.

T or F   5.   Many students with AD/HD have seriously impaired social relationships.

MULTIPLE CHOICE

6.   What percentage of young children with AD/HD have speech and language disorders?
   a.   25%
   b.   35%
   c.   50%
   d.   65%

7.   Which of the following commonly used acronyms match the corresponding type of AD/HD?
   a.   Inattentive: ADD, ADD-WHO, AD/HD-I
   b.   Hyperactive/impulsive: AD/HD, ADD-H, AD/HD-2
   c.   Inattentive: AD/HD-NOS, ADD, AD/HD-C
   d.   Hyperactive-impulsive: AD/HD, AD/HD-HI, AD/HD-NOS

8.   Blaine has been diagnosed with AD/HD. He has trouble paying attention in class, is easily distracted, and cannot seem to sit still. What type of AD/HD does he most likely have?
   a.   Predominantly inattentive
   b.   Predominantly hyperactive-impulsive
   c.   Predominantly neurologically kinesthetic
   d.   Combined type

9.   Kara is 13 and has lost interest in all classes except art since entering junior high school. She cannot seem to concentrate, her grades have plummeted, and she appears bored. She stares out the window much of the time and seems to have no friends. Can she be diagnosed with AD/HD?
   a.   No, because she did not exhibit these symptoms early enough.
   b.   No, because most adolescents go through this stage.
   c.   Yes, because she is obviously inattentive, at risk, and needs special help.
   d.   Yes, because otherwise she is not eligible for the help she needs to get the most appropriate education.

10.   What are current estimates of the ratio of boys to girls who have AD/HD?
   a.   9:1
   b.   6:1
   c.   4:1
   d.   3:1

11.   Which of the following is true about ADD?
   a.   Of the three types, it contains the largest percentage of girls.
   b.   It is associated with a core problem of poor goal-directed persistence.
   c.   The children with this condition tend to be more often accidentally poisoned than other children.
   d.   It is seen more in young children who have not attended school.

12. Of the 52 children identified with AD/HD in the town of Juniper, how many probably have relatives with the condition?
    a. About 5
    b. About 16
    c. About 27
    d. More than 35

13. Victoria suspects that a child in her first grade class has AD/HD. What should be her first step?
    a. Talk to the child's physician
    b. Keep a record of characteristics that she notices in the classroom
    c. Ask the child's parents to request a screening
    d. Request a referral

14. Which of the following is not mentioned as a component of multimodal treatment?
    a. Organizational training
    b. Medication
    c. Education
    d. Diet

15. Which of the following is not a common side effect of stimulants?
    a. Insomnia
    b. Increased heart rate
    c. Dizziness
    d. Decreased appetite

SHORT ANSWER

16. What four specific skill deficits are mentioned which relate to behavioral issues for students with AD/HD?
    a. _____
    b. _____
    c. _____
    d. _____

17. What can you as a teacher do to help a student with AD/HD who needs help in improving peer relationships?

    _____
    _____
    _____

18. List at least five suggestions for an effective preschool program for children with AD/HD.
    a. _____
    b. _____
    c. _____
    d. _____
    e. _____

ESSAY

19. Compare and contrast the three types of AD/HD in relation to characteristics and accommodations for the classroom.

20. Discuss the causes of AD/HD as are presently understood. Describe the influence of both environmental and biological explanations. Include a discussion of the relationship of medical management to the causes of AD/HD.

CHAPTER 7: GIFTEDNESS

CHAPTER OVERVIEW

The nature of giftedness is a subject that has intrigued educators and philosophers in every generation. Although IDEA does not cover students who are gifted and talented, they too need special services not ordinarily provided by the school. This chapter explores the nature of giftedness by examining changes in definition, the controversy over characteristics, and a discussion of the causes and prevalence rates. It also examines assessment tools unique to giftedness, such as Torrance's tests for creativity and Maker's DISCOVER assessment for determining multiple areas of giftedness. Product and process measures, including reflective assessment, are examined as a means to involve students who are gifted in the evaluation of the nature and extent of special education services needed. The chapter concludes by probing benefits and concerns with inclusion and collaboration along with a description of some excellent program options being utilized in today's schools and communities.

The life of ten-year-old Nadine Cambridge helps demonstrate and clarify issues revolving around students who daily experience both the benefits and the challenges of being gifted. Nadine was selected because she represents both the typical student who is gifted as well as demonstrating some unexpected characteristics. She is typical because of her high test scores and deep academic interest in geography and social studies. She is atypical because she often appears bored and lazy in her general education classroom. Her life and daily circumstances form a platform for evaluating the many and varied dimensions of what it means to be gifted today.

CHAPTER AT-A-GLANCE

Chapter Outline	Instructional Goals	Key Concepts
WHAT IS GIFTEDNESS?		
Defining Giftedness • Historical Overview • Recent Perspectives • Multicultural Perspectives	• Differentiate among models for defining giftedness in today's classrooms	• Definitions of giftedness vary according to whether they are based on a conceptual model or a domain-specific model. Definitions also vary by culture.
Describing the Characteristics Expected Characteristics • General Intellect • Specific Academic Aptitude • Creative Productive Thinking • Leadership Ability • Visual and Performing Arts Unexpected Characteristics Unexpected Behavioral Characteristics Unexpected Gender-Related Characteristics	• Describe key characteristics of expected aspects of giftedness • Identify unexpected characteristics of giftedness	• The federal definition lists five expected characteristics associated with giftedness. • Giftedness is not always easily recognized. Some behavior associated with AD/HD is also typical of giftedness. In addition, gender bias also hides girls' giftedness.
Identifying the Causes of Giftedness	• Discuss the nature vs. nurture explanation of causes of giftedness	• Most researchers attribute giftedness to a combination of genetic and psychosocial factors.
Identifying the Prevalence of Giftedness	• Apply prevalence figures to an average classroom	• If an IQ of 125-130 is the standard, then 2% to 3% of the population are gifted. If a "talent pool" is the standard, then 15% to 20% of students may be considered gifted.

WHAT ARE EVALUATION PROCEDURES?		
Determining the Presence of Giftedness • Multiple Intelligences • DISCOVER Assessment • Creativity Assessment	• Compare the characteristics of different assessment tools used to determine the presence of giftedness	• A balance of IQ and creativity tests along with rating scales and documentation helps determine the presence of giftedness.
Determining the Nature and Extent of Special Education and Related Services • Product Evaluation • Process Evaluation	• Recognize the need for culture-fair tests for students from different backgrounds • Analyze the nature and extent of special education needed	• Standardized tests are biased against culturally diverse groups, low socioeconomic groups, and English as a second language students. New assessment tools such as DISCOVER help to alleviate this bias. • Student responsibility for the nature and extent of special education can be built into IEP goals with product and process evaluation measures.
WHAT AND HOW DO PROFESSIONALS TEACH?		
Curriculum • Higher Level Thinking Curricula • Whole Language Interdisciplinary Curricula • Differentiated Reading Curricula	• Differentiate curriculum options available for use with students who are gifted	• Three types of curriculum modifications are a benefit: integrated curriculum studies in areas of interest, modification of the pace of learning, and modification of the depth of content coverage.
Methods • Acceleration • Content Enrichment • Magnet Schools	• Evaluate how different methods are most effective for varied student needs	• Proven methods include acceleration, content enrichment with pull-out programs, and magnet school programs.
HOW IS PARTICIPATION ENCOURAGED?		
Inclusion	• Summarize benefits and problems associated with inclusion for students who are gifted	• Inclusion means more work for the general educator, but collaboration with mentorship and in-service programs can strengthen the program that is offered for all children.
Collaboration • Professional Collaboration • Family Collaboration • Peer and Community Collaboration	• Explore ways to collaborate on behalf of students who are gifted	• Professional, family, and peer collaboration each contribute much toward successful student learning.
Careers	• Examine careers available that work with students who are gifted	• General and special educators and gifted education specialists are only a few who enjoy careers that touch the lives of students who are gifted.
WHAT ARE PROGRAM OPTIONS?		
Early Intervention and Preschool Years	• Describe characteristics of effective preschool gifted programs	• Montgomery Knolls Elementary School serves underserved preschoolers who are gifted.
Elementary Years	• Describe characteristics of effective elementary school gifted programs	• The Kids' Development Corporation has elementary students build a functional community by each taking an occupational role within a corporation.

Middle and Secondary Years	• Describe characteristics of effective gifted programs for middle and secondary students	• The Purdue Three Stage Model at the secondary level focuses on core content and critical thinking skills applied to real-life problems.
Transitional and Postsecondary Years	• Describe characteristics of effective program options for adults who are gifted	• MENSA is a social organization for people of all ages who are gifted. It sponsors programs to benefit these individuals and their endeavors.

PROJECT OPTIONS

1. Obtain a checklist of characteristics to assess giftedness from a local school. Complete this checklist for three students. Ask the cooperating teacher to fill them out on the same students. Then, based on your evaluations, discuss the areas of giftedness in terms of one of the models discussed in this chapter along with their potential for positive contributions to society.

2. Along with several other students in this class, read works by Glenn Doman and David Elkind on causes of giftedness and structure a debate based on the best arguments of each side. Present your debate to the class and ask the class to assess your arguments.

3. Find and research as many types of creativity tests as you can, including Torrance's two main tests. Take each test yourself and then create a chart to compare the strengths and weaknesses of each one. Or you may choose to do this with different IQ tests.

4. From the program options discussed, create a new program model for students who are gifted that would amplify on the best of each program model as well as build on involvement and collaboration across age levels and the community.

KEY TERMS

Acceleration	Genius
Collaboration	Gifted
Creativity	Inclusion
Documentation	Magnet schools
Domain-specific giftedness	Multiple intelligences
Evaluation	Prodigy
Expertise	Talent pool

CHAPTER 7 GUIDED REVIEW

Teaching Prodigies

"Prestige has nothing to do with anything," Itzhak Perlman's violin teacher Dorothy DeLay comments. Children realize that their parents are happiest when they are the best. Therefore, they fear losing love if they do not perform well. Outstanding performance may bring admiration, power, or influence, but not love. "I'm always hunting around for whatever is tying children up so that they are not free," she says.

Delay emphasizes that highly gifted children need to learn three things: no matter what happens, you can always build; curiosity should always be the motivating force to learn and grow; and give something to people that they can value, rather than focusing on pleasing them.

See U.S. News and World Report, 103, p. 59.

What Is Giftedness?

1. Although IDEA (does, does not) cover gifted and talented, many states have shown their priority for students who are gifted by providing quality programs. (See Defining Giftedness; Historical Overview)

2. Write out the definition that, in 47 states, provides the foundation for guiding programs for students who are gifted. (See Defining Giftedness; Historical Overview)

   _____

   _____

   _____

3. What two misconceptions arose from Terman's important studies of individuals who are gifted? (See Defining Giftedness; Historical Overview)

   a. _____

   b. _____

4. Compare the traditional understanding of giftedness with today's emerging paradigm by filling in the characteristic differences. (See Defining Giftedness; Recent Perspectives)

	Traditional Paradigm	*Emerging Paradigm*
Basis for giftedness		
Potential for trait changes		
Identification basis		
Social orientation		
Influences on expression		
Model for instruction		
Location orientation		
Cultural diversity		

5. What are the five categories of giftedness specified in the federal definition? (See Defining Giftedness; Recent Perspectives)

   a. _____   d. _____

   b. _____   e. _____

   c. _____

6. Match the classification system for identifying students who are gifted with the researcher: (See Defining Giftedness; Recent Perspectives)

a. _____ Gardner	1. Above-average ability + creativity + task commitment
b. _____ Clark	2. Five areas of giftedness: general intellect, specific academic, performing/visual arts, leadership, creative
c. _____ Renzulli	3. Giftedness expressed in 8 different domains: linguistic, musical, bodily-kinesthetic, spatial, logical-mathematical, intrapersonal, interpersonal, and naturalist
d. _____ Sternberg and Zhang	4. Different processing of information based on the four major functions of the brain: cognitive, affective, physical, intuitive
e. _____ Federal definition	5. Pentagonal theory: excellence + rarity + productivity + demonstrability + value

7. According to Howard Gardner, complete these four statements. (See Defining Giftedness; Recent Perspectives)
   a. The difference between giftedness and prodigiousness is _____.
   b. _____ is the technical mastery of skills and lore.
   c. _____ is a unique expression within a domain of giftedness.
   d. _____ is when a person's works assume a universal significance.

8. Name four examples of unexpected characteristics of giftedness. (See Describing the Characteristics; Unexpected Characteristics)
   a. _____   c. _____
   b. _____   d. _____

Whiz Kid with Dyslexia

Identifying students who are gifted can be a complex process. Many unexpected characteristics can hide giftedness. The giftedness of Benjamin Bolger could easily have been overlooked and undeveloped, if not for a mother who recognized his unique abilities.

Benjamin graduated from the University of Michigan at age 17 and at 19 was the youngest student at Yale Law School. However, Benjamin has dyslexia and cannot read. Although he's a member of MENSA, he can't read a menu at a restaurant. Benjamin has a hard time reading a number from a phone book or keeping track of time. Sometimes he has to ask strangers for help.

As a child, his teachers didn't understand his problem and labeled him as lazy or stupid. In fourth grade, his mom, a former teacher, began teaching him herself because she couldn't find a school that could help her son. He flourished under her tutelage, and at age 13 Benjamin entered the University of Michigan.

How does Benjamin keep up with the reading required in his demanding program? His mother reads his assignments to him. Frequently they're in the library until 3 a.m. due to this laborious task. His friends know about his problem and also help—with encouragement as well as academic support.

Despite the challenges he experiences, Benjamin says, "I've learned not to look at dyslexia as a liability."

See Jill Johnson, "Not Your Typical Whiz Kid," *React,* January 15-21, 1996, p. 10.

See also http://www.react.com for more information about Benjamin.

---

9. Most researchers agree that giftedness is the result of a combination of _____
   (or _____) and _____ (or _____). (See Identifying the Causes of Giftedness and Promoting Them)
10. What two levels of giftedness are recognized by most researchers? _____ and
    _____ (See Identifying the Prevalence of Giftedness)

11. Traditional definitions usually assume that giftedness includes the top _____% to _____% of the population, or IQs starting at _____ to _____. (See Identifying the Prevalence of Giftedness)

12. Currently, many states determine giftedness from a talent pool with IQs of _____ or above. This results in gifted services for the top _____% to _____% of all students, or _____ to _____ students per class. (See Identifying the Prevalence of Giftedness)

Two Gifted Talkers

Maria Sansome, at age 12, is a sports reporter for NJET-TV in Erie, PA. Jennifer Hawkins, age 16, hosts a one-hour radio call-in program for teenagers on WBZT-AM in West Palm Beach, FL. How would Gardner, Clark, Renzulli, Sternberg. and Zhang, and the federal definition classify their giftedness?

See *People Weekly*, May 16, 1994, and August 12, 1993.

What Are Evaluation Procedures?

13. African-Americans, Hispanics, and Native Americans are underrepresented by _____% to _____% in gifted programs. (See Determining the Presence of Giftedness)

14. What forms of documentation can be used to ensure that assessments do not discriminate against students from culturally diverse backgrounds? (See Determining the Presence of Giftedness)
   a. _____   c. _____
   b. _____   d. _____

15. The DISCOVER performance-based assessment evaluates students in which six of Gardner's eight domains of intelligence? (See Determining the Presence of Giftedness; Multiple Intelligences; DISCOVER Assessment)
   a. _____   d. _____
   b. _____   e. _____
   c. _____   f. _____

Ayinde Jean-Baptiste

When he was four years old, Ayinde Jean-Baptiste memorized Martin Luther King's "I Have a Dream" speech and was delivering original speeches to school assemblies at Marva Collin's West Side Preparatory School. At age 6, Ayinde appeared on the Oprah Winfrey Show. At age 12, he spoke to more than a million Black men. This highly sought-after high school sophomore, who at the age of 6 was testing at eleventh- and twelfth-grade levels in some subjects, enjoys friends, sports, and collecting comic books. He hopes to be a lawyer or a scientist, but whatever career he chooses, he will continue to use his oratorical abilities to better the lives of others. "It's not a performance," he comments. "It comes from the heart....I have an ability to get a message out and have people act on it. That's what's important."

See J.B. Kinnon. (1997). "Ayinde Jean-Baptiste: Superstudent." *Ebony, 52*(4), 148-152.

---

16. What criteria does Maker use for evaluating giftedness? _____ (See Determining the Presence of Giftedness; Multiple Intelligences; DISCOVER Assessment)

_____

_____

17. Name Torrance's two creativity tests. Tell what domain of giftedness is assessed for each of these tests. (See Determining the Presence of Giftedness; Creativity Assessment)
   a. _____; _____
   b. _____; _____

18. Reflective assessment helps students take responsibility for measuring their own progress for both the _____ and _____ of learning. (See Determining the Nature and Extent of Special Education and Related Services; Process Evaluation)

What and How Do Professionals Teach?

19. Identify three types of curriculum modification that instill critical and creative thinking. Then give at least one example for each type. (See Curriculum)

    a. _____; _____

    b. _____; _____

    c. _____; _____

The Link Between Geography and Mortality

When Nadine's parents travel, she is very concerned about their safety. One of her dad's trips took him to Entrea when she was eight years old. Because of her knowledge of geography and the problems being experienced in that area at the time, she was almost inconsolable and was very concerned about his safety both in the plane and in Entrea. Her mother was very surprised at Nadine's awareness of mortality. Building on Gardner's model of multiple intelligences, what does Nadine's behavior in this situation indicate about her giftedness?

---

20. List the levels of Bloom's taxonomy from easiest to most challenging: (See Curriculum)

    a. _____   d. _____

    b. _____   e. _____

    c. _____   f. _____

21. Match the type of teaching used with students who are gifted with the identifying method. (See Methods)

1. Acceleration	a.____ A school with an instructional emphasis on a specific domain of talent such as math
2. Content enrichment	b.____ Compacting or telescoping the curriculum
3. Magnet school	c. ____ Pull-out programs
	d. ____ Moving faster through the grades or mastery of a particular subject area
	e. ____ Revolving Door Model

How Is Participation Encouraged?

22. List at least two benefits and two concerns of inclusion for students who are gifted. (See Inclusion)

    Benefits: _____

    _____

    Concerns: _____

    _____

23. Identify at least four key collaborators who may be involved in adapting the classroom environment for helping an unproductive student who is gifted. (See Collaboration)

    a. _____   c. _____

    b. _____   d. _____

24. Based upon Peterson's model of successful inclusion and collaboration, identify four characteristics of successful programs for working together on behalf of students who are gifted. (See Collaboration)

    a. _____   c. _____

    b. _____   d. _____

25. Mentorships are a good example of _____. (See Collaboration)

Doctor Doctor Kloor

Henry Kloor is the first known American to get two simultaneous Ph.D.s in chemistry and physics--and he did it by the age of 31. Kloor says he decided as a kid that he wanted to have multiple degrees because "so many comic-book scientist -heroes seemed to have them."

Despite being born with his feet pointing backward and having to wear metal braces and special shoes as a child, his mother said, "Nothing ever got him down."

Along with comic heroes, Henry was also inspired by a fireman who told his class that they could do anything they set their minds to. Henry commented, "That just stayed with me."

See *People Weekly*, August 22, 1994, p. 120.

What Are Program Options?

26. What three types of underserved children are offered opportunities to develop their gifts at the Montgomery Knolls preschool program? (See Early Intervention and Preschool Years)

    a. _____

    b. _____

    c. _____

27. In the elementary school "Kids Development Corporation," how did students' questions and thinking change from the beginning of the program to the end? (See Elementary Years)

    Before: _____

    After: _____

28. Name at least four types of programs available for middle- or secondary-level students. (See Middle and Secondary Years)

    a. _____   c. _____

    b. _____   d. _____

29. In the Purdue Three Stage Model for secondary students, teachers move from acting as the _____ to acting as a _____ for the students. (See Middle and Secondary Years)

30. Name the one requirement for membership in MENSA, the international organization primarily for adults who are gifted. _____ (See Transitional and Postsecondary Years)

An Update on Michael Kearney and Others

Michael and his family spent the year after college graduation exploring Michael's interest in a television career. He appeared on many national talk shows and performed in one made-for-television movie. He decided that show business wasn't the best career move. So now Michael, at age 13, is completing a master's degree in Biochemistry at Middle Tennessee State University. He plans to continue his graduate studies in biochemistry with a doctoral degree. Michael continues to enjoy academic pursuits, video games, and reading good books.

Maeghan, at age 11, also has made great strides. She completed high school and is presently working on a B.S. in veterinary medicine. She's enjoying learning about the animals she loves, but is also facing some difficult situations being not only young and gifted, but also a girl.

Kevin and Cassidy have purchased a home in Middlesboro, Tennessee, and continue to pursue their interest in the connection between giftedness and AD/HD. Their goal continues to be to have two children who are happy and well adjusted, both now and at the age of 25 and beyond.

APPLICATION EXERCISES FOR CHAPTER 7

Application Exercise 7a. Identifying Multiple Intelligences

After rereading the "Recent Perspectives" section of the text chapter, identify which category of giftedness is most evident in each of the following students.

1. Jodi can't seem to sit still; she stretches her teacher's patience with her constant activity. She loves playing out of doors. While many consider her a tomboy, she wins every relay race and is always chosen first for sports events.

    Category: _____

2. Susie is quick to recognize what pleases both her teachers and her peers. She also recognizes when other students' actions and motives are going the wrong direction – even before the teacher notices. Her friendship is sought after and she works to make the classroom a real community.

    Category: _____

3. Jack talks all the time. He loves to explain everything to everyone. Some peers call him "motormouth" while others ignore him because they don't understand the long words he uses. When he's not talking, he's writing poetry.

    Category: _____

4. When the teacher needs help organizing things in the classroom, he enlists Jacob's assistance. Jacob can see how things fit. He even comes up with original and useful designs that simplify classroom layouts and events.

    Category: _____

5. Darlene spends a lot of time doodling. Even when she's supposed to be taking notes, her pages are cluttered with pictures – many of which relate to the topic of the lesson.

    Category: _____

6. Jimmy is the class detective. He figures out complex problems before others. He has invented his own secret code that he uses with a few buddies.

    Category: _____

7. Roberta loves cars. She knows every make and model on the road. She can tell you the differences between very similar models and is always looking at car magazines.

    Category: _____

8. Rachel comes to school wearing a headset and complains when she has to turn it off. Even after it's turned off, her body still seems to move with the rhythm of the last song she heard and later she sings the song for her friends.

    Category: _____

9. Betsy cries every time someone gets in trouble. She is always first to offer help to someone in need. She spends more time looking out for others than attending to classwork.

    Category: _____

Application Exercise 7b. IQ Scores in the Classroom

Reread the section "Identifying the Prevalence of Giftedness." Using expected frequencies for IQ scores, compute how many students in a classroom of 40 students have IQs in the following ranges. Note that an IQ beyond 130 is very rare.

1. Sam's IQ is about 100.   Total in class with similar IQ: _____
2. Julie's IQ is about 107.   Total in class with similar IQ: _____
3. Mary's IQ is about 115.   Total in class with similar IQ: _____
4. Andrew's IQ is about 122.   Total in class with similar IQ: _____
5. Helen's IQ is about 130.   Total in class with similar IQ: _____

Application Exercise 7c. Mapping Giftedness in Action

Based upon the five major questions* addressed in this chapter, select your favorite domain of giftedness and create a written or visual schema representation to summarize the major concepts affecting gifted education today for each of these questions.

*Five Major Questions: What is giftedness? What are evaluation procedures? What and how do professionals teach? How is participation encouraged? What are program options?

ANSWERS TO MARGIN QUESTIONS

Page 276	Concern with values, ethics, or justice may reveal intrapersonal giftedness, though these characteristics may also describe someone with interpersonal and leadership abilities.
Page 277	Build on her inherent strengths. Allow her to develop ideas for classroom social studies activities. Encourage positive contributions in subjects she most dislikes by asking her to find connections between those subjects and her areas of expertise. Then give her choices for integrated class projects that allow her to work in both subject areas..
Page 278	Inherent strengths that demonstrate the potential to make positive contributions are described as "Early Indicators of Giftedness" in Table 7-4. Examples include such things as the ability to sing or play an instrument at an early age, the ability to figure things out without paper, the ability to see many perspectives, as well as to motivate, encourage, and help others.
Page 281	This information is consistent with information in Chapter 8 as well as other chapters in this text, indicating that causes of disabilities and giftedness, whether biomedical or psychosocial, are not always fully understood. Yet nurture, collaboration, and psychosocial factors can play a significant role in the development of any child.
Page 283	The major reason for underrepresentation of culturally diverse groups in gifted programs is test bias. Additionally, students from other races or cultures might be gifted in different domains than those normally assessed. To encourage their full participation, use several types of measurement for determining the presence of giftedness in various domains.
Page 290	Give the student a set of geometric shape patterns and have her create and explain different series of patterns. For instance, with her shapes, she may form a line of 2 triangles, 3 squares, 4 circles, 5 hexagons demonstrating sequential increases of one OR she may form a line of 3 squares, 2 circles, 4 triangles, 1 hexagon demonstrating that a increase in the first number indicates a similar decrease in the second number.
Page 290	Teaching students to use higher level thinking skills is a productive way to scaffold information progressively and allow students to view information and learning from varying perspectives. Thus, expectations by teachers can be met in multiple ways and learning can be broadened.
Page 294	Giving students choices means that students have opportunities to direct their own lives and act on their preferences and interests. The revolving door model invites students to choose topics of their own interest to explore. It allows them to do it in a way that is comfortable to them. It not only acknowledges these specialized interests, but helps students broaden their interests and talents there.
Page 296	To serve students who are gifted more effectively, schools with full inclusion might also (1) broaden their basis for evaluation to additional domains, (2) focus on cooperative learning and collaboration during implementation, (3) build on group interests of students, and (4) provide a broader range of opportunities.
Page 300	All of the values are evidenced in one form or another. Full citizenship is realized when Joan focuses on students who are underachieving; Relationships are an integral part of the whole program, not just with students but the faculty as she seeks to use as little pull-out time as possible as well as through her newsletters; Positive contributions are acknowledged when she affirms student accomplishments; Inherent strengths are key to the programs and activities she develops in order to entice students to come before and after school; Great expectations are demonstrated toward students, faculty and parents; Choices are seen not only in content, but time for programs and level of involvement.
Page 302	Outcomes might include greater confidence in the student's own abilities, clearer focus for future goals, and greater understanding of human relationships. These connections will add to the quality of life in the present and the future.

SAMPLE QUIZ FOR CHAPTER 7

Circle the correct answer.

TRUE OR FALSE

T or F   1.   Definitions of giftedness vary according to whether they are based on a conceptual model or a domain specific model of giftedness.

T or F   2.   Most researchers today attribute giftedness to genetic factors.

T or F   3.   Many schools today use acceleration because research tends to favor it.

T or F   4.   A student who is gifted may be a discipline problem in the classroom.

T or F   5.   Pull-out programs are the most common type of program option for preschool students who are gifted.

MULTIPLE CHOICE

6.   Considering what we now understand about giftedness, identify the characteristic of Terma''s groundbreaking work that most contributed to this understanding.

    a.   The notion that genius is closely tied to IQ

    b.   The extensive data provided on individuals with high IQs

    c.   The connection of genius with genetics

    d.   Highly intelligent people tend to be high strung or neurotic

7.   While the federal definition is instrumental in guiding programs for students who are gifted, it does not address one important concern. Which concern is <u>not</u> true?

    a.   Giftedness is stated as worthy of federal attention.

    b.   Areas and characteristics of giftedness are described.

    c.   States are required to establish programs for students who are gifted.

    d.   It is stated that students who are gifted require services.

8.   Although only eight years old, Tracina wins adult performing arts contests in violin. These contests are governed by official standards. Which of the following is one of Sternberg and Zhang's criteria for identifying this aspect of giftedness?

    a.   Value

    b.   Productivity

    c.   Usefulness

    d.   Demonstrability

9.   Which of the following researchers has developed a model of domain-specific giftedness?

    a.   Sternberg

    b.   Gardner

    c.   Renzulli

    d.   Terman

10.   Samantha's judgment seems to lag behind her development of intellect. She often struggles with authorities and questions rules, customs, and traditions. She has poor attention when bored and has a low tolerance for tasks that seem irrelevant. Which one of the following choices does this type of behavior characterize?

    a.   Giftedness

    b.   Attention-deficit/hyperactivity disorder

    c.   A combination of both giftedness and attention-deficit/hyperactivity disorder

    d.   Neither giftedness nor attention-deficit/hyperactivity disorder

11. If IQ is used as the basis for assessing giftedness, then what is the proportion of the population considered gifted?
    a. 1% to 2%
    b. 2% to 3%
    c. 3% to 4%
    d. 4% to 5%

12. The DISCOVER assessment process has evaluated a number of potentially gifted students. Which of the following students was considered a superior problem-solver and referred for placement into a gifted program?
    a. Suzy scored one definite in linguistics and one in spatial testing.
    b. Leah scored two definites in logical-mathematical testing.
    c. Tom scored one definite in spatial and one in logical-mathematical testing.
    d. Ralph scored two definites in spatial testing.

13. Ms. Beach recognizes that Bethany is far beyond her other students in math. In order to provide her with opportunities for more challenging projects, Ms. Beach allows Bethany to test out of the material and only do assignments she finds interesting. Which of the following methods is Ms. Beach using?
    a. Compacting the curriculum
    b. The Revolving Door Model
    c. Magnet schools
    d. Acceleration

14. Which one of the following situations best reflects the benefits and goals of inclusion for students who are gifted?
    a. The understanding of giftedness is more easily certified.
    b. More students benefit from ability development.
    c. More help is given by the general education teacher, including "differentiated" activities.
    d. Students who are gifted can provide information for their teachers.

15. Finding the best support for children who are gifted is not always easy. What additional option are more and more parents using to help students who are gifted achieve their potential?
    a. Critical counseling
    b. Family mentors
    c. Home schooling
    d. Resource consultation

SHORT ANSWER

16. What are the five federal classifications for students who are gifted?
    a. _____   d. _____
    b. _____   e. _____
    c. _____

17. Identify three types of curriculum modifications for students who are gifted.
    a. _____   c. _____
    b. _____

18. State two items that could be included in a reflective learning portfolio.
    a. _____   b. _____

ESSAY

19. Assess and prioritize different identification assessments used for students who are gifted according to how they build on the inherent strengths of these students.

20. Compare and contrast the characteristics of program options for students who are gifted at the four different age levels. Evaluate the strengths and weaknesses at each level.

CHAPTER 8: MENTAL RETARDATION

CHAPTER OVERVIEW

Mental retardation is a social concept derived from society's views about people with intellectual challenges. This chapter explores the identification, characteristics, causes, and prevalence of mental retardation as a social construct. An overview of assessment focuses on adaptive skills to determine the presence of mental retardation while a description of assessments such as The Arc's Self-Determination Scale establishes a means for determining the nature and extent of special education services. Curriculum options for remedial, general classroom support are explored as beneficial plans. Additional program options at each level are described to provide an overview of effective practices for serving these students.

The life of twenty-year-old Ryan Banning provides an illustration of a student with mental retardation who has experienced tremendous challenges when the school district was not prepared to provide a state-of-art inclusive program. The vignette highlights the frustrating impact that this creates for Ryan and his family. Through Group Action Planning, system changes have occurred that not only enable better support for Ryan but for other students with disabilities as well. One of the special challenges that Ryan faces at this time is preparation for his life after high school. Successful outcomes for students with disabilities is a major national priority.

CHAPTER AT-A-GLANCE

Chapter Outline	Instructional Goals	Key Concepts
WHAT IS MENTAL RETARDATION?		
Defining Mental Retardation • Mental Retardation as a Social Construct • The Evolving Definition • The 1992 AAMR Definition	• Differentiate among models for defining mental retardation	• Definitions of mental retardation have evolved to include not only permanent intellectual impairment, but also a student's educational performance and potential, focusing on three areas: capabilities, environments, and functioning.
Describing the Characteristics • Limitations in Intellectual Functioning • Limitations in adaptive skill areas • Need for supports • Using the AAMR Approach in Schools	• Describe key characteristics of mental retardation • Identify diagnostic criteria for describing characteristics of mental retardation	• The three main characteristics of mental retardation relate to intelligence, adaptive skills, and need for supports. • The diagnosis of mental retardation requires an IQ score of 70 to 75 or below.
Identifying the Causes of Mental Retardation • Biomedical Causes • Psychosocial Disadvantage • Interaction of Biomedical and Psychosocial Causes • Preventing Mental Retardation	• Categorize causes of mental retardation • Explain levels of prevention for mental retardation	• Two ways to categorize causes of mental retardation include timing and type. • Mental retardation typically results from interactions among multiple causes. • Prevention encompasses primary, secondary, and tertiary prevention.
Identifying the Prevalence of Mental Retardation	• Recognize prevalence rates and recent trends	• Prevalence is less than 1% to 3% of the general population. • Prevalence is declining while increasing for students identified with learning disabilities.

WHAT ARE EVALUATION PROCEDURES?		
Determining the Presence of Mental Retardation	• Compare the characteristics of different assessment tools used to determine the presence of mental retardation	• AAMR proposes a comprehensive assessment. • The AAMR Adaptive Behavior Scale-School is a frequently used assessment tool.
Determining the Nature and Extent of Special Education and Related Services	• Recognize the possibilities for developing a specialized needs based program	• Developing a profile that includes intensities of needed supports is a high priority.
WHAT AND HOW DO PROFESSIONALS TEACH?		
Curriculum	• Differentiate curriculum options available for use with students with mental retardation	• Three major curriculum options are remedial, general classroom support, and adult outcomes. • Professionals emphasize a life-skills curriculum.
Methods	• Evaluate different methods that are effective for varied student needs	• A current emphasis for secondary students is instruction to enhance self-determination.
HOW IS PARTICIPATION ENCOURAGED?		
Inclusion	• Identify trends for inclusion of students with mental retardation	• Trends indicate that 8.69% of students with mental retardation receive inclusive education in general education classrooms.
Collaboration	• Explore ways to collaborate on behalf of students with mental retardation	• Person-centered planning approaches bring together family, professionals, and friends for problem solving and social support.
Careers: Who Are the Professionals?	• Examine careers available that work with students with mental retardation	• Opportunities can be found at early intervention, elementary, secondary, and postsecondary levels.
WHAT ARE PROGRAM OPTIONS?		
Early Intervention and Preschool Years	• Describe characteristics of effective preschool programs	• Project EAGLE is designed to provide comprehensive services to families and to prevent psychosocial disadvantages.
Elementary Years	• Describe characteristics of effective elementary programs for students with mental retardation	• Morristown Elementary School attributes success to the school's underlying values and beliefs, responses to educational initiatives, school and classroom climate, the model of shared leadership, capacity building, and community connections.

Middle and Secondary Years	• Describe characteristics of effective programs for middle and secondary students	• The Birmingham Public Schools provide both inclusive experiences as well as teaching functional outcomes.
Transitional and Postsecondary Years	• Describe characteristics of effective program options for adults with mental retardation	• Collaboration between schools and industry is used by Project TASSEL to ensure that their students are prepared for competitive employment.

PROJECT OPTIONS

1. Interview and research the history of two students with mental retardation. Using the AAMR definition of mental retardation explained in Figure 8-2, provide an overview of capabilities, environments, and functioning for each of the two students selected.

2. Compile a listing of characteristics and causes for learning disabilities and for mental retardation. Create a diagram that proposes reasons for the decrease in students identified with mental retardation and the increase in the number of students identified as having learning disabilities.

3. Write a "Choose Your Own Adventure" short story using Ryan or another student featured in this chapter as your main character. Tell his/her life story and as each negative factor arises, create an alternate choice that would have made a positive influence in his/her life.

4. Design your own evaluation form for students with mild or moderate retardation based on the best aspects of the IEP and GAP.

KEY TERMS

Amniocentesis

Anoxia

Augmentative communication device

Biomedical causes

Chromosomes

Educable students

EMR classroom

Hypoxia

Karyotyping

Learned helplessness

Outer-directedness

Psychosocial disadvantage

Social construct

Tertiary prevention

Trainable students

CHAPTER 8 GUIDED REVIEW

The Most Valuable Player on Stallings' Team

Retired University of Alabama coach Gene Stallings hoped for a son who could play football. Instead, his son Johnny was born with Down syndrome in 1963, 12 years before IDEA was enacted in 1975. His doctors recommended institutionalization, and the family received little support when they decided to take Johnny home with them. Johnny could not even attend public school until he was 10.

Despite the challenges the family faced, they believe that Johnny provided them with something far more valuable than the ability to play football. "Johnny has given us love—total, unconditional love—and joy," Gene Stallings said in an interview with *People* magazine. Johnny attended games with his father and spent time with the players, teaching them to do their best with what they have. You can read more about Johnny and his family in Gene Stallings' book *Another season: A coach's story of raising an exceptional son* and in *People* (February 2, 1998, pp. 40-45).

What Is Mental Retardation?

1. Why is mental retardation considered a social construct? (See Defining Mental Retardation; Mental Retardation as a Social Construct) _____

2. What has been the distinguishing characteristic over the years for the AAMR's definition of mental retardation? (See Defining Mental Retardation; The Evolving Definition)
   _____

3. Write out IDEA's definition of mental retardation and then explain how IDEA's definition of mental retardation differs from the AAMR's definition. (See Defining Mental Retardation; The Evolving Definition)

   IDEA's definition:
   _____
   _____

   Differences between IDEA's and AAMR's definitions:
   _____
   _____
   _____

4. Complete the following chart to demonstrate the AAMR's 1983 classification system. (See Defining Mental Retardation; The Evolving Definition.)

AAMR 1983 Classification	IQ Range	Educational Classification
a.		
b.		
c.		
d.		

5. The 1992 AAMR definition changed the perspective of mental retardation as an inherent trait to one that encompasses three elements. What are they? (See Defining Mental Retardation; The 1992 AAMR Definition.)
   a. _____
   b. _____
   c. _____

Up Syndrome

"I have a slight case of Down syndrome," Chris Burke once said in an interview for *Life* magazine. "I call it 'up syndrome'" (November 1991, p. 70). Chris's family maintained high expectations for him, and Chris achieved more than even they could have imagined. Perhaps you will remember that Chris acted in the television drama *Life Goes On*, making television history. Previously, actors without disabilities played the roles of series characters with mental retardation. Chris has also acted in other television programs. Since his pioneering work, more people with Down syndrome have found their way into television and movie roles. Chris, with co-author Jo Beth McDaniel, wrote a book about his life. (*A Special Kind of Hero: Chris Burke's Own Story*, Dell, 1991).

---

6. Match the definitions for identifying students with mental retardation with the source: (1) 1983 AAMR; (2) 1992 AAMR; or (3) 1997 IDEA. (See What Is Mental Retardation?; Defining Mental Retardation)

	(a) Recognizes both intellectual and adaptive behavior limitations and their effects on the person
	(b) Mental retardation means significantly subaverage general intellectual functioning existing concurrently with deficits in adaptive behavior and manifested during the developmental period that adversely affects a child's educational performance.
	(c) Holds the environment responsible for providing needed supports for greater inclusion of individuals with disabilities.
	(d) Mental retardation refers to significantly subaverage general intellectual functioning existing concurrently with deficits in adaptive behavior and manifested during the developmental period.
	(e) Includes the four levels of mild, moderate, severe, and profound.
	(f) Includes four assumptions essential to its application: cultural and linguistic diversity, assessing adaptive behavior within typical environments, recognizing strengths as well as needs, and expressing great expectations for people with mental retardation.

7. What is the new title of the AAMR manual and what new component has been added that reflects the new understanding of mental retardation? (See Defining Mental Retardation; The 1992 AAMR Definition)

_____

_____

Best Buddies

Anthony Kennedy Shriver wants to make sure that people with mental retardation are included in mainstream society. He founded an innovative program called Best Buddies to help that happen. As a result of his efforts, thousands of people with mental retardation and people without mental retardation are enjoying close friendships. The buddies may go to sporting events, movies, or the mall—any event that friends typically enjoy together. "Part of our mission," Shriver comments, "is to make it so people won't stare [because they are used to seeing people with mental retardation in these settings].

See *People*, February 27, 1995, pp. 57+. You can call 1-800-89-Buddy for more information.

---

8. What are the three main characteristics of mental retardation? (See Describing the Characteristics)

   a. _____

   b. _____

   c. _____

9. Regardless of IQ score, what two areas are affected in students with mental retardation? (See Describing the Characteristics; Limitations in Intellectual Functioning)

   a. _____

   b. _____

10. Identify the four areas of difficulty for each limitation in intellectual functioning and describe the main identifying characteristic: (See Describing the Characteristics; Limitations in Intellectual Functioning)

Area of Difficulty in Intellectual Functioning	Identifying Characteristic
a.	
b.	
c.	
d.	

Count Us In

Two friends, Jason Kingsley and Mitchell Levitz, wrote the book *Count Us In* (Harcourt Brace & Company, 1994). The book records a number of conversations the young men had with their parents, grandfathers, and Jason's girlfriend. Jason and Mitchell openly discuss their viewpoints about having Down syndrome, friendships, going to school, enjoying leisure activities, sex, marriage and children, personal beliefs, politics, grief, and living independently.

---

11. Students with mental retardation often lack motivation. Identify how to help students to learn through The Efficacy Model. (See Describing the Characteristics; Limitations in Intellectual Functioning)
    a. Decrease learned helplessness or outer-directedness:

    _____

    b. Increase learned capacity or inner-directedness:

    _____

12. In addition to significant subaverage intelligence, how many adaptive skill areas must be significantly affected before a student can be identified as having mental retardation? (See Describing the Characteristics; Limitations in Adaptive Skill Areas)

    _____

13. What are the four areas in which students may need varying systems of support? (See Describing the Characteristics; Limitations in Intellectual Functioning)
    a. _____
    b. _____
    c. _____
    d. _____

14. Four levels of intensities of support have been identified. First, identify these four levels. Second, identify the variables that must be considered within each level. (See Describing the Characteristics; Need for Supports)
    a. Levels: _____ _____ _____ _____
    b. Variables: _____ _____

    _____ _____ _____

15. How many causes of mental retardation have been identified? (See Identifying the Causes of Mental Retardation.)_____

16. How does the AAMR categorize causes of mental retardation? (See Identifying the Causes of Mental Retardation.)

Timing	Types
a.	d.
b.	e.
c.	

What Will Happen When I Die?

Despite laws such as IDEA and ADA, many adults with mental retardation continue to depend on their parents to care for them. Many of these parents are at a stage in their life when they need the type of nurturing and care they have bestowed on their children. For these elderly parents, the strain can be enormous. "I worry all the time," one parent shares. "What will happen when I die?"

Adults with mental retardation find financial and housing obstacles to achieving independence. For example, a parent who loved her son and wanted him to gain the independence he was capable of achieving had to disown him, the only way he could receive Medicaid and afford to live in an apartment with a roommate. Her son who is deaf and mentally retarded signed, "All of this has helped me to have good goals and to be successful in independent living."

Many adults with mental retardation have been on waiting lists for over a decade to be placed in group homes that could provide them with independence and opportunities for meaningful employment. Instead of planned, careful, individualized placement of these adults, much of the placement in group homes has been crisis-oriented, based on who is most desperate for care, usually when a caregiver becomes extremely ill or dies.

One major cause for the lack of group homes is neighborhood resistance. Why do neighbors resist? Part of it is fear and part of it is financial (concern about property values). How would you feel about a group home being constructed in your neighborhood?

See *Cleveland Jewish News*, May 16, 1997, and *Newsday*, May 2, 1994, p. A05.

---

17. Chromosomal disorders and oxygen deprivation are associated with which type of causes? (See Identifying the Causes of Mental Retardation)

18. What is the frequency of occurrence for Down syndrome, one of the most common chromosomal disorders? (See Identifying the Causes of Mental Retardation; Biomedical Causes)

19. How are chromosomal disorders identified? Name and describe the process. (See Identifying the Causes of Mental Retardation; Biomedical Causes)

20. Name the most common cause of mental retardation and list at least three possible influencing factors. (See Identifying the Causes of Mental Retardation; Psychosocial Disadvantage)
    Most common cause: _____

    Influencing factors: _____

21. Out of a school of 500 students, probably _____ to _____ would have mental retardation. (See Identifying the Prevalence of Mental Retardation)

22. Why is it believed that more students are being diagnosed with learning disabilities than mental retardation? (See Identifying the Prevalence of Mental Retardation)

23. List the three levels of prevention, the time of intervention, and at least one example of each. (See Identifying the Causes of Mental Retardation; Psychosocial Disadvantage.)

Level	Time of Intervention	Example
a.		
b.		
c.		

What Are Evaluation Procedures?

24. An important type of evaluation for students who might have mental retardation is the _____, which is completed by parents, teachers, or others who work closely with the student. (See Determining the Presence of Mental Retardation)

Include Us

Christy Johnson searched diligently and in vain for an entertainment video that featured children with disabilities like her daughter Tiffani, who has mental retardation. When Christy attended the National Down Syndrome Congress's annual conference in 1995, she shared her frustration with Lou Shaw, a Hollywood producer whose daughter Hillary also has mental retardation. Together, they formed TiffHill Productions, named for their daughters, and created the video *Include Us*, which features children at a playground, forming a rainy-day band from kitchen utensils, and enjoying a magic show. Some national video store chains now carry *Include Us*, and sales have been strong. An educator's guide comes with the video, in case you want to purchase it for your classroom.

Christy cried when she learned that one five-year-old had befriended a classmate with Down syndrome after watching the video. "It's so important for typical children to know they can have friendships with people like my daughter," Christy says.

See *Good Housekeeping*, June 1997, p. 36, and the web site http://IncludeUs.com for more information.

---

25. What four domains of essential characteristics of self-determination are measured by The Arc's Self-Determination Scale? (See Determining the Nature and Extent of Special Education and Related Services)
   a. _____
   b. _____
   c. _____
   d. _____

What and How Do Professionals Teach?

26. Identify the three major curriculum options for students with mild and moderate mental retardation and describe their focus. (See Curriculum)

Curriculum Option	Curriculum Focus
a.	
b.	
c.	

The Rehabilitation Research and Training Center on Improving Community Integration for Persons with Mental Retardation is located at the University of Minnesota. Its goal is to improve community integration by conducting applied research, training, and dissemination activities in each of five areas: community living arrangements, financial support, extended service options and opportunities for community integration, social skills and interpersonal relationships, and personal independence and choice. A wealth of useful and relevant material is available by contacting the Center at 612/624-6328 or 612/625-6619 (fax).

27. Methods that focus on the importance of self-determination include instruction in which seven basic skills? (See Methods)

a._____   e. _____

b. _____   f. _____

c. _____   g. _____

d. _____

28. Match the percentages of students with their education placements. (See Inclusion)

a. _____ 8.6%	1. Separate class
b. _____ 26.1%	2. Residential facility
c. _____ 0.5%	3. Resource room
d. _____ 7.0%	4. Regular class
e. _____ 0.7%	5. Separate school
f. _____ 57 %	6. Homebound/ hospital

29. What is the difference between the term *optimal inclusion* and *full inclusion*? (See Inclusion)
_____

30. What is the chief benefit of the Group Action Planning Process? (See Collaboration)
_____

31. List key features for each of the following programs. (See What Are Program Options?)

Program	Key Features
Project EAGLE, Kansas City	
Morristown, Vermont, Elementary School	
Birmingham, Michigan Public Schools	
Project TASSEL, Shelby, NC	

Appropriate Candidate

Sandra Jensen has faced many challenges as a result of having Down syndrome and a congenital heart defect. "She's a real warrior, a real role model," comments a rehabilitation administrator and a friend. Sandra had an apartment, worked in a cafeteria, and advocated for the rights of the disabled. But her health began to slow her down, and doctors told her that her only chance to survive was to have a heart-lung transplant.

Administrators at two university hospitals refused her cardiologist's request, stating that people with Down syndrome are not "appropriate candidates." One hospital specified that Sandra's memory and recall problems might affect her ability to adhere to a medical regimen. However, Sandra's attendant who started assisting Sandra when her health failed, said that Sandra took her own medication and blood pressure without assistance.

Previously, Sandra had experienced another refusal from doctors. They denied her an operation after she was born because she was mentally retarded. It is likely that that surgery would have prevented her adult health problems.

"I wanted to live," Sandra said about her desire to have the transplant. After a year, Sandra finally received her new heart and lungs. As a result of her advocacy, Congress enacted a bill forbidding health care providers from denying transplant requests from people with disabilities. Sandra says about her new chance at life, "I may be retarded and only 35 years old. But I know how good it is to be alive."

See *Good Housekeeping*, February 1997, pp. 90-96, and *People*, October 16, 1995, p. 67+.

APPLICATION EXERCISES FOR CHAPTER 8

Application Exercise 8a. Identifying Limitations in Intellectual Functioning

Identify which area related to intellectual limitations is affected in the following situations:

1. Juanita doesn't respond when people call her name. _____

2. Shawn learned how to work subtraction problems on paper, but he can't figure out how much change he should get at the store. _____

3. Natisha isn't interested in doing anything after school except watching TV. _____

4. Maria learns to spell her name one day, but she can't remember how to spell it on the next day. _____

Application Exercise 8b. Adaptive Behavior Limitations

Identify which adaptive behavior limitation is being remediated in the following situations:

1. Mohammad is learning to look both ways before crossing the street. _____

2. Lettie is learning not to grab things away from other students. _____

3. Jose is learning to read the words "men" and "women" on restroom signs. _____

4. Sharon's teacher is encouraging her not to limit her responses to one or two words. _____

5. Alonzo is learning to dress himself. _____

Application Exercise 8c. Obstacles to Learning Challenge

Based upon the five major questions* addressed in this chapter, summarize the major concepts concerning mental retardation. For each major chapter question, describe how you personally dealt with (a) attention, (b) memory, (c) generalization, and (d) motivation problems in learning the concepts of this chapter.

*Five Major Questions: What is mental retardation? What are evaluation procedures? What and how do professionals teach? How is participation encouraged? What are program options?

ANSWERS TO MARGIN QUESTIONS

Page 319   To define mental retardation taking a strengths perspective, AAMR might state that mental retardation refers to significant limitations in present functioning "but does not exclude the existences of strengths and capacities in adaptive skill areas across various life domains." (The text inside the quotation marks represents the addition of a strengths perspective to the present definition.) This approach is consistent with AAMR's stated assumption that "specific adaptive limitations often coexist with strengths in other adaptive skills or other personal capacities."

Page 322   Many people remember the numbers by grouping digits in chunks, actively repeating the digits in correct sequence in their minds, and/or associating the numbers with numbers that are memorable (e.g., number on the uniform of a favorite athlete).

Page 346   Full inclusion refers to placement in general education classrooms with the appropriate support so that the student can meaningfully benefit from the curriculum and instruction. Optional inclusion suggests that there are various points on the continuum of services that are appropriate for placement given the student's needs for intensive instruction. It does not suggest that placement should always be in general education classrooms. Likely, The Arc would object to the concept of optimal inclusion. They believe that intensity of instruction can be brought into general education classes so that goals of placement with chronological-age peers and appropriate instruction are delivered in the same setting.

Page 346   Contributions might include developing a friendship with the individual with the disability and hanging out together, suggesting community resources that might be helpful, coming up with creative ideas when brainstorming current problems, and working to take "next steps" to help implement preferred alternatives. Benefits might include gaining friends, developing and refining skills related to inclusion and collaboration, learning more about the community, deriving a stronger sense of self-esteem, and knowing that personal actions have genuinely made a difference in another person's quality of life.

SAMPLE QUIZ FOR CHAPTER 8

Circle the correct answer

TRUE OR FALSE

T or F   1.   Mental retardation is a social construct.

T or F   2.   It was generally believed that a student who was "educable" would be able to develop functional academic skills at a fourth- or fifth-grade level while those who were "trainable" would be able to learn self-care and social skills but not be able to learn to read.

T or F   3.   According to the 1992 AAMR definition, mental retardation manifests before age 18.

T or F   4.   Samantha's recent IQ score was 78. This score enabled her to receive a diagnosis of mental retardation with appropriate services.

T or F   5.   Although many causes of mental retardation are known, it is often not clear which causes apply to a particular individual.

MULTIPLE CHOICE

6.   Which of the following is the new phrase in the title of the AAMR's recent manual that reflects a new perspective in the definition of mental retardation?

   a.   Definition
   b.   Classification
   c.   Characteristics
   d.   Systems of support

7.   Sharla, a student with mental retardation, often experiences frequent failure. In order to prevent future failure she sets low goals. Which of the following is <u>not</u> true about Sharla?

   a.   She distrusts her own solutions.
   b.   She seeks cues from others.
   c.   She lacks motivation to learn or act.
   d.   She is inner-directed.

8.   A person identified with mental retardation must have limitations in how many of the 10 adaptive skill areas essential for daily functioning?

   a.   A minimum of two
   b.   A minimum of three
   c.   A minimum of four
   d.   A minimum of five

9.   Bill lacks skills related to making choices. Which characteristic of mental retardation is associated with this limitation?

   a.   Limitations in intellectual functioning
   b.   Limitations in academic functioning
   c.   Limitations in adaptive skill areas
   d.   Need for supports

10.   With which type of mental retardation are biomedical causes most frequently associated?

   a.   Slight
   b.   Moderate
   c.   Severe
   d.   Profound

11.   Approximately how many known causes of mental retardation have been identified?

   a.   400
   b.   600
   c.   800
   d.   1000

12. Which of the following interventions are best addressed with tertiary prevention?
    a. Good nutrition during pregnancy
    b. Lead screening
    c. Medical control of seizure disorders
    d. Special education to reduce the effects of a present disability

13. Which of the following is not true about Down syndrome?
    a. It occurs in approximately one in seven hundred live births.
    b. Karyotyping shows that the individual has 46 chromosomes.
    c. It can be identified as early as the first few hours after birth.
    d. Three separate chromosomal aberrations are associated with Down syndrome.

14. Jimmie's curriculum focuses on basic academic and social skills. He receives intensive programming in reading, math, and language arts. Which type of curriculum option is this?
    a. Remedial
    b. General classroom support
    c. Adult outcomes
    d. Life-skills preparation

15. Which of the following most accurately portrays where most students with mental retardation are placed in school: from most frequently to least frequently?
    a. Separate school, separate class, resource room
    b. Separate class, resource room, regular class
    c. Regular class, separate school, resource room
    d. Resource room, regular class, separate class

SHORT ANSWER

16. What are the four areas of impairment in the learning process that students with mental retardation typically experience?

    a. _____   c. _____
    b. _____   d. _____

17. Students with mental retardation need varying intensities of support. Identify the four levels of intensities and explain each one briefly.

    a. _____
    b. _____
    c. _____
    d. _____

18. Why is there an increasing curricular emphasis on a life-skills orientation from the early years?

    _____

    _____

ESSAY

19. Explain the changes in the definition of mental retardation over time. Discuss how the latest changes offer new benefits to students like Ryan.

20. Compare and contrast major differences between GAP and IEP on the basis of short-term and long-term benefits.

CHAPTER 9: SEVERE AND MULTIPLE DISABILITIES

CHAPTER OVERVIEW

Students with severe and multiple disabilities typically have severe mental retardation and other accompanying disabilities. This chapter examines the categories of characteristics of these students in relationship to the causes and prevalence as understood today. Various evaluation tools are explored, with a particular focus on Making Action Plans (MAPs). Innovative curriculum and methods are examined to see what possibilities are being utilized for students with severe and multiple disabilities. Important aspects of inclusion and collaboration are presented in the context of real life applications. Some strong program options tie together the chapter's contents, demonstrating that students with severe and multiple disabilities have many options and possibilities.

The life of eight-year-old Joshua Spoor provides an illustration of a student with very severe disabilities who has the benefit of attending one of the country's premier inclusion programs—the Johnson City, New York school program. Joshua's story also illustrates that special challenges can arise within families that require families to find additional support in order to meet the 24-hour needs of their children. In Joshua's case, he lives at a residential program, but he still has the opportunity to be included in one of his community's schools.

CHAPTER AT-A-GLANCE

Chapter Outline	Instructional Goals	Key Concepts
WHAT ARE SEVERE AND MULTIPLE DISABILITIES?		
Defining Severe and Multiple Disabilities	• Recognize that the term defines a very diverse group of people	• IDEA has two separate definitions, one for multiple disabilities and one for severe disabilities.
Describing the Characteristics • Intellectual Functioning • Adaptive Behaviors • Motor Development • Sensory Impairments • Health Care Needs • Communication Skills	• Describe key characteristics of severe and multiple disabilities	• Two indications of intellectual function include limited academic skills and levels of awareness. • Deficits in adaptive behavior include a lack in self-care skills, a lack of typical social interactions, and challenging behaviors. • Delayed motor development often results in abnormal muscle tone. • Two out of five students with severe and multiple disabilities typically have sensory impairments. • Health care needs include procedures such as clean intermittent catheterization, gastrostomy tube feeding, and respiratory ventilation. • The critical factor in communication is to identify and interpret a student's particular method of communication.
Identifying the Causes of Severe and Multiple Disabilities • Genetic Metabolic Disorders • Disorders of Brain Formation • Preventing Severe and Multiple Disabilities	• Identify causes of severe and multiple disabilities • Explain ways to prevent severe and multiple disabilities	• Etiology is unknown in 40% of this population. • Most known causes are due to prenatal biomedical factors. • Some severe and multiple disabilities are preventable through medical technology, maternal education, and genetic counseling.

Identifying the Prevalence of Severe and Multiple Disabilities	• Recognize prevalence rates	• Prevalence rates vary between 1% and 1.6% of all students in IDEA programs.
WHAT ARE EVALUATION PROCEDURES?		
Determining the Presence of a Disability	• Explain how major assessment tools are used to determine the presence of severe and multiple disabilities	• Screening tests such as the Apgar determine the type and extent of the disability. • While controversial, IQ tests and adaptive behavior scales are most often used to make classification decisions.
Determining the Nature and Extent of Special Education and Related Services • Developmental Model • Ecological Model • Behavior States • Making Action Plans (MAPs)	• Compare the characteristics of different approaches for determining special education and related services	• Approaches to assessing skills for curriculum and program development, including the developmental model, the ecological model, assessment of behavior states, and Making Action Plans, offer different perspectives to assess skills.
WHAT AND HOW DO PROFESSIONALS TEACH?		
Curriculum	• Differentiate curriculum options available for use with students with severe and multiple disabilities	• Most recently, curriculum has focused on the environmental ecological approach. • Multilevel instruction and curriculum overlapping are effective to participate in shared activities with peers without disabilities.
Methods • Systematic Instruction • Partial Participation and Adaptations	• Examine effective methods for teaching students with severe and multiple disabilities	• Systematic instruction includes procedures to teach skills and the ways to reinforce correct responses. • Effective instruction is enhanced by providing opportunities to participate in activities partially when full participation is not possible.
HOW IS PARTICIPATION ENCOURAGED?		
Inclusion	• Identify appropriate settings for students with severe and multiple disabilities	• The majority of students are taught in separate facilities or programs, yet a variety of setting are used according to the student's needs and abilities.
Collaboration • Professional collaboration • Family collaboration • Students and community collaboration	• Explore ways to collaborate for students with severe and multiple disabilities	• Because of medical and health care needs, families, educators, physicians and occupational therapists, speech and language pathologists, and medical personnel, must work collaboratively together.
Careers	• Examine careers available that work with students with severe and multiple disabilities	• Many career options are available, such as a pediatrician, nurse, speech-language pathologist, rehabilitation counselor or special education teacher.

WHAT ARE PROGRAM OPTIONS?		
Early Intervention and Preschool Years	• Describe characteristics of effective preschool programs	• Twenty-three preschool programs have successfully included infants, toddlers, and preschoolers through the Circle of Inclusion Program.
Elementary Years	• Identify effective elementary school programs for students with severe and multiple disabilities	• The Johnson City schools provide an excellent model of inclusion and collaboration.
Middle and Secondary Years	• Describe characteristics of effective programs for middle and secondary students	• Whittier High School made positive changes as part of a schoolwide improvement plan. Negative special education labels were removed and all students grouped heterogeneously.
Transitional and Postsecondary Years	• Identify effective program options for adults with severe and multiple disabilities	• One effective school for students with severe and multiple disabilities is the University Connection in Washington, D.C.

PROJECT OPTIONS

1. Do a library search of children's literature to find as many books as possible that relate to students with severe and multiple disabilities. Classify the books according to the amount of inclusion in typical settings experienced by the individuals with disabilities.

2. Design your own evaluation for students with severe and multiple disabilities based on the best aspects of the models presented in this chapter.

3. Research different support systems and organizations available in your community. Based on all you learn, create a plan for one student that would incorporate the best advantages offered within your community.

4. In a local school or institution, get to know one student and do a case study using an ecological inventory. Include a "Vision for the Future" statement to summarize your findings.

KEY TERMS

Amniotic band syndrome

Augmentative and alternative communication

Authentic assessment

Clean intermittent catheterization

Ecological assessment

Ecological curriculum

Encephalocele

Enzymes

Functional academic skills

Gastrostomy tube feeding

Metabolism

Muscle atrophy

Reciprocal friendship

Respiratory ventilation

CHAPTER 9 GUIDED REVIEW

> ### Kenny
>
> Can students with severe and multiple disabilities be successfully included in general classrooms? Kenny's story suggests that it can happen. Kenny has severe and multiple disabilities, including emotional and behavioral disorders. To make inclusion work, Kenny's principal and teacher asked for and received the following services: speech-language specialist, learning consultant, special education teacher, school psychologist, and an aide. Staff-wide training prepared the school to meet Kenny's needs, and Kenny received a modified curriculum. Now, Kenny is exceeding academic expectations, behaves more appropriately, and enjoys the acceptance and friendship of his peers. Inclusion can be a positive experience for all involved, but it requires commitment, collaboration, and financial resources to be successful.
>
> See *CEC Today*, September 1994.

What Are Severe and Multiple Disabilities?

1. According to the definitions discussed for severe and multiple disabilities, list five types of disabilities that are included in this category. (See What Are Severe and Multiple Disabilities?; Defining Severe and Multiple Disabilities)

    a. _____

    b. _____

    c. _____

    d. _____

    e. _____

2. What two characteristics pervade these different definitions? (See Defining Severe and Multiple Disabilities)

    a. _____

    b. _____

3. Which level of mental retardation do the vast majority of students who are served in programs for students with severe and multiple disabilities have? (See Defining Severe and Multiple Disabilities)

    _____

4. Identify the six categories of characteristics that help describe students with severe and multiple disabilities. Then describe key identifying features of that characteristic. (See Describing the Characteristics)

Characteristic Category	Key Identifying Features
a.	
b.	
c.	
d.	
e.	
f.	

5. What are the two indicators of intellectual functioning in students with severe and multiple disabilities? (See Describing the Characteristics)

    a. _____

    b. _____

6. What two adaptive behaviors are especially relevant for individuals with severe and multiple disabilities? (See Describing the Characteristics)

   a. _____

   b. _____

Many children with severe and multiple disabilities die young as a result of their medical conditions. Carol Abbot's son Brian died when he was six. She says that, despite his young death, the significance of his life was universal. Everyone who knew him "found that they were moved and changed for the better by their encounters with Brian. . . . People were impressed with his *being*. Brian radiated peaceful acceptance of life."

See *Exceptional Parent*, October 1993, p. 24.

---

7. Hearing and vision impairments are so common among individuals with severe and multiple disabilities that _____ out of every _____ students have sensory impairments. (See Describing the Characteristics)

8. What are three examples of health care needs of students with severe and multiple disabilities that now are being met by teachers and other school staff? (See Describing the Characteristics)

   a. _____

   b. _____

   c. _____

9. The majority of known causes for severe and multiple disabilities relate to prenatal biomedical factors. Give four examples of these factors. (See Identifying the Causes of Severe and Multiple Disabilities)

   a. _____

   b. _____

   c. _____

   d. _____

10. Abnormalities in a parent's genes can cause a disorder in a child's metabolism. The two types of hereditary genetic transmissions discussed in the chapter are _____ and _____. In recessive disorders, when both parents have the gene, the children have a _____ % chance of being affected by the disorder. In dominant disorders, when a carrier and a noncarrier have children, the children have a _____ % chance of developing the disorder. If both the parents have the dominant gene, the disease can be _____ for a child. (See Identifying the Causes of Severe and Multiple Disabilities)

11. Identify and explain with examples current techniques to identify and possibly prevent multiple disabilities. (See Identifying the Causes of Severe and Multiple Disabilities)

Technique	Explanation and Examples
a. Prenatal fetal therapy	
b. Routine postnatal screenings	
c. Maternal education	

12. The prevalence of severe and multiple disabilities appears to be between _____ percent and _____ percent. (See Identifying the Prevalence of Severe and Multiple Disabilities)

What Are Evaluation Procedures?

13. Newborns are screened with a(n) _____ test which measures the following five physical traits: (See What Are Evaluation Procedures?; Determining the Presence of Severe and Multiple Disabilities)

   a. _____

   b. _____

   c. _____

   d. _____

   e. _____

14. What four approaches are more beneficial for evaluation than standardized measures? (See What Are Evaluation Procedures?; Determining the Nature and Extent of Special Education and Related Services)

   a. _____ measures focus on predetermined skill checklists.

   b. _____ measures focus on functional skills needed within the student's particular environments.

   c. _____ measures focus on identifying a student's level of awareness and responsiveness at different times of the day.

   d. _____ measures focus on comprehensive lifestyle enhancement.

We encourage you to contact The Association for Persons with Severe Handicaps (TASH), a professional organization that advocates inclusion for people with severe disabilities into family, educational, and community settings. TASH sponsors conferences, a journal, a newsletter, and a range of educational opportunities. They can be reached at 11201 Greenwood Avenue North; Seattle, WA 98133; 206-361-8870.

What and How Do Professionals Teach? Curriculum and Methods

15. Explain the emphasis of the ecological curriculum approach. (See What and How Do Professionals Teach?; Curriculum)

   _____

   _____

   _____

16. Name and describe the two ways for adapting the general education curriculum so that students can participate fully. (See What and How Do Professionals Teach?; Curriculum)

Curriculum Adaptation	*Identifying Characteristic*
a.	
b.	

17. During systematic instruction, teachers verbally or manually _____ students to demonstrate steps in a skill sequence. These _____ help students make correct responses. Rewarding _____ _____ is another important part of systematic instruction. (See What and How Do Professionals Teach?; Methods)

18. Identify eight levels of prompts and create as many examples for each level of prompt as you can. (See Figure 9-7 in What and How Do Professionals Teach?; Methods)

Level of Prompt	Examples of Behaviors
a.	
b.	
c.	
d.	
e.	
f.	
g.	
h.	

19. List and define the six types of partial participation that students with severe and multiple disabilities may learn. (See What and How Do Professionals Teach?; Methods)

a. _____

b. _____

c. _____

d. _____

e. _____

f. _____

The Research and Training Center on Improving Supported Employment Outcomes for Individuals with Developmental and Other Severe Disabilities is located at Virginia Commonwealth University in Richmond, Virginia. The goal of this Center is to increase employment options for individuals with severe disabilities. This Center serves as a national clearinghouse of research and best practice information. Their telephone number is 804-367-1851. Their fax number is 804-828-2521.

20. Match the four instructional strategies for individualized adaptations for students with severe and multiple disabilities to examples of adaptations. (See What and How Do Professionals Teach?; Methods)

Instructional Strategy	Examples of Adaptations
a. Adapting Skill Sequences	1. _____ Allowing a longer lunch period so student who has difficulty eating quickly can eat with peers in cafeteria
b. Adapting Rules	2. _____Asking a friend to help turn pages for a student who has poor fine motor skills

c. Utilizing Personal Assistance d. Materials and Devices	3. _____ Using color-coded home phone numbers for a student who has low reading ability 4. _____Sitting on floor before picking up puzzle pieces from the floor for a student who is unable to balance when bending and reaching 5. _____Using enlarged game pieces for a student with poor fine motor skills 6. _____Asking someone to push out-of-reach elevator button for a student in a wheelchair 7. _____ Writing name with a rubber stamp for a student unable to write name 8. _____Tagging clothes that match with coded labels for a student who has difficulty matching colors

How Is Participation Encouraged?

21. What percentage of students identified as having multiple disabilities are taught in residential facilities, special schools, and separate classes within a regular school? (See How Is Participation Encouraged?; Inclusion)
_____%

22. There are six themes related to the successful inclusion of students with disabilities. Rank and explain your ranking for these six themes as they apply to students with severe disabilities. (See How Is Participation Encouraged?; Inclusion)
    a. (Highest priority) _____
    b. _____
    c. _____
    d. _____
    e. _____
    f. _____

23. Explain the different roles for each of the following collaborators in the life of a student with severe and multiple disabilities. (See How Is Participation Encouraged?; Collaboration)
    Professional Collaborator: _____
    _____

    Family Collaborator: _____
    _____

    Student and Community Collaborator: _____
    _____

Consider the community in which you are living. What are some of the recreational opportunities in which you think Joshua Spoor and his family could participate as a family unit? What changes do you think might be made in community services and support so that they might be more responsive to him and his family?

---

24. Of the many career opportunities for working with individuals who have severe and multiple disabilities, list three of your own preferences. (See How Is Participation Encouraged?; Careers)
    a. _____
    b. _____
    c. _____

What Are Program Options?

25. What type of placement does IDEA favor for students with severe and multiple disabilities? (See What Are Program Options?)

   _____

26. List key features for each of the following programs. (See What Are Program Options?)

Program	Key Features
The Circle of Inclusion Program, Kansas	
Johnson City Central District, New York	
Whittier High School, Southeast Los Angeles	
University Connection, George Washington University	

I Love My Brother James

Siblings often benefit from having a brother or sister with severe and multiple disabilities. Fourth-grader Carlo Testa-Aviles writes that he loves his brother James. And when people call James retarded, Carlo says he doesn't care, or even listen. "I don't believe that there is any label that can be put on my brother or anyone else's. We are all alike in this world, and we are all different." (See _Exceptional Parent_, May 1994, p. 68.)

A resource that can help you explain disabilities to siblings is _Sib Shops: Workshops for Siblings of Children with Special Needs_ (Baltimore: Paul H. Brookes Publishing Company).

APPLICATION EXERCISES FOR CHAPTER 9

Application Exercise 9a. Determining the Likelihood of a Disability in a Newborn

Based on Apgar evaluations, identify which infants are at risk for disabilities. Rank the infants in order of risk and defend your ranking.

	Heart Rate		Respiratory Effort		Muscle Tone		Gag Reflex		Color	
	1 min	5 min	1 min	5 min	1 min	5 min	1 min	5 min	1 min	5 min
1. Miguel	2	2	2	2	2	2	2	2	1	2
2. Susannah	1	1	1	1	0	0	0	0	1	1
3. Vishnu	2	2	2	2	2	2	1	2	2	2
4. Felicia	0	1	0	1	0	0	0	0	0	1
5. Chin-Cheng	2	2	1	1	2	2	1	1	2	2

Application Exercise 9b. Assessment Methods for Student Learning and Performance

Identify which assessment method is being used for the students described below.

Assessment Model	Student's Performance Activity
a. Developmental Model	1. _____ Zubaidah is putting pegs in a pegboard to demonstrate eye-hand coordination.
b. Ecological Model	2. _____ Khaldoun is learning to dance to popular music, thus learning to spend time after school with friends.
c. Behavior States	3. _____ Daniela is vocalizing when asked direct questions in order to stay alert for 10 minutes.
d. Making Action Plans	4. _____ Janis is locating an item on a grocery shelf to demonstrate a knowledge of shopping.

Application Exercise 9c. Concept Application in Context

Discuss the life of Joshua Spoor as you summarize each of the five major questions* addressed in this chapter. Summarize the major concepts concerning severe and multiple disabilities as you integrate your knowledge about Joshua with the chapter contents for students with severe and multiple disabilities.

*Five Major Questions: What are severe and multiple disabilities? What are evaluation procedures? What and how do professionals teach? How is participation encouraged? What are program options?

ANSWERS TO MARGIN QUESTIONS

This chapter included only a few reflective questions, asking for personal perspectives.

SAMPLE QUIZ FOR CHAPTER 9

Circle the correct answer.

TRUE OR FALSE

T or F 1. Deaf-blindness is considered a multiple disability.

T or F 2. Many students with severe disabilities function at the early childhood sensorimotor stage of development.

T or F 3. Over one-third of students with severe and multiple disabilities have sensory impairments.

T or F 4. Prenatal biomedical factors are responsible for the majority of severe and multiple disabilities in individuals.

T or F 5. Rewarding correct performance is the first step in ensuring successful skill attainment.

MULTIPLE CHOICE

6. What are the four intensity levels of support for students with multiple and severe disabilities?
    a. Intermittent, limited, extensive, pervasive
    b. Minimal, maintenance, major, intensive
    c. Minimal, limited, profound, extensive
    d. Episodic, transitional, constant, permanent

7. Which of the following is <u>not</u> mentioned by the authors as a category of characteristics which describes students with multiple and severe disabilities?
    a. Health care needs
    b. Sensory functioning
    c. Adaptive behavior
    d. Functional needs

8. For what percentage of children born with severe or multiple disabilities is there no identifiable cause?
    a. 25%
    b. 40%
    c. 55%
    d. 70%

9. Tommy has an Apgar score of 6 five minutes after birth. What will most likely happen next?
    a. Diagnostic testing over several years
    b. Nothing, as long as he seems aware
    c. Prereferral in an early childhood program
    d. Referral to a residential facility for children with severe disabilities

10. Which assessment method for educational program development uses a "bottom-up" approach that uses sequenced skills checklists?
    a. Behavior states
    b. Ecological model
    c. Developmental model
    d. Environmental model

11. What is the key to an ecological curriculum approach?
    a. Identifying the adult domains, subdomains, and specific life-skills as a basis for organizing instruction
    b. Adapting rules to individualize the curriculum
    c. Community collaboration
    d. A comprehensive analysis of the disability and how it can be overcome in the student's natural environment

12. What is the level of the prompt that occurs when the teacher positions Kasey's hand directly over the correct silverware bin?
     a. Gestural
     b. Full physical
     c. Minimal physical
     d. Partial physical

13. Devon has poor motor skills and cannot handle a broom. He is allowed to use a cordless vacuum cleaner instead. What adaptation has occurred?
     a. Adapting rules
     b. Using materials and devices
     c. Adapting skill sequences
     d. Incorporating personal independence

14. Since the passage of IDEA, where is the largest percentage of students with multiple disabilities now placed?
     a. Regular classroom
     b. Separate class
     c. Residential facility
     d. Homebound

15. Which of the following is true about Libby's "head cheerleaders"?
     a. They include the principal, general education teacher, special education teacher, paraprofessional, and school counselor.
     b. They meet weekly to discuss her progress.
     c. They collaborate by having the same goals for Libby.
     d. They address her needs holistically, with literal and figurative support.

SHORT ANSWER

16. What two major characteristics pervade the definitions of multiple and severe disabilities?
     a. _____
     b. _____

17. List four approaches that can be used to assess a student's skills for specific curriculum goals and program development.
     c. _____
     d. _____
     e. _____
     f. _____

18. Identify three problems that occur when using the developmental model of assessment with students who have severe and multiple disabilities.
     a. _____
     b. _____
     c. _____

ESSAY

19. Compare and contrast the benefits to students for the four approaches used to assess a student's skills for specific curriculum goals and program development: developmental model, the ecological model, the behavior states, and Making Action Plans (MAPs).

20. Describe the factors that make the Circle of Inclusion Program effective. Compare these factors with those of other program options described in this chapter.

CHAPTER 10: AUTISM

CHAPTER OVERVIEW

Autism, the disability that affects verbal and nonverbal communication and social interaction, was not recognized as a separate IDEA disability until 1991. This chapter examines how our understanding of autism has changed in many areas. It traces how autism's definition has emerged and the typical characteristics, causes, and prevalence rates associated with people with this disability. Various evaluation procedures are explored as well as successful curriculum and methods. Special attention is given to the methods of positive behavioral support and social stories. Issues surrounding successful inclusion and collaboration on behalf of students with autism are also discussed, with several important strategies highlighted. Key factors of successful program options for students with autism are presented along with the stories of how students Sam and Amro overcame great difficulties.

This chapter examines autism through the life of fourth-grade student A.J. Poston. A.J. spends the majority of his time in a "magnet" special classroom for students with autism but is included in a general education classroom for a portion of the school day. His school district is moving in the direction of inclusion, having bused all students with autism to a nearby school district several years ago. The collaboration box in chapter 3 illustrates an example of how his school might take the next step in implementing inclusion by doing away with the "magnet" special classroom and including students with autism in their neighborhood schools.

CHAPTER AT-A-GLANCE

Chapter Outline	Instructional Goals	Key Concepts
WHAT IS AUTISM?		
Defining Autism	• Recognize the diverse factors defining autism	Autism is a developmental disability significantly affecting verbal and nonverbal communication and social interaction.
Describing the Characteristics • Language Development • Social Interaction • Stereotypical Behavior • Behavioral Challenges • Need for Environmental Predictability • Sensory and Movement Disorders • Intellectual Functioning	• Identify the key characteristics of autism • Explain the role of facilitative communication	• The seven main characteristics of autism, are listed in the first column. • Two language impairments associated with autism are delayed language and echolalia. • Facilitative communication is a training method that involves supporting a person who does not speak or has highly repetitive speech to use a facilitator and keyboard to communicate. • People with autism often have fewer and weaker social skills. • Stereotypical behaviors (inappropriate and repetitive acts are displayed) are typical. • Behavioral challenges include self-injurious behavior, aggression, tantrums, and property destruction. • Predictability and structure are important sources of security. • Sensory disorders often result in under- or overresponsiveness to sensory stimuli. • The majority of people with autism function in the IQ range of mental retardation.

Identifying the Causes of Autism • Historical Perspective on Causes • Biomedical Causes	• Trace the changes in explanations for causes of autism • Explain biomedical causes	• Although parents have historically been seen as the cause of their child's autism, this viewpoint is totally unwarranted. • Autism is biologically caused, but the specific biological trigger is unknown at this time.
Identifying the Prevalence of Autism	• Recognize prevalence rates for people with autism	• The prevalence of autism is approximately one person per 1,000.

WHAT ARE EVALUATION PROCEDURES?

Determining the Presence of Autism	• Explain how major assessment tools are used to determine the presence of autism	• The Childhood Autism Rating Scale (CARS) is an assessment tool that is frequently used as part of the multidisciplinary process for identifying students as having autism.
Determining the Nature and Extent of Special Education and Related Services	• Recognize the possibilities for developing a functional assessment with tailored intervention	• A functional assessment identifies specific relationships between environmental events and a student's problem behavior and tailors intervention accordingly.

WHAT AND HOW DO PROFESSIONALS TEACH?

Curriculum	• Differentiate among domains of curricular options for students with autism	• The typical curriculum domains include life skills for integrated community living, vocational preparation, and functional academics.
Methods • Positive Behavioral Support • Social Stories	• Evaluate different methods that are effective for varied student needs	• Positive behavioral support seeks to create a personally tailored responsive environment. • Social stories describe social situations in terms of important social cues and appropriate responses to those cues.

HOW IS PARTICIPATION ENCOURAGED?

Inclusion	• Examine how inclusion is viewed for students with autism	• There are many different viewpoints on the appropriateness of inclusion for students with autism.
Collaboration • Professional Collaboration • Family Collaboration • Student and Community Collaboration	• Explore ways to collaborate on behalf of students with autism	• Collaboration with professionals, families, students, and communities can significantly increase successful inclusion for individuals with autism.
Careers	• Examine careers available that work with students with autism	• Music therapy is a promising career option offering opportunities to work with students with autism.

WHAT ARE PROGRAM OPTIONS?		
Early Intervention and Preschool Years	• Describe characteristics of effective preschool programs	• A model early intervention program emphasizes family support, communication, and community and preschool inclusion.
Elementary Years	• Describe characteristics of effective elementary programs for students with autism	• Positive behavioral support can be used to promote model elementary school practices and to aid students with autism to "get a life" within and outside of school.
Middle and Secondary Years	• Describe characteristics of effective programs for middle and secondary students	• Systematic school reform at the secondary level can result in successful inclusion for students with autism.
Transitional and Postsecondary Years	• Describe characteristics of effective program options for adults with autism	• Community Services for Autistic Adults and Children (CSAAC) has demonstrated that adults with autism can live in typical homes and work in typical jobs when state-of-the-art training and supports are provided.

PROJECT OPTIONS

1. Investigate how your school system educates students with autism. Describe and then evaluate how this schooling lines up with the six values guiding special education.

2. Interview a family with a member who has autism. Get to know each member of the family and ask each to help you draw up a plan for this student that will emphasize the place of the six values guiding special education.

3. Identify one of your own problems related to learning or behavior and complete the five steps of a functional assessment. Construct a scatter plot similar to the one in Figure 10-3 to diagram the assessment. Collaborate with a family member or friend to brainstorm ideas and make plans.

4. Based on the characteristics of as many successful program models for students with autism that you can find, create the ideal program for A. J. Poston, or another student with autism that you personally know. Describe this program at each of the four levels: early childhood, elementary, secondary, and postsecondary years.

KEY TERMS

Asperger disorder

Echolalia

Facilitated communication

Higher functioning autistic disorder

Neuromotor impairment

Positive behavioral support

Savant syndrome

Social stories

Stereotypical behaviors

Pervasive developmental disorder

CHAPTER 10 GUIDED REVIEW

What Is It Like to Have Autism?

Imagine that you enter your classroom and your teacher tells you that you will have only three things to do to get along well in your new room: sit still in your seat, follow simple directions, and be reasonably quiet. It sounds simple, but in a simulation experience designed by Susan Moreno, a parent of a child with autism, these three tasks become very difficult. Participants are in a room where all lights are turned out except a strobe light. A radio is blaring white noise (static). The teacher wears a cotton glove while shaking hands to greet students and varies his voice pitch and volume while speaking. He stands uncomfortably close to each student while conversing. When a student responds by pulling away or making noise, the teacher pats her face with a dampened luffa sponge and screams, "It's all right! Don't be so nervous!"

Students with autism, according to current theory, are overstimulated or understimulated by information they receive through their senses. Thus, a gentle touch could be painful for these students. Words spoken softly may seem loud or not be heard at all. As you continue this review, think about the challenges these students are facing and how you might try to make their school environment more conducive to learning.

What Is Autism?

1. When autism was first identified, why was this condition called early infantile autism? (See Defining Autism)

   _____

2. Autism is a severe form of a broader group of disorders referred to as _____
   _____ _____. (See Defining Autism)

3. Name and describe two common forms of language impairments experienced by students with autism. (See Describing the Characteristics; Language Development)

   a. _____

   b. _____

4. Complete the following chart to demonstrate your knowledge of the major characteristics of autism. (See Describing the Characteristics)

Area Affected	Identifying Characteristics	Appropriate Responses to Students with These Characteristics
a. Language development		
b. Social interaction		
c. Stereotypical behavior		
d. Behavioral challenges		
e. Need for environmental predictability		
f. Sensory and movement disorders		
g. Intellectual functioning		

5. When is language intervention most successful for students with autism? (See Describing the Characteristics; Language Development)

   _____

6. Facilitated Communication is a training method that involves using a human facilitator and keyboard to communicate. Match the element of facilitated communication with its identifying characteristics. (See Describing the Characteristics; Language Development)

1. Physical support	a. _____ Provides emotional support or encouragement, knowing the person's thinking and literacy will reveal themselves over time.
2. Initial training/ introduction	b. _____ Reminds student to keep eyes on the communication aid, use index finger for pointing, reduce extraneous actions, and type what he or she intends to communicate.
3. Maintaining focus	c. _____ Helps student isolate index finger and stabilize student's hand or arm during typing.
4. Avoiding competence testing	d. _____Works on fading physical support as student becomes more independent.
5. Generalization	e. _____ Provides encouragement and repeated attempts to generalize to more facilitators.
6. Fading	f. _____Provides initial activities with fairly predictable answers and encourages progress to open-ended conversation.

7. Define *echolalia* and then tell why children and youth with autism may use echolalia. (See Describing the Characteristics; Language Development)

   _____

   _____

8. List the four categories of behavioral challenges encountered by students with autism and the identifying characteristics for each one. (See Describing the Characteristics; Behavioral Challenges)

   a. _____   _____

   b. _____   _____

   c. _____   _____

   d. _____   _____

Who Are People with Autism?

We experience things holistically. The sight, sound, smell, feel, and emotional tone of a situation hits us all at once. It's hard to filter anything out. Sometimes one sensation seems to trigger all our senses, making it difficult to tell where the real signal came from. We may be alert to information others miss, but the task of processing and dealing with it can be overwhelming.

We are visual learners with good memories. We tend to notice and remember visual details. Often this is very useful, but we may need help to separate what's important from what is not. While others see larger patterns emerge from details, for us these are like hidden pictures that *stay* hidden. The unseen future is difficult to grasp.

We are straightforward and honest. We expect people's words and behavior to mean exactly what they seem, and not to have multiple or covert meanings. The language of emotions can prove especially tricky.

We have specialized interests. We avidly pursue and thoroughly enjoy what appeals to *us*, not just the latest syle or fad.

We prefer routines. Sudden changes are too unnerving. You might say we are traditionalists.

Our friends are very important to us. Being a friend takes a lot of effort and energy. Some people think we don't care about having a social life, but we do.

From Look Again: An Inside View of Autism/PDD by The Autism National Committee.

9. Name and describe two variations of intellectual function associated with students with autism. (See Describing the Characteristics; Intellectual Functioning)

    a. _____

    b. _____

10. How has the perception of the causes of autism changed over time? (See Identifying the Causes of Autism and Preventing Them; Historical Perspective on Causes)

    _____

    _____

11. If a school district has 40,000 students, how many are likely to have autism? _____ How many of those students with autism would be male? _____ (See Identifying the Prevalence of Autism)

What Are Evaluation Procedures?

12. What three areas are most frequently assessed to determine eligibility for the diagnosis of autism? (See What Are Evaluation Procedures?; Determining the Presence of Autism)

    a. _____

    b. _____

    c. _____

13. What is (a) the name for one of the most frequently used diagnostic scales and (b) how many areas of behavioral observations does it require? (c) On what two items do the ratings depend? (See What Are Evaluation Procedures?; Determining the Presence of Autism)

    a. Name: _____

    b. Number of areas: _____

    c. Ratings depend on: 1. _____

       and 2. _____

14. One kind of ecological assessment is functional assessment. Identify the five steps for conducting a functional assessment. (See What Are Evaluation Procedures?; Determining the Nature and Extent of Special Education)

    a. _____

    b. _____

    c. _____

    d. _____

    e. _____

Facilitated Communication

Is facilitated communication a new way to allow people with autism to express themselves, is it a sham, or can it be either, depending on who the facilitator is? If you want to read some articles that support or raise concerns about facilitated communication, you might find the following helpful:

Child Abuse and Neglect, Vol. 18

Choice, Vol. 31, no. 1, p. 222

Mental Retardation, Vol. 32, no. 4, pp. 299-318

New York Times, Vol. 143, p. 21

Newsweek, Vol. 120, no. 12, p. 75

U.S. News & World Report, Vol. 113, no. 4, pp. 63-65

---

15. List examples of circumstances that influence problem behaviors associated with autism. Then propose modifications for intervention. (See What Are Evaluation Procedures?; Determining the Nature and Extent of Special Education)

Factors	Circumstances	Proposed Modifications
Physiological Factors		
Classroom Environment		
Curriculum and Instruction		

What and How Do Professionals Teach?

16. What is the key to appropriate, beneficial education for students with autism? (See What and How Do Professionals Teach?; Curriculum)

    _____

17. Compare and contrast how curriculum options differ for students who function at higher cognitive levels and those who have mental retardation. Give specific examples appropriate to each one. (See What and How Do Professionals Teach?; Curriculum)

Curriculum for Students at Higher Cognitive Levels	Curriculum for Students Who Have Mental Retardation

18. What three areas are typically included in a curriculum for students with autism who also have mental retardation? (See What and How Do Professionals Teach?; Curriculum)

    a. _____

    b. _____

    c. _____

Ah-Kheem?

Cathy Copeland, a school counselor, visited a classroom with a seven-year-old boy with autism throughout one school year. Ben had many challenging as well as appealing behaviors. When Cathy stroked her guitar, he placed his hands on the strings and cocked his head to one side, connecting with her through the music. She noticed that he also seemed to try to connect with his teacher by repeating the question "Ah-kheem? Ah-kheem?" Sometimes Cathy observed the teacher stroking Ben's arms and repeating "Ah-kheem, Ah-kheem" to him, as though in a lullaby.

Cathy began to give meaning to Ben's word. "Ah-kheem" means "Help," she says. Help, ... love..., and accept me. See me as I am, not as you are; ... realize... I need calmness in a chaos over which I have no control."

See *Journal of Emotional and Behavioral Problems* (1994), *3*(3), pp. 67-68

---

19. Identify and briefly describe two frequently used instructional methods for students with autism. (See What and How Do Professionals Teach?; Methods)

    a. _____

    _____

    b. _____

    _____

20. Describe how social stories can decrease aggressive behavior and help students with autism learn how to handle specific social situations. (See What and How Do Professionals Teach?; Methods)

    _____

    _____

How Is Participation Encouraged?

21. What percentage of students with autism are educated in separate environments? (See How Is Participation Encouraged?; Inclusion) _____

22. What percentage of students with autism receive the majority of their education in a general education classroom? (See How Is Participation Encouraged?; Inclusion) _____

23. When is inclusion for students with autism unwarranted? (See How Is Participation Encouraged?; Inclusion)

    _____

24. Identify at least four characteristics of successful inclusion programs for students with autism. (See How Is Participation Encouraged?; Inclusion)

    a. _____

    b. _____

    c. _____

    d. _____

25. Describe at least three things each different collaborator can do to encourage the success of students with autism in a school inclusion model. (See How Is Participation Encouraged?; Collaboration)

Collaborator	Contributions to Student Success
Professional collaborators	1. 2. 3.
Family collaborators	1. 2. 3.
Student and community collaborators	1. 2. 3.

26. In addition to a career as a teacher of students with autism, what other caceer might you also consider? (See How Is Participation Encouraged?; Careers) _____

Two Views from Within

You read part of Temple Grandin's story in this chapter. Temple writes about her experiences growing up with autism in two books: *Emergence: Labeled Autistic* (1996, Warner Books) and *Thinking in Pictures: And Other Reports from My Life with Autism* (1996, Vintage Books).

Another author who writes about her experiences with autism is Donna Williams. As a child, Donna was misdiagnosed as having deafness, mental retardation, and emotional disturbance. Donna chronicles her life, which includes work as a teacher of students with autism, in three books: *Nobody Nowhere: The Extraordinary Life of an Autistic* (1994, Avon), *Somebody Somewhere: Breaking Free from the World of Autism* (1995, Times Books), and *Like Color to the Blind* (1996, Times Books).

What Are Program Options?

27. The importance of early intervention for young children with autism is clear. Compare and contrast the characteristics, goals, and outcomes of the "Lovaas Model" and the program at the Florida Mental Health Institute. (See What Are Program Options?; Early Intervention and Preschool Years)

	Lovaas Model	*Florida Mental Health Institute Program*
Characteristics		
Goals		
Outcomes		

28. Identify the five characteristics of the TEACCH model for elementary students with autism. Star (*) the ones you think were also involved in Sam's successful program. (See What Are Program Options?; Elementary Years)

a. _____

b. _____

c. _____

d. _____

e. _____

29. Explain how excellence and equity are demonstrated in the University of New Hampshire's School Restructuring and Inclusive Education Project. (See What Are Program Options?; Middle and Secondary Years)

_____

_____

30. The success of individuals involved with Community Services for Autistic Adults and Children can be traced to several key factors. Identify at least three factors leading to the success of individuals with autism. (See What Are Program Options?; Middle and Secondary Years)

    a. _____

    b. _____

    c. _____

"When people with autism succeed, it's not because some professor's theory worked to a 't', but because real-life people with real-life common sense did what they had to do with what they got. And no theory can replace that."

KL, a person with autism

APPLICATION EXERCISES FOR CHAPTER 10

Application Exercise 10a. Identifying Characteristics of Autism

Identify which characteristic of autism is in focus for the following students:

a. Language development	1. _____ Bob frequently rocks back and forth, attempting to communicate his boredom with certain situations.
b. Social interaction	2. _____ Malik experiences great anxiety whenever his expected television shows are not on.
c. Stereotypical behavior	3. _____ Shan is in the majority of students with autism, in that her IQ registers below 50.
d. Behavioral challenges	4. _____ Julian screams whenever he has to wear formal clothes to church because they feel scratchy and different.
e. Need for environmental predictability	5. _____ Marga's family saw significant changes in Marga's communication with the use of facilitated communication.
f. Sensory and movement disorders	6. _____ Jimmy has a pattern of not making eye contact with others and chooses to spend large amounts of time alone.
g. Intellectual functioning	7. _____ Eduardo demonstrates aggressive behavior that, with positive behavioral support, is potentially harmful to others.

Application Exercise 10b. Functional Assessment: Matching Situation and Intervention

Identify which intervention is most suited to the situation described.

a. Intersperse an easy activity with the more difficult activity	1. _____ Jemima demands her own way during reading circle and will kick and bite to sit by the teacher.
b. Make sure she eats breakfast and/ or has an early snack.	2. _____ Shanti cries when she is asked to complete a fairly lengthy assignment.
c. Give her a specific place to sit all her own and you the teacher change places each time.	3. _____ Alvara is off task for most of the science class assignment.
d. Ask her to monitor her own corrections or give her an easier assignment.	4. _____ Emily slaps her arm and sometimes others around 10:30 every day because she is hungry.
e. Give her clear instructions about a select portion of the work she is to complete.	5. _____ Samantha argues with the teacher about correcting her mistakes and then refuses to make corrections on daily worksheets.

Application Exercise 10c. Social Stories to Convey Conceptual Understanding

Based upon the five major questions* addressed in this chapter, summarize the major concepts concerning autism. For each major chapter question, create a social story to explain the main concepts in each section.

*Five Major Questions: What is autism? What are evaluation procedures? What and how do professionals teach? How is participation encouraged? What are program options?

ANSWERS TO MARGIN QUESTIONS

Page 406 Different individuals reconcile the difference between research and the perspectives of those people who are very close to the issues in various ways depending upon their philosophy of science. Personally, we try to strike a balance in giving credence to empirical *and* experiential knowledge. There are many family members and teachers who "vouch" for the authenticity of facilitative communication. We would like to see research carried out using collaborative teams involving families, teachers, and researchers to try to understand the source of discrepant perspectives.

Page 412 It has been a traditional belief that asthma in children is caused by living in a stressful environment. Parents with mental health problems are also often blamed for creating emotional disorders within their children. Furthermore, it is not unusual to hear gay and lesbian parents blamed for creating emotional problems within their children. It's clear that parents who feel judged and blamed by professionals often experience intense levels of anger, frustration, and low self-esteem. Consequently, it becomes very difficult for these families to form trusting partnerships with professionals.

Page 413 In A.J.'s community, one would expect about 42 individuals with autism and four or five students with autism in his school district. (Interestingly, there are approximately 12 children who have been identified in the school district.) In terms of promoting relationships, one of the most important things to do is to identify common interests among a group of children who live in close enough proximity so that they have an opportunity to get together both in and outside of school. For A.J., one might identify the other children in his school and neighborhood who share similar interests to his and look for ways to bring them together and to foster a sense of connection.

Page 417 There are almost twice as many problems with hitting in the afternoon as contrasted to the morning. It's important to find out what's going on in the time block for vocational activities, since this is definitely the most problematic time of day.

Page 421 A.J.'s teacher might help create opportunities for A.J. to develop some soccer skills. This might be done through going to soccer games, practicing soccer in physical education classes, and identifying some other children with particularly good soccer skills who might help A.J. develop his own skills. The teacher might also talk with the soccer coach of a community children's soccer league about the possibility of involving A.J. The teacher might work with the coach in creating peer understanding and support so that teammates would know how to help build on A.J.'s strengths.

Page 426 The earlier approach advocated by Bettelheim focused very much on judging and blaming parents for causing the problem. This collaboration model respects parents' expertise and involves them in collaborative educational activities. The early childhood program helps children develop functional language in their interactions in inclusive preschool settings and within their family relationships. We particularly concentrate on identifying the communication needs associated with challenging behavior and teaching children to use communication rather than engaging in inappropriate behavior. In terms of environmental productivity, the early childhood program helps children gain some control over their lives by learning to complete tasks and ask/or get what they want.

Page 432 1. Language development—uses functional communication approaches in teaching children to communicate in their natural environments with family, friends, and teachers.

2. Social interaction—focuses on including children in typical child care, preschool, and community settings and facilitating the social interactions and friendships between children with autism and significant others.

3. Behavioral challenges—uses positive behavioral support in conducting a functional assessment and developing an intervention plan aimed at teaching children meaningful alternative behaviors to replace their challenging behavior and to help them gain access to meaningful social and inclusive opportunities.

SAMPLE QUIZ FOR CHAPTER 10

Circle the correct answer.

TRUE OR FALSE

T or F   1.   Challenging behavior serves as a communicating function.

T or F   2.   The key to appropriate education for students with autism is individualization.

T or F   3.   A high percentage of individuals with autism attain an independent lifestyle.

T or F   4.   IDEA requires the parents of a student with autism to be part of the evaluation and IEP teams.

T or F   5.   Echolalia happens with most children under the age of three, even those without autism.

MULTIPLE CHOICE

6.   Rocking back and forth and hand flapping are examples of what behavioral challenge?

    a.   Stereotypical behavior

    b.   Aggression

    c.   Tantrums

    d.   Self-injury

7.   A.J. participates in a general education fourth grade classroom part of the day. Why do his mother and teachers feel this is not an ideal situation?

    a.   He doesn't like to be with other students with disabilities.

    b.   He thinks the other fourth graders are too rough on the playground.

    c.   The classroom is not predictable enough for him to feel comfortable.

    d.   He does not have enough opportunities to develop his potential.

8.   Sarah, age 7, has autism. Which of the following is most probably true of her?

    a.   She runs to her mother for a hug and bandage when she skins her knee.

    b.   She does not like to spend time alone.

    c.   She always takes her teddy bear with her whenever she leaves the house.

    d.   She greets strangers without prompting but keeps shaking their hand too long.

9.   Jim is a 5-year-old boy with autism who is very sensitive to sensory stimuli. According to Temple Grandin, how can his mother best help Jim when she takes him grocery shopping?

    a.   Calmly describe everything he sees.

    b.   Let him know in advance that a shopping trip will occur.

    c.   Provide him with headphones and a favorite cassette.

    d.   Let him choose a favorite treat to distract him.

10.   Your friend Kristen, who is talented both in athletics and in the fine arts, is thinking about working with children with autism, but she does not want to be a classroom teacher. What might be another appropriate career option you might suggest to her?

    a.   Music therapist

    b.   Lovaas therapist

    c.   CSAAC staff worker

    d.   Bettelheim Project employee

11.   Which of the following most commonly provides security for many individuals with autism?

    a.   Cattle squeeze chutes

    b.   Security blankets

    c.   Rigid routines and patterns

    d.   Loving support of peers

12. Which of the following is <u>not</u> a benefit of social stories for students with autism?

    a. They help in focusing on relevant social cues.

    b. They help in achieving better scores on tests and evaluations.

    c. They help in learning new routines and rules.

    d. They help in expanding social skills.

13. How common is inclusion of students with autism in general education K-12 classrooms?

    a. About 9% of such students receive the majority of their education in a general education classroom.

    b. About 50% of such students are in a general education classroom.

    c. About 27% of such students are in cluster classes, which are considered inclusion.

    d. About 80% of such students are in separate inclusion environments.

14. Laurie, a 10-year-old with autism, has just finished the school year. Her family is packing for a vacation to Disney World. What is Laurie most likely to exhibit?

    a. Anxiety

    b. Sensory disorders

    c. Nonchalance

    d. Happiness

15. What is savant syndrome?

    a. An individual with autism who displays extraordinary ability in one area

    b. An individual with autism who has an IQ above 90

    c. An individual with autism who has Asperger disorder

    d. An individual with autism who has higher functioning autistic disorder

SHORT ANSWER

16. Name two common language impairments in students with autism.

    a. _____ b. _____

17. What is a neuromotor impairment? _____

    _____

18. What is CARS and how is it used? _____

    _____

    _____

ESSAY

19. Discuss principles of positive behavioral support.

20. How has IDEA helped students with autism?

CHAPTER 11: OTHER HEALTH IMPAIRMENTS

CHAPTER OVERVIEW

The category of other health impairments includes disabilities with many diverse characteristics that can be either easy or difficult to identify. The factors common to all health impairments include limitations in strength, vitality, or alertness. Students served under IDEA are those whose educational needs have been adversely affected by the condition. This chapter investigates the multifaceted characteristics, causes, and prevalence of six specific health impairments. Different evaluation processes that can be used for determining the presence of health impairments and the nature and extent of special education needed are discussed. Use of service dogs, handling insensitivity, and coping with grief are topics covered in this chapter that apply to other exceptionalities as well. The place of inclusion and collaboration for students with a chronic illness in the classroom is described, followed by a discussion of various program options currently available in schools and communities today.

The life of eleven-year-old Jacob Empey helps demonstrate and clarify issues revolving around students with other health impairments. Jacob has epilepsy. His condition is classified as "other health impairment" under IDEA because his alertness, vitality, and strength are adversely affected. Jacob frequently experiences generalized tonic-clonic and absence seizures at school. His family, teachers, paraprofessionals, and peers work closely to provide Jacob with an inclusionary school environment that is accommodated to meet his needs.

CHAPTER AT-A-GLANCE

Chapter Outline	Instructional Goals	Key Concepts
WHAT ARE OTHER HEALTH IMPAIRMENTS?		
Defining Other Health Impairments	• Clarify distinctions in defining other health impairments	• The conditions and definitions in this category vary widely in symptoms and prognosis.
Describing the Characteristics • Human Immunodeficiency Virus • Prenatal Substance Exposure • Asthma • Cancer • Juvenile Diabetes • Epilepsy	• Describe key characteristics of other health impairments • Recognize unifying criteria for inclusion as a health impairment	• Students with health impairments have limitations in strength, vitality, or alertness. The condition can be chronic or acute. • To be served under IDEA, educational needs must be adversely affected by the condition. • The conditions vary widely and are condition-specific, but their unifying criteria are limits in strength, vitality, and/or alertness.
Identifying the Causes of Other Health Impairments • Infections • Genetic Factors • Environmental Influences	• Explain causes of other health impairments	• Health impairments can be caused by infections, genetic factors, and environmental factors, including prenatal teratogens and postnatal influences.
Identifying the Prevalence of Other Health Impairments	• Identify prevalence figures for other health impairments and where these students are served	• Schools served 1.9% of students in 1995, but approximately 3% of all students have some type of health impairment that does not qualify them for IDEA special education. • Many IDEA-eligible students are served in the general classroom.

WHAT ARE EVALUATION PROCEDURES?		
Determining the Presence of Other Health Impairments	• Recognize who determines the presence of other health impairments	• A physician usually makes a diagnosis.
Determining the Nature and Extent of Special Education and Related Services	• Identify who decides the nature and extent of special education and how it is decided.	• School personnel have to decide if the student can be served under IDEA evaluation measures.
WHAT AND HOW DO PROFESSIONALS TEACH?		
Curriculum	• Explain how curriculum needs are met for students with other health impairments	• The curricular needs for most students with health impairments are similar to those for students without disabilities.
Methods • Including Service Dogs • Handling Insensitivity • Grief in the Classroom	• Evaluate effective methods for students with other health impairments	• Standard methods work for students with health impairments, though the teacher makes accommodations as necessary. • When a student is dying, teachers should provide honesty and support to the students, family, and classmates.
HOW IS PARTICIPATION ENCOURAGED?		
Inclusion	• Summarize importance of inclusion for students with other health impairments	• Forty percent of students with other health impairments benefit greatly from the acceptance and support of being included in the general education classroom.
Collaboration • Collaboration with Parents and Professionals • Collaboration with Students and Peers	• Explore how collaboration benefits students with other health impairments	• Close communication among all collaborators promotes learning and wholeness for students with other health impairments.
Careers	• Examine careers available that work with students with other health impairments	• Many careers, including homebound education, are available to those who want to work with students with other health impairments.
WHAT ARE PROGRAM OPTIONS?		
Early Intervention and Preschool Years	• Describe characteristics of effective preschool programs	• Preschool intervention begins as soon as needs are identified and services are provided in community-based settings.
Elementary Years	• Describe characteristics of effective elementary school programs	• Children at the elementary level become more concerned about relationships with peers, so inclusive school settings can benefit them.

Middle and Secondary Years	• Describe characteristics of effective programs for middle and secondary students	• "Meeting the Challenge" was developed to improve five social skills of adolescents with health impairments: self-awareness, social imitation and conversational skills, assertion or direct communication, empathy or active listening, and conflict resolution and problem solving.
Transitional and Postsecondary Years	• Describe characteristics of effective program options for adults with other health impairments	• During the postsecondary years, programs work to help individuals find meaningful employment and leisure activities and to know and advocate for their rights to full citizenship.

PROJECT OPTIONS

1. Write a play that demonstrates the importance of strength, vitality, and alertness to all of life and how people with health impairments are affected by their absence. Show how these three characteristics are tied to the six values guiding special education.

2. Visit a local nursing home and interview three people older than 75 about people they have known with health impairments (which might include the people you're interviewing). Ask each person to describe the difficulties these people overcame and the positive contributions they made to their families, schools, friends, and communities. Then compare and contrast findings from the three people you interviewed.

3. Select one of the health impairments discussed in this chapter and research options in your community that specifically work with and help people with this impairment. Prepare a descriptive brochure highlighting your findings.

4. Plan and present a puppet show for students to teach them (a) the characteristics of students with the health impairments discussed in this chapter, and (b) ways they can support and help these students in a school setting.

KEY TERMS

Absence seizure

Acquired Immune Deficiency Syndrome (AIDS)

AIDS-related Complex (ARC)

Acute condition

Asymptomatic or latency stage

Chronic condition

Focal sensory seizures

Generalized seizures

Health care plan

Hyperglycemia or ketoacidosis

Hypoglycemia

Myclonic seizures

Opportunistic infections

Other health impairments

Partial seizures

Symptomatic stage

Temporal lobe or psychomotor seizure

Tonic-clonic or grand-mal seizure

CHAPTER 11 GUIDED REVIEW

The Bald Eagles

Ian O'Gorman, age 11, didn't feel out of place with his bald head when he returned to his fifth-grade class after cancer treatments. All 13 of the boys in his class shaved their heads so he wouldn't feel different. The boys now refer to themselves as the Bald Eagles. Ian said, "What my friends did really made me feel stronger. It helped me get through all this."

See *People Weekly*, April 11, 1994, p. 60.

What Are Other Health Impairments?

1. How does IDEA define other health impairments? (See Defining Health Impairments)

   _____
   _____
   _____

2. What three limitations are central to the other health impairments category? (See Defining Health Impairments)

   a. _____
   b. _____
   c. _____

3. The IDEA definition emphasizes that conditions can be chronic or acute. Explain the differences between these two conditions. (See Defining Health Impairments)

   Chronic condition: _____

   Acute condition: _____

HIV

4. HIV gradually infects and destroys important cells in the _____ system. T4 _____ cells are a major target of HIV. (See Describing the Characteristics of Other Health Impairments; Human Immunodeficiency Virus; What Is HIV?)

5. People with HIV are susceptible to _____ infections that generally do not affect otherwise-healthy people. (See Describing the Characteristics of Other Health Impairments; Human Immunodeficiency Virus; What Is HIV?)

6. Name and describe the stages of HIV. (See Describing the Characteristics of Other Health Impairments; Human Immunodeficiency Virus; Stages of HIV)

Stage	Symptoms

A New Face

"This is the new face of AIDS," comments correspondent Leslie Stahl. Magic Johnson, after living with HIV for years, is robust, healthy, and vigorous. In 1998, the virus was virtually undetectable in his bloodstream. Hoping that his exercise regime and positive attitude were the causes of his progress, Magic was inconsistent with his medication for a time. The result? The virus made a comeback. Realizing his need to continue taking his medication cocktail, Magic now has the energy and health to continue his work improving the quality of life for people in poor neighborhoods. He comments, "I'm not cured, I'm healed."

See *60 Minutes* transcript, May 10, 1998.

7. A person has AIDS when he or she is in the _____ stage. The CDC identifies AIDS as when a person has a T4 cell count less than _____ and has developed one or more specified _____ infections. (See Describing the Characteristics of Other Health Impairments; Human Immunodeficiency Virus; Stages of HIV)

8. Describe the two issues involved with HIV in the classroom. (See Describing the Characteristics of Other Health Impairments; Human Immunodeficiency Virus; HIV and the Classroom)

    a. Transmission and spread of HIV in schools:

    _____

    _____

    b. How the condition can affect learning and behavior of students with HIV:

    _____

    _____

You can read an account of Ryan White's final days in *People Weekly* (April 23, 1990). His mother Jeanne now travels the country continuing Ryan's quest for AIDS awareness.

Prenatal Substance Exposure

9. Of children exposed to cocaine in utero, _____% appear to have been seriously damaged, and _____% to _____% seem unscathed. (See Describing the Characteristics of Other Health Impairments; Prenatal Substance Exposure)

10. Children of mothers who use drugs or alcohol have a higher risk of developing _____. _____(See Describing the Characteristics of Other Health Impairments; Prenatal Substance Exposure; What Is Prenatal Substance Exposure?)

11. What percentage of congenital abnormalities are caused by fetal alcohol syndrome and fetal alcohol exposure? _____% What percentage of mild mental retardation? _____% (See Describing the Characteristics of Other Health Impairments; Prenatal Substance Exposure; At or Before Birth)

12. Identify the three groups children with prenatal substance exposure can be divided into. (See Describing the Characteristics; Prenatal Substance Exposure; Later Years)

    a. _____

    b. _____

    c. _____

Asthma

13. How often does asthma begin before age three? _____ What is the ratio of boys to girls with asthma?_____ (See Describing the Characteristics of Other Health Impairments; Asthma; What Is Asthma?)

14. List the three primary features of asthma. (See Describing the Characteristics of Other Health Impairments; Asthma; What Is Asthma?)

    a. _____

    b. _____

    c. _____

15. Describe the circumstances when medical help should be sought for students with asthma. (See Describing the Characteristics of Other Health Impairments; Asthma; What Is Asthma?)

    _____

    _____

    _____

16. Identify four preventions and treatments that you as a teacher need to know to help students with asthma. (See Describing the Characteristics; Asthma; What Is Asthma?)

    a. _____

    b. _____

    c. _____

    d. _____

Cancer

17. Cancer is a condition that causes _____. In 1993, approximately _____ children and adolescents died from cancer with _____ of those from leukemia. Approximately _____% of all children survive cancer today. (See Describing the Characteristics of Other Health Impairments; Cancer; What Is Cancer?)

18. Why should all children reentering school after cancer have an IEP completed? (See Describing the Characteristics of Other Health Impairments; Cancer; Cancer in the Classroom)

    _____

    _____

The Jester Has Lost His Jingle

Not long after his twenty-third birthday and soon after graduating from Yale with honors in art and English, David Saltzman died from Hodgkin's Disease. Before his death, he wanted to leave a legacy. Combining his love for words and art, David wrote and illustrated a children's book titled *The Jester Has Lost His Jingle* (call 800-9-JESTER or contact your local bookseller to order). In the story, the Jester looks for someone who can still laugh, despite the difficulties of life. He finds the laughter from a little girl with cancer. You can read more about David and his book at http://www.chnms.com/jester/index.html.

David wrote, "The best we can do is live life, enjoy it and know it is meant to be enjoyed—know how important and special every time . . . moment . . . person is."

Juvenile Diabetes

19. Juvenile diabetes results when the _____ stops producing or produces too little of the hormone _____. Juvenile diabetes (Type I) begins before age _____ and onset is most common in young people between _____ and _____. (See Describing the Characteristics of Other Health Impairments; Juvenile Diabetes; What Is Juvenile Diabetes?)

20. Describe the two serious medical conditions that can occur in the classroom if the student's diabetes is not under good control. (See Describing the Characteristics of Other Health Impairments; Juvenile Diabetes; Juvenile Diabetes and the Classroom)

Name of Condition	Medical Description and Symptoms	Treatment
Hyperglycemia/ Ketoacidosis		
Hypoglycemia		

Epilepsy

21. How can students usually reduce the number of seizures? (See Describing the Characteristics of Other Health Impairments: Epilepsy; Epilepsy and the Classroom)

    a. _____

    b. _____

22. Students sometimes experience a(n) _____ that lets them know that they are about to have a seizure. After a seizure, a student often needs to _____. (See Describing the Characteristics of Other Health Impairments; Epilepsy; Epilepsy and the Classroom)

23. Fill in the information about the types and subtypes of seizures associated with epilepsy (See Describing the Characteristics of Other Health Impairments; Epilepsy; What Is Epilepsy?)

Types	Characteristics	Subtypes	Characteristics of Subtypes
Generalized seizures		a. b.	a. b.
Partial seizures		a. b. c.	a. b. c.

Describing the Causes of Other Health Impairments

24. Three causes of other health impairments include _____, _____, and _____. (See What Are Other Health Impairments?; Describing the Causes of Other Health Impairments)

25. Approximately _____ % of students have health impairments, though only _____% are served under IDEA. (See What Are Other Health Impairments?; Identifying the Prevalence of Other Health Impairments)

What Are Evaluation Procedures?

26. Perhaps the most important part of the diagnostic procedure is to_____ _____. Following this, the student should receive an IEP if _____. An attached _____ allows coordination and dissemination of essential medical information among family and medical and school staffs. (See What Are Evaluation Procedures?)

What and How Do Professionals Teach?

27. Teachers can modify curriculum for students who must be absent often by asking what three questions? (See Curriculum)

    a. _____

    b. _____

    c. _____

What's So Funny?

How do you handle disability humor? Where do you draw the line between finding a joke amusing and being appalled by it? Robin Smith, who uses a wheelchair because of her disability, asks these questions in her article "Offensive Humor: Can I Handle It?" (*Tuesday's Child Magazine*, March/April 1998, pp. 30-31). Robin suggests asking yourself: "Does this joke laugh at or with? Is there a cost? Is it exploitative? Who benefits?" She also discusses ways to confront inappropriate jokes. We highly recommend that you read this article.

---

28. Describe three important methods associated with helping students with other health impairments described in this chapter. Describe classroom benefits for each method. (See Methods)

Method	Key Characteristics	Classroom Benefits
Including service dogs		
Handling insensitive comments and teasing		
Understanding the grief process		

29. When a student is dying, teachers need to develop support systems for whom? (See Methods; Grief in the Classroom)

      a. _____   c. _____

      b. _____   d. _____

How Is Participation Encouraged?

Ending the Isolation

What would you do if your children had a rare disorder and research was limited because of the unavailability of people with the condition? Patrick and Sharon Terry, whose two children have pseudoxanthoma elasticum, decided to be proactive. They formed an international PXE registry, linked together by the Internet. Thanks to their efforts, medical researchers now have ready access to blood samples and people willing to participate in studies. Recently, the gene that causes PXE was identified. Moreover, people with the condition no longer feel isolated; they support each other through an e-mail forum. Their informal dialog is also providing new insights into the condition.

30. Why are inclusion and collaboration inseparable issues for students with health impairments? (See Inclusion)

      _____

      _____

31. What are the three primary educational placements for students with other health impairments? List them from greatest to least placements. (See Inclusion)

      a. _____

      b. _____

      c. _____

32. Identify key collaborators and the contribution they can make when collaborating on behalf of students with other health impairments. (See Collaboration)

Collaborator	Contributions

33. List four career opportunities for working with students with other health impairments. List them in order of your own preferences. (See Careers)

    a. _____   b. _____

    b. _____   d. _____

What Are Program Options?

34. Describe key characteristics of successful program options available for individuals with health impairments at each of the 4 life-span stages described in the textbook. (See What Are Program Options?)

Life-span Stage	Key Characteristics
Early Intervention and Preschool Years	
Elementary Years	
Middle and Secondary Years	
Postsecondary Years	

"I Want To Be Left Alone"

Should young people be given the right to decide when they will stop life-prolonging treatments? Benito Angelo, who underwent two liver transplants, decided he had had enough. When social workers tried to force him to go to the hospital, Benny told them to leave him alone. Finally, a judge ruled that he could have his wish. For Benny, the medications and treatments were destroying his quality of life. He wanted to have some time to play Nintendo, read books, enjoy his friends, and discover at least for a brief time how it felt to be like other teenagers.

See *Time*, June 27, 1994, p. 65.

APPLICATION EXERCISES FOR CHAPTER 11

Application Exercise 11a. Identifying Conditions and Symptoms of Health Impairments

Try to match the physical symptoms experienced with the associated health impairment.

a. Stage 2 of HIV	1. _____ Khaldoun often feels dizzy, sweaty, and shaky when he forgets to take his medicine. Sometimes he has blurred vision and headaches, too.
b. Prenatal substance exposure	2. _____ Josephina's treatment has many side effects, and may even lower her white cell count, but the survival rate is 72%.
c. Hypoglycemia	3. _____ Jamie's tiredness is accompanied by frequent fevers. Just recently her glands have been swelling and she has had night sweats.
d. Asthma	4. _____ Maria has a low tolerance for change, cannot read social cues, and has not developed good friends. She also experiences poor ability to pay attention and concentrate.
e. Temporal lobe or psychomotor seizure	5. _____ Joan picks at her clothes and repeats a sentence several times, but has no memory of doing these things.
f. Stage 3 of HIV	6. _____ Tomatillo is extra sensitive to physical changes. He takes medication daily to maintain routine activities and to help him when he has difficulty breathing.
g. Hypoglycemia	7. _____ Steve is experiencing excessive thirst, urination and blurred vision. He appears to be drunk.
h. Childhood leukemia	8. _____ Elissa is critically ill. Eating is not only difficult, but her body isn't able to obtain nutrients from food. She's lost much weight and therapies have only minimal effect.

Application Exercise 11b. Developmental Responses to Death

See if you can match the child's understanding of death with the appropriate age range.

a. Newborn to age three	1. _____ Omar thinks he can handle the grief himself so doesn't express his feelings to anyone, but he really needs help from adults.
b. Ages three to six	2. _____ Rebecca understands that death is final, but needs a detailed explanation of how the person died.
c. Ages six to nine	3. _____ Olga thinks she is responsible for the death.
d. Ages nine to twelve	4. _____ Wanda shows more anger, guilt, and grief than adults.
e. Teenagers	5. _____ Keith needs to have his routine maintained as much as possible and be given extra affection and attention.
	6. _____ Timothy doesn't seem affected by the death of his brother because he expects him to return.
	7. _____ Deirdre needs to be reassured that it is okay to express emotions she is feeling, and that crying and feeling bad or mad are normal.
	8. _____ Darlene thinks that death is contagious and doesn't want to go to the house or funeral home.

<u>**Application Exercise 11c. Medical Vocabulary Applications**</u>

Based upon the five major questions* addressed in this chapter, review all the major concepts by listing and reviewing key medical vocabulary for each section. Use each word in a sentence to summarize each important aspect of each question and subheading.

*<u>Five Major Questions</u>: What are other health impairments? What are evaluation procedures? What and how do professionals teach? How is participation encouraged? What are program options?

ANSWERS TO MARGIN QUESTIONS

All margin notes provided information or asked reflective questions rather than asking questions needing answers.

SAMPLE QUIZ FOR CHAPTER 11

Circle the correct answer.

TRUE OR FALSE

T or F   1.   In an acute condition the symptoms are intense and develop quickly but last for a relatively short period of time.

T or F   2.   According to the CDC, universal precautions are not necessary for contact with body fluids unless blood is visible.

T or F   3.   Most infants with prenatal substance exposure do not differ significantly from other infants on standardized developmental tests.

T or F   4.   Hypoglycemia occurs when a person has too much sugar in his or her bloodstream due to a lack of insulin.

T or F   5.   An IFSP can be developed soon after birth for an infant with special health needs.

MULTIPLE CHOICE

6.   Which of the following children is <u>not</u> a possible candidate for services under the IDEA category of OHI?

    a.   Jeri, who has sickle cell anemia

    b.   Ulan, who has nephritis

    c.   Roger, who has tuberculosis

    d.   Ellyn, who has muscular sclerosis

7.   Paula is in the middle stage of HIV. What is the most appropriate educational placement for her?

    a.   The general classroom is always the most appropriate placement unless she has a secondary impairment causing academic limitations that cannot be met in the general education classroom, because students with HIV should be welcomed.

    b.   If she is under age eight, a resource room is the most appropriate placement so that universal health precautions can be carefully observed to protect other students.

    c.   If she easily contracts infections from other people, she should be educated at home or in an individualized setting.

    d.   If she has been involved in drugs or sexual activity, she should be educated in a resource room so that she does not negatively influence other students who are susceptible to peer pressure.

8.   Shoshanna has ADD, microcephaly, and facial deformities. Which of the following conditions does she most likely have?

    a.   Ketoacidosis

    b.   Fetal alcohol syndrome

    c.   ARC

    d.   Cerebral palsy

9.   Which of the following is <u>not</u> true about asthma?

    a.   About twice as many boys have asthma than girls.

    b.   In about half the childhood cases, asthma begins before age 1.

    c.   Boys are more likely to have severe asthma.

    d.   Asthma is the most prevalent chronic illness of children.

10.   Yang Yang died of the most common fatal disease among children ages one to fourteen. What caused her death?

    a.   AIDS

    b.   Asthma

    c.   Heart disease

    d.   Cancer

11. Usha is experiencing a dreamlike state with random actions such as picking at clothes or repeating a sentence over and over. Which of the following medical conditions might you suspect?

    a. Grand mal seizure

    b. Absence seizure

    c. Myclonic seizure

    d. Temporal lobe seizure

12. Which of the following diseases does not appear to have a genetic component?

    a. Diabetes

    b. Asthma

    c. Epilepsy

    d. HIV

13. What is the most common environmental disease of childhood?

    a. Radon-caused cancer

    b. Obesity

    c. Lead poisoning

    d. Fetal alcohol syndrome

14. Lidscott Elementary is in a wealthy school district, but does not serve all of its students who have health impairments. What is the most likely reason?

    a. The students' conditions do not have an adverse educational effect.

    b. IDEA only funds school districts where at least 10% of the students are below the poverty line.

    c. Parents who are from higher socioeconomic levels do not want IEPs attached to their children.

    d. IEPs are not necessary for children with chronic illnesses.

15. Rhett, a student in your class, has died of cancer. Identify the appropriate response to students after informing them of his death.

    a. Focus their attention on schoolwork so they do not dwell on morbid thoughts.

    b. Express your own grief and answer questions.

    c. Do not directly talk about it so emotions have a chance to heal.

    d. Use euphemisms to get it out in the open.

SHORT ANSWER

16. List the three major criteria of OHI according to IDEA.

    a. _____

    b. _____

    c. _____

17. You are the teacher of Corwin, who uses an assistance dog. Briefly describe what you as a teacher could say to a parent of another student who objects to having an assistance dog in the same classroom as her child.

_____

_____

18. List two ways that you as a teacher can help prevent the spread of HIV.

    a. _____

    b. _____

ESSAY

19. Explain how the three major criteria for other health impairments are evident in HIV, asthma, cancer, and juvenile diabetes.

20. Differentiate between the characteristics of two health impairments discussed in this chapter and describe how you would support students with these impairments in the classroom.

CHAPTER 12: PHYSICAL DISABILITIES		

CHAPTER OVERVIEW

Physical disabilities have the potential to severely limit an individual's mobility and ability to perform educationally. This chapter investigates the characteristics, causes, and prevalence of physical disabilities, with a detailed look at cerebral palsy, spina bifida, and muscular dystrophy. It also examines how to determine the presence of physical disabilities as well as the nature and extent of special education, with a special look at the role of the occupational therapist and physical therapist. Project MOVE represents a curriculum focused on mobility. Several assistive technologies are examined as effective methods for helping students with physical disabilities. Successful program options at four levels are highlighted for their unique contributions to students with physical disabilities.

The life of thirteen-year-old Rommel Nanasca provides an example of extraordinary team cooperation. Rommel's spinal muscular atrophy requires extensive physical supports both at home and at school. The degenerative nature of Rommel's disability along side his exemplary perseverance has special implications for classroom accommodations and emotional support.

CHAPTER AT-A-GLANCE

Chapter Outline	Instructional Goals	Key Concepts
WHAT ARE PHYSICAL DISABILITIES?		
Defining Physical Disabilities	• Examine different models for defining physical disabilities	• A physical disability is often referred to as an orthopedic impairment that affects a student's mobility and educational performance.
Describing the Characteristics • Cerebral palsy • Spina bifida • Muscular dystrophy	• Describe characteristics and causes for some of the most typical physical disabilities	• Cerebral palsy describes a group of disabling conditions characterized by nonprogressive and nonhereditary brain damage; it is commonly characterized by spastic, athetoid, ataxic, or mixed movement patterns. • Spina bifida is a malformation of the spinal cord and is often accompanied by hydrocephalus. • Muscular dystrophy designates a group of nine hereditary muscle-destroying disorders. • A physical disabiity is caused by congenital anomaly, disease, or other causes.
Identifying the Prevalence of Physical Disabilities	• Identify prevalence rates for physical disabilities	• Approximately 1.2% of all students receiving special education services have physical disabilities.
Preventing Physical Disabilities	• Understand how physical disabilities can be prevented	• Primary prevention of physical disabilities includes educating pregnant women about risk factors. • Other types of prevention include trying to reduce the effect of a disability or trying to prevent a related disability from occurring.
WHAT ARE EVALUATION PROCEDURES?		
Determining the Presence of Physical Disabilities	• Recognize the most appropriate times and ways for determining the presence of physical disabilities	• Screening may take place before or after birth or at a later date when an infant fails to meet developmental milestones.

Determining the Nature and Extent of Special Education and Related Services	• Identify principal ways to plan for special education and related services for students with physical disabilities • Describe the roles of two principal professionals in providing related services	• A functional assessment leads to a plan designed to overcome or compensate for discrepancies between student performance and performance expected from peers without disabilities. • Occupational and physical therapists play pivotal roles in the assessment of motoric abilities.
WHAT AND HOW DO PROFESSIONALS TEACH?		
Curriculum	• Differentiate curriculum options available for use with students with physical disabilities	• Curriculum varies according to the students' individual strengths and needs. • Mobility should be fostered as early as possible to ensure richness of experience.
Methods • Adapted Equipment • Computers • Medical Technology Assistance • Augmentative and Alternative Communication	• Evaluate different methods that are effective for varied student needs	• Some students rely on assistive technology, adaptive equipment, or medical technology assistance. • Augmentative and alternative communication techniques and devices supplement students' naturally acquired speech.
HOW IS PARTICIPATION ENCOURAGED?		
Inclusion	• Identify challenges for inclusion to benefit students with physical disabilities	• Inclusion challenges professionals to provide a balance between fully including students and providing them with the fundamentals they need to succeed.
Collaboration • Professional Collaboration • Family Collaboration • Student and Community Collaboration	• Explore people and ways to collaborate on behalf of students with physical disabilities	• Collaboration involves the efforts of professionals, family, student with a disability, peers, and community to work together as a team to deliver services.
Careers	• Examine careers available that work with students with physical disabilities	• Professionals include dually certified teachers, rehabilitation engineers, computer software specialists, occupational therapists, physical therapists, physicians, and nurses.
WHAT ARE PROGRAM OPTIONS?		
Early Intervention and Preschool Years	• Describe characteristics of effective preschool programs	• The Savick School combines inclusion, parent participation, a curriculum to foster mobility, interagency collaboration and technical assistance.
Elementary Years	• Describe characteristics of effective elementary programs for students with physical disabilities	• One model includes the use of itinerant teachers for able students and the use of resource centers and teachers for students who have not yet learned the enabling skills necessary for a lower level of service.
Middle and Secondary Years	• Describe characteristics of effective programs for middle and secondary students	• A program which facilitates a mentor relationship can help increase students' self-determination, confidence, independent living skills, and community participation.

Transitional and Postsecondary Years	• Describe characteristics of effective program options for adults with physical disabilities	• The Disabled Students' Program at UC–Berkeley offers programs that assist students in gaining personal and academic independence.

PROJECT OPTIONS

1. Read at least one recent (1980-1998) adolescent's or children's book dealing with one of the disabilities discussed in this chapter. Write a description of (a) what types of evaluation took place in the main character's life, (b) what types of curriculum and methods were used with him or her, and (c) the role of inclusion and collaboration in the life of the main character.

2. Select the physical disability most interesting to you and interview two individuals with this disability. Develop a questionnaire based on the six values guiding special education to ask each one and compare and contrast your findings.

3. Compare and contrast the strengths of the four program options in this chapter with the program options available in your community. Analyze and present your findings to your local community for each of the four levels.

4. Research three forms of assistive technology. Then learn how to use one of them and write a description for others to learn how to use this type of assistive technology. Share the difficulties and joys.

KEY TERMS

Assistive technology	Perinatal
Clean intermittent catheterization	Postnatal
Colostomy	Prenatal
Hypertonia	Pulseoximeter
Incontinence	Quadriplegia
Intermittent Position Pressure Breathing Machine (IPPB)	Scoliosis
Jejunum	Speech recognition technology
Neonatal Intensive Care Unit (NICU)	Tracheostomy
Paraplegia	Topographical classification system

CHAPTER 12 GUIDED REVIEW

Tarah Gets to Sesame Street

As a fourth grader, Tarah Lynne Schaeffer beat out 70 other kids to become Sesame Street's first fulltime neighbor with a disability. She has osteogenesis imperfecta. Tarah knew her ABCs at 10 months and watched Sesame Street loyally. Although she has had more than 90 fractures in her young life, she maintains an upbeat attitude and a sense of humor. Tarah's father says the family taught her skills that helped her get the role. "We've pushed her to lead, not to follow, and not to be afraid to speak up."

See *People Weekly*, May 2, 1994, p. 109.

What Are Physical Disabilities?

1. IDEA refers to physical disabilities as orthopedic impairments. Provide IDEA's definition of "orthopedic impairment." (See Defining Physical Disabilities)

   _____

   _____

   _____

   _____

2. While IDEA uses the term "orthopedic impairment," educators typically use what term?
   _____ (See Defining Physical Disabilities)

3. Define the terms "cerebral" and "palsy." (See Describing the Characteristics; What Is Cerebral Palsy?)
   a. Cerebral: _____

   _____

   b. Palsy: _____

   _____

4. What two characteristics distinguish cerebral palsy? (See Describing the Characteristics; What Is Cerebral Palsy?)
   a. _____

   b. _____

5. Identify the four movement terms that characterize individuals with cerebral palsy. Put an "X" after the most prevalent movement pattern. (See Describing the Characteristics; What Is Cerebral Palsy?)
   a. _____ c. _____

   b. _____ d. _____

A Model Child

Talent scouts said that Stephanie Hammerman, born with cerebral palsy, is a natural model. The pretty eight year old is never seen at a photo shoot without her crutches. "It's easy to model," she says, "because I like having my picture taken."

Great expectations are the rule in her family. "In this family, we try not to accept the easy way out," her mother says. When Stephanie was five, her teacher asked her mother to get her a wheelchair, but her mother refused. Stephanie could walk using a walker, but it took her longer. Mrs. Hammerman believes Stephanie is able to use crutches today because using the walker strengthened her legs. Stephanie is included in general education— even in physical education. Although Stephanie is the only student who uses crutches, she keeps up with her peers. Stephanie also insists on dressing herself each morning. Her mother says that if it takes her a half hour to button her shirt, she just determines to wake up earlier.

See "Strutting Her Stuff" by Lynda Spiegel in *Exceptional Parent* (1998), *28*(5), 58-61.

---

6. Cerebral palsy is also characterized by the area of the brain affected. Identify and tell what is affected by damage to each of the three motor systems of the central nervous system. (See Describing the Characteristics What Is Cerebral Palsy?)

Area of the Brain Affected	*Specific Effect on an Individual*
a.	
b.	
c.	

7. Match the form of cerebral palsy with its primary characteristics. (See Describing the Characteristics; What Is Cerebral Palsy?)

1. Spastic or hypertonic form	a. _____ Abrupt involuntary movements of the head, neck, face, and extremities, particularly the upper ones.
2. Athetoid or low-tone form	b. _____ Spastic muscle tone and the involuntary movements of athetoid cerebral palsy.
3. Ataxic form	c. _____ Tightness in one or more of the muscle groups which causes limited movement.
4. Mixed form	d. _____ Unsteadiness, lack of coordination and balance, and varying degrees of difficulty with standing and walking.

8. Cerebral palsy is also classified by referring to the area of the body that is affected. Name and describe the seven areas of the body that are affected. (See Describing the Characteristics; What Is Cerebral Palsy?)

Classification	Area of Body Affected
1.	
2.	
3.	
4.	
5.	
6.	
7.	

9. What are some identified causes of cerebral palsy? (See Describing the Characteristics; What Is Cerebral Palsy?)

a. _____

b. _____

c. _____

10. Spina bifida refers to a(n) _____ or _____ spine. In a person with spina bifida, the spinal column does not _____.

The higher the spinal defect, the more _____ is the loss of function. (See Describing the Characteristics; What Is Spina Bifida?)

My Wheelchair Is Not an Issue

John Hockenberry, who has had paraplegia since the age of 19, is a news reporter for National Public Radio. He has traveled all over the world, taking on some of the most dangerous assignments. John says that he decided when he was in rehab that "Nothing's going to stop me. I can do anything." John comments about the chair that is his constant companion, "My wheelchair is not an issue with people—unless I run over their feet"

See *People Weekly*, June 6, 1994, pp. 101-102.

---

11. Identify the three most common forms of spinal bifida and describe the degree of severity and typical characteristics. (See Describing the Characteristics; What Is Spina Bifida?)

Form of Spina Bifida	Degree of Severity	Typical Characteristics
a.		
b.		
c.		

12. To date, what is known about the causes of spina bifida? (See Describing the Characteristics; What Is Spina Bifida?) _____
_____

13. What does the term "muscular dystrophy" designate? (See Describing the Characteristics; Muscular Dystrophy)
_____
_____

14. What is spinal muscular atrophy characterized by? (See Describing the Characteristics; Muscular Dystrophy)
    a. _____
    b. _____

15. Three types of spinal muscular atrophy have been identified. Identify the type and list the accompanying symptoms. (See Describing the Characteristics; Muscular Dystrophy)
    a. _____
    b. _____
    c. _____

16. What is the cause of spinal muscular atrophy? (See Describing the Characteristics; Muscular Dystrophy)_____

17. Identify three conditions that often accompany spinal muscular atrophy and describe how these conditions can be treated or prevented. (See Describing the Characteristics; Muscular Dystrophy)

Conditions Accompanying Spinal Muscular Atrophy	Treatment and/or Prevention
1.	
2.	
3.	

18. What percentage of all students who receive special education services have physical disabilities? (See Identifying the Prevalence of Physical Disabilities) _____%

19. Identify at least two ways physical disabilities can be prevented. (See Preventing Physical Disabilities)

    a. _____

    b. _____

What Are Evaluation Procedures?

20. At what times can screening take place for physical disabilities? (See Determining the Presence of Physical Disabilities)

_____

21. Two professional disciplines are concerned with movement in the assessment of students with physical disabilities. Identify them and describe each one's role in intervention. (See Determining the Nature and Extent of Special Education)

Professional Discipline	Intervention Role of This Professional Discipline
a.	
b.	

Liberation Technology

People with physical disabilities are plugging into the Internet. Besides being able to talk to people with and without disabilities throughout the world from their wheelchairs, they can access disability databases. Jack Nelson, who has written the book *The Disabled, the Media, and the Information Age*, says that computers and modems have given people with physical and other disabilities a "virtual community" where they can participate without barriers. Mark Geisler, who has muscular dystrophy, is a desktop publisher. He says that his connections with people online have "literally opened the whole world. I hardly even notice that I am primarily housebound."

See *U.S. News and World Report*, September 12, 1994, p. 85.

---

22. Explain how to carry out an ecological inventory for a student with physical disabilities and how it can enhance this student's daily living experiences. (See Determining the Nature and Extent of Special Education)

_____

_____

_____

What and How Do Professionals Teach?

23. Mobility impairments require significant intervention. Describe how the curriculum "Project MOVE." (Mobility Opportunities via Education) is designed to teach students motor skills needed for adult life. Describe both the skills and levels for this curriculum. (See What and How Do Professionals Teach?; Curriculum)

    Description: _____

    _____

    Types of Skills: _____

    _____

    Levels: _____

    _____

24. Identify examples for four different assistive technologies/ methods and tell how they enable students with physical disabilities to be full participating members of their schools. (See What and How Do Professionals Teach?; Methods)

Type of Assistive Technology	Examples	How Each One Accommodates the Student
a. Adapted Equipment		
b. Computers		
c. Medical Technology Assistance		
d. Augmentative and Alternative Communication		

25. Identify some of the complicated issues raised by the use of medical technology assistance. (See What and How Do Professionals Teach?; Methods; Medical Technology Assistance)

    _____

    _____

    _____

26. To what does "augmentative and alternative communication" refer? (See What and How Do Professionals Teach?; Methods; Augmentative and Alternative Communication)

    _____

    _____

Why Do You Use a Wheelchair?

John Dybala, who has spondiloephiphysial dysplasia, is a junior at Colorado State University. John has had over 40 operations in his lifetime. But that hasn't stopped him from having great expectations for himself. He is preparing to be a teacher. He shares the following advice about how you can help students feel comfortable with people who have disabilities:

As a person with a disability, I have never experienced anything other than natural curiosity from children. Answer the question: "Why do you use a wheelchair?" or "Why does he walk funny?" or "What's that plastic thing in her ear?" Once that is answered, they ask other questions: "What's your favorite food?" "Did you watch TV last night?" "Do you like football?" This is more interesting to them.

We, as teachers, have a tremendous impact on students. We have the power—we really do—to show them which set of questions is more important. And we can model that.

—John Dybala

How Is Participation Encouraged?

27. When assistive technology became available, what happened to students with physical disabilities who became able to independently initiate both movement and speech? (See How Is Participation Encouraged?; Inclusion)

_____

_____

28. Match the percentages of students with their education placements. (See How Is Participation Encouraged?; Inclusion)

1. Separate class	a. _____ 7.0%
2. Residential facility	b. _____ 20.7%
3. Resource room	c. _____ 0.5%
4. General education class	d. _____ 33.3%
5. Separate school	e. _____ 2.9%
6. Homebound/ hospital	f. _____ 37.4%

One Less Scholarship

Unfortunately, people with physical disabilities are still facing attitudinal as well as physical barriers in some institutions of higher education. Ryan Martin is a champion tennis player who has won six national championships, visited the White House by invitation for his skills, and was voted his high school's best athelete. Yet, when he applied for a tennis scholarship at one university in 1992, he was turned down because he is paralyzed from the waist down as a result of a gunshot wound. The university wrote him a letter telling him that giving him a scholarship would adversely affect the program because it would mean one less scholarship for the men's tennis team. Ryan comments, "The problem is that many people just don't get it. A person with a disability can be an athlete in the true sense of the word."

See _The Chronicle of Higher Education_, May 18, 1994, p. A34.

29. Explain the role of the individuals who collaborate on behalf of Rommel. (See How Is Participation Encouraged?; Collaboration as well as Determining the Nature and Extent of Special Education)

School district resource nurse, Cathy Schmitz: _____

_____

Registered nurse, Rebecca Draper:_____

_____

Robin, his physical therapist: _____

_____

Karen, his occupational therapist: _____

_____

Lorna and Romy, Rommel's parents: _____

_____

30. List, in order of your own preference for a career, five career options discussed in this chapter. Explain your ranking. (See How Is Participation Encouraged?; Careers)

a. _____

b. _____

c. _____

d. _____

e. _____

31. List key features for each of the following program options. (See What Are Program Options?)

Program	Key Features
Sevick School, El Cajon, California	
Madison, Wisconsin, School District	
Mentoring in the Pacific Northwest	
The Disabled Students' Program at UC–Berkeley, California	

Still Me

Christopher Reeve, the star of the *Superman* movies, who was paralyzed in an horseback riding accident, chose this title for his book for two reasons: he wants people to realize he is still the same person; and his paralysis causes him to live a life of physical stillness. But his life is active in other ways. Besides becoming an author, Reeve is a sought-after speaker, a film director, and an advocate for people with disabilities. When *Superman* previewed, people asked Reeve what he thought a hero was. He told them that a hero "commits a courageous act without considering the consequences." He has a new definition of hero now: "I think a hero is an ordinary individual who finds strength to persevere and endure despite overwhelming obstacles."

See Christopher Reeve, *Still Me* (Random House, 1998).

APPLICATION EXERCISES FOR CHAPTER 12

Application Exercise 12a. Identifying Forms of Cerebral Palsy by Movement Difficulties

Identify which form of cerebral palsy each individual has: spastic, athetoid, ataxic, or mixed.

1. Miguel has difficulty with coordination and balance. Often he has difficulty with standing and walking.

   _____

2. Karim has abrupt, involuntary movements of his neck and arms. Sometimes it's more frequent than other times. He doesn't have trouble initiating movement, but rather has difficulty controlling movement and maintaining posture.

   _____

3. Nadia is a quadriplegic who often has involuntary movements of her upper limbs. She sometimes finds her limbs becoming rigid and tight.

   _____

4. When Abram is transferred from his bed to his wheelchair, his body straightens out and becomes extremely rigid.

   _____

Application Exercise 12b. Identifying Characteristics of Spina Bifida

Match the characteristic of spina bifida with the common forms.

1. Spina bifida occulta	a. _____ The covering of the cord protrudes through the opening created by the defect in the spine.
2. Meningocele	b. _____ This is the mildest and most common form.
3. Myelomeningocele	c. _____ More than 90% of people with this type of spina bifida have an inability to control their bowels or bladder.
	d. _____ In this form of spina bifida, the protrusion contains the cord's covering and a portion of the spinal cord or nerve roots.
	e. _____ The spinal cord or its covering do not protrude.
	f. _____ This form is not detectable by physical exam and is not disabling.
	g. _____ This form is the most severe form of spina bifida.
	h. _____ Four out of five children born with this kind of spina bifida also develop hydrocephalus.

Application Exercise 12c. The Conceptual Impact of Inclusion and Collaboration on Physical Disabilities

Based upon the five major questions* addressed in this chapter, summarize the major concepts concerning physical disabilities. Explain the role and/or impact of inclusion and collaboration as it applies to each major chapter question.

*Five Major Questions: What are physical disabilities? What are evaluation procedures? What and how do professionals teach? How is participation encouraged? What are program options?

ANSWERS TO MARGIN QUESTIONS

This chapter did not include specific questions.

SAMPLE QUIZ FOR CHAPTER 12

Circle the correct answer.

TRUE OR FALSE

T or F   1.   Cerebral palsy is a nonprogressive disease in which the nerves connecting the muscles to the spinal cord are damaged, resulting in a loss of muscle control.

T or F   2.   Individuals with the mixed form of cerebral palsy usually have quadriplegia.

T or F   3.   Almost 3% of all children served by special education in the United States have physical disabilities.

T or F   4.   There is no single disease by the name of muscular dystrophy.

T or F   5.   Almost all students who are ventilator assisted have physical disabilities.

MULTIPLE CHOICE

6.   About how many people in the United States have cerebral palsy?
   a.   100,000
   b.   500,000
   c.   1,000,000
   d.   1,500,000

7.   What condition can be caused by bleeding in the brain of a newborn?
   a.   Spina bifida
   b.   Cerebral palsy
   c.   Spinal muscular atrophy
   d.   Muscular sclerosis

8.   Ty has spina bifida and is paralyzed from the waist down. What does this indicate?
   a.   A saclike bulge occurred fairly high in his spine.
   b.   He has meningocele spina bifida.
   c.   He has a progressive condition.
   d.   Only the covering of the spinal cord protruded.

9.   What can be done for a child born with hydrocephalus?
   a.   Nothing, because it is progressive and the child will die at a young age.
   b.   A shunt can be implanted to remove excess fluid.
   c.   Physical therapy can overcome most problems associated with hydrocephalus.
   d.   Brain surgery is required to remove the frontal lobe and prevent further damage from the disease.

10.   What problem associated with spinal muscular atrophy can an initial screening at birth indicate?
   a.   Respiratory
   b.   Vitamin deficiency
   c.   Cerebral malfunctioning
   d.   Incontinence

11.   For what condition can electromyography and muscle biopsies establish a diagnosis?
   a.   Cerebral palsy
   b.   Spinal muscular atrophy
   c.   Spina bifida
   d.   Multiple sclerosis

12. You have a student, Una, in your class who uses a wheelchair. What can happen to her if she is not properly positioned in her wheelchair?

    a. Her mobility can be curtailed.

    b. She can become incontinent.

    c. Her colostomy can become infected.

    d. She can get sores and need a J-tube.

13. What caused educational expectations for students with physical disabilities to rise dramatically?

    a. More teachers were trained to work with children who had disabilities.

    b. IDEA mandated all students be treated without discrimination.

    c. Assistive technology allowed students to move and speak independently.

    d. Parents demanded a role in collaboration.

14. Which of the following is not a component of the Sevick program?

    a. Interagency collaboration

    b. Technical assistance

    c. Implementation of the MOVE curriculum

    d. Transitional skills for adult living

15. How does UC Berkeley support students with physical disabilities?

    a. It provides a special dorm with adapted architectural features.

    b. It provides an attendant referral service and special recreation program.

    c. It provides full-time aides for every student with physical disabilities.

    d. It guarantees federally subsidized jobs for its graduates.

SHORT ANSWER

16. What is the term used by IDEA for physical disabilities?

_____

17. List the four forms of cerebral palsy.

_____

_____

_____

_____

18. Name two professional people who are keys to the assessment of students with physical disabilities but who are not as important for students with most other disabilities.

    a. _____

    b. _____

ESSAY

19. Compare and contrast the ways to classify physical disabilities as they relate to cerebral palsy, spinal bifida, and muscular dystrophy.

20. Discuss the role of inclusion and collaboration in the lives of students with physical disabilities. Include a discussion of different careers available for working with these students and their families.

CHAPTER 13: TRAUMATIC BRAIN INJURY

CHAPTER OVERVIEW

Traumatic brain injuries can cause dramatic changes in a person's intellectual, emotional, linguistic, social, and/or physical functioning. This chapter presents important information about the definition, characteristics, causes, and prevalence rates for traumatic brain injury. It describes the many dimensions of the evaluation process to determine its presence as well as the process to ensure academic and social success with appropriate special education. A discussion of the cognitive retraining curriculum and various effective methods is presented along with the place of inclusion and collaboration on behalf of these students. Emphasis is placed on the importance of collaboration between the rehabilitation program and the school for this population. This chapter concludes with a discussion describing factors critical to helping students at each age level.

The life of twelve-year-old Jimmie Eagle McVay demonstrates and clarifies issues revolving around students who have experienced brain injuries. Jimmie, a Native American, was struck by a drunk driver when he was eight years old. He sustained open and closed traumatic brain injuries, leaving him in critical condition. Jimmie recovered, but as is typical of students who sustain traumatic brain injuries, he experienced changes in his intellectual, emotional, linguistic, social, and/or physical function. Although he has regained many of his pre-injury skills, Jimmie continues to face challenges in these areas.

CHAPTER AT-A-GLANCE

Chapter Outline	Instructional Goals	Key Concepts
WHAT IS TRAUMATIC BRAIN INJURY?		
Defining Traumatic Brain Injury Types of Traumatic Brain Injury —Closed Head Injury —Open Head Injury	• Differentiate among types of traumatic brain injuries	• IDEA's definition includes acquired injuries to the brain caused by an external force. It does not include brain injuries caused by anoxia or disease or congenital brain injuries. • Closed head injuries and open head injuries are the two types under IDEA.
Relationship of Brain Injury to Other Disabilities	• Differentiate between traumatic brain injury and other disabilities	• Traumatic brain injury differs from other disabilities in onset, complexity, and prognosis.
Describing the Characteristics • Physical Changes • Cognitive Changes • Linguistic Changes • Social, Behavioral, and Personality Changes • Prognosis	• Describe key characteristics seen in students with traumatic brain injury	• Students with brain injury often experience physical, cognitive, linguistic, and social, behavioral, or personality changes. • No generalizations can be made about prognosis based on the injury's mildness or severity.
Identifying the Causes of Traumatic Brain Injury	• Identify the major causes and effects of traumatic brain injury	• Three major causes include accidents, sports and recreational injuries, and violence. • Shaken impact syndrome is a dangerous form of child abuse that can cause brain injuries or death. • Called the silent epidemic, the effects of brain injury are widespread but often unrecognized.

Identifying the Prevalence of Traumatic Brain Injury	• Recognize prevalence rates of traumatic brain injuries	• Approximately 0.5% to 1% of school-age students have sustained a traumatic brain injury. • About 3% of adolescents have sustained head injuries that are severe enough to cause school problems.
WHAT ARE EVALUATION PROCEDURES?		
Determining the Presence of Traumatic Brain Injury	• Describe key characteristics in successful evaluation of brain injuries	• Because the needs of students with traumatic brain injury are diverse and rapidly changing, evaluation needs to be comprehensive and ongoing. • The multidisciplinary team should evaluate the students in all areas of functioning, including cognitive processes such as problem solving and memory.
Determining the Nature and Extent of Special Education and Related Services	• Analyze unique education needs and services for students with traumatic brain injury	• The IEP team should update the student's document frequently, probably every six to eight weeks initially.
WHAT AND HOW DO PROFESSIONALS TEACH?		
Curriculum	• Differentiate curriculum needs for students with traumatic brain injury	• Students receive three forms of cognitive retraining: component retraining, compensatory strategy training, and functional training.
Methods • Instructional Methods • Methods to Improve Behavior • Methods to Improve Self-esteem	• Evaluate how different methods are most effective for varied student needs	• Computer-assisted instruction helps students develop cognitive skills. • Methods for improving behavioral and social skills include differential reinforcement of other behaviors, stimulus control, environmental control, and self-control techniques. • Professionals can improve self-esteem by fostering a sense of significance, competence, power, and virtue.
HOW IS PARTICIPATION ENCOURAGED?		
Inclusion	• Explain the best educational placement for students with traumatic brain injury	• The general education classroom is the least restrictive environment in most cases.
Collaboration • Collaboration Among Professionals • Collaboration with Family • Collaboration with Peers	• Explore the role of collaboration on behalf of students with traumatic brain injury	• Close collaboration among rehabilitation staff, school personnel, family, peers, and the student is essential to meet the diverse, ever-changing needs of individuals with brain injury.
Careers	• Examine careers available that work with students with traumatic brain injury	• An important career for this field is the school reentry specialist.

WHAT ARE PROGRAM OPTIONS?		
Early Intervention and Preschool Years	• Describe characteristics of effective preschool programs	• Since abuse accounts for 90% of brain injury in children under three, bonding with a nanny helps children make the transition. • Language development is particularly important during these years.
Elementary Years	• Describe characteristics of effective elementary school programs	• Providing an educational environment much like a real school makes the transition easier for students with brain injury.
Middle and Secondary Years	• Describe characteristics of effective programs for middle and secondary students	• Counseling and support groups, focusing on social skills and self-acceptance are particularly important to the success of students in the middle and secondary years.
Transitional and Postsecondary Years	• Describe characteristics of effective program options for adults with traumatic brain injury	• Vocational training and preparation for independence are key factors in the success of postsecondary students.

PROJECT OPTIONS

1. Research the different areas of the brain that can be affected during a traumatic brain injury. Construct three creative charts comparing (a) the sections of the brain and what they control, (b) the characteristics for injuries centered in each section of the brain (including things to watch for in the classroom), and (c) the recovery prognosis for injuries in each section of the brain.

2. Find out your state's requirement for brain injury and your school district's means for assessment and on-going evaluation. Then interview two people with brain injury and evaluate how their experience has been coordinated with the state and local school district. From your findings, create a drama presentation that demonstrates the needs of students with brain injury.

3. Explore the types of brain injury programs available in your community. Then create a presentation comparing and contrasting local programs with programs such as Hilltop Manor's program. Write up your findings and share them with both Hilltop Manor and your local programs.

4. Keep a journal for one week. For each entry, speculate about how your day would have been different if you had a brain injury.

KEY TERMS

Acquired brain injury

Aphasia

Closed head injury

Cognitive retraining

Compensatory strategy training

Component training

Congenital condition

Differential reinforcement of other behavior

Functional retraining

Open head injury

Personal Intervention Plan

Postconcussional syndrome, or mild traumatic brain injury (MRBI)

Traumatic brain injury

CHAPTER 13 GUIDED REVIEW

I Wish I Could Go Home

In this chapter, you will learn about the changes that people with traumatic brain injury experience. In his own words, Richard Browning compares his experience to *The Wizard of Oz*:

1. Do you remember the early part of the movie? Just as the house is getting picked up by the tornado, Dorothy gets hit in the head by a storm shutter and is knocked unconscious. (*To me that sounds like a person knocked unconscious into a "coma."*)

2. When she wakes up, she is in a place she is not familiar with at all. Everything is new and different. (*That seems like after a person comes out of their coma most everything appears the same but in a different way. "Where am I?"*)

3. As she walks out of her house, she finds herself in a new and different place surrounded by many little people. [*This could be symbolic of (people with traumatic brain injury) thinking that they are bigger and better than the average person around them.*]

4. Then she starts her long walk down the yellow brick road. (*This could be the start of the long road to a complete recovery!*)

5. As she goes down the road, she meets the Scarecrow—the man with no brain. (*Or, in other words, a person with no cognitive thinking abilities!*)

6. As she goes farther down the road, she then meets the Tin Man—the man with no heart. (*To me that sounds like that could be a person that is self-centered that doesn't care for anyone else except for themselves—but as you know, the Tin Man is a very caring person.*)

7. Then she meets the Cowardly Lion. (*The person with no self-esteem afraid to do anything on his own.*)

8. As she is going along the yellow brick road, she meets the Wicked Witch. (*That is like meeting a person that wants to take advantage of you in your situation.*)

9. As she is going along the yellow brick road, she eventually makes it to Oz. (*Where they teach her what she really wants to know to get back to where she wants to be—to me, that sounds like a person going through vocational rehabilitation.*)

If you remember, throughout the entire movie all she wants to do is to go back home. (*Or become herself again.*) Then she says to herself, "I want to go home, I want to go home, etc." Then she is back where she wants to be.

But through the entire ordeal she learns love, caring, and compassion for others that are going through what she is going through.

At the end of the movie, the Wizard gives them all awards, diplomas, or medals to show that they really can do what they have been doing all along.

See *Alabama Head Injury Foundation Newsletter*, vol. 22, pp. 4-5.

What Is Traumatic Brain Injury?

1. How does IDEA define traumatic brain injury? (See Defining Traumatic Brain Injury)

2. Describe the two causes of traumatic brain injury served under the IDEA category of other health impairments. (See Defining Traumatic Brain Injury)
   a. Anoxia:
   b. Disease:

3. Explain the difference between an acquired brain injury and a congenital brain injury. (See Defining Traumatic Brain Injury)

4. Compare and contrast the two types of traumatic brain injury served under IDEA (See Defining Traumatic Brain Injury; Types of Traumatic Brain Injury)

	What Causes the Brain Injury?	*What Areas of the Brain Are Damaged?*	*Resulting Behavior or Academic Problems*
Closed Head Injury			
Open Head Injury			

Much More Than a Statistic

John Dybala, whom you also read about in Chapter 12 of this study guide, shares what he experienced when his sister was involved in a car accident:

In 1990, my sister became a statistic. She was hit by a car as she tried to cross the street. My sister was but one of the many thousands of people injured in car accidents that year. Happily, she survived and is doing well.

I suspect that some people who read the brief account of the accident in the newspaper sighed and commented on what a shame it was, then went on with their day and forgot all about it. She was a number to them. A statistic. They could depersonalize it as being something that happened to someone else. It didn't affect them; therefore, it was not their concern.

For my sister, her family, and her friends, this accident was more than just one statistic. It was several frantic hours in the emergency room. It was a weekend of keeping a bedside vigil. It was a year of slow recovery, and nearly three years fighting to recover damages from the driver's insurance company.

—John Dybala

5. Even mild closed head injury, sometimes called _____ or _____ can seriously impact a person's ability to enjoy life and work and earn a living. (See Defining Traumatic Brain Injury; Types of Traumatic Brain Injury; Closed Head Injury)

6. Name and describe the three ways students with brain injury differ from students with other disabilities. (See Relationship of Brain Injury to Other Disabilities)

Type of Difference	*Description of Difference*

7. The number and magnitude of changes vary according to _____ and _____ of injury, as well as the length of time the student was in a _____ and the student's _____ at the time of the injury. (See Describing the Characteristics)

8. Discuss the four areas of changes that are often experienced by students with traumatic brain injury by providing examples and a description of the characteristics. (See Describing the Characteristics)

Area of Change	Examples of Changes	Characteristics/Outcomes
1. Physical Changes	a. b. c.	
2. Cognitive Changes	a. b. c.	
3. Linguistic Changes	a. b. c.	
4. Social, Behavioral, and Personality Changes	a. b. c.	

Every Day Gets Better

One of the physical changes Mike Euler experienced as a result of his traumatic brain injury after being in a car accident was loss of hearing. Mike was one of the first people with traumatic brain injury to receive a cochlear implant. Now he hears sounds that are changed into electrical signals by a small speech processor. The processor sends the signals to a device that is similar to a hearing aid. When Mike was in rehab, he often spoke of when he was a "regular man" and a "normal person." Today he credits his recovery to faith in God. Mike is looking forward to the future and enjoys his hobby of bowhunting from his wheelchair. He explains, "Every day gets better, like steps on a ladder. I just gotta keep going up."

See *The Charleston Gazette*, November 24, 1994.

9. In _____% of traumatic brain injuries, the student experiences seizures, which often decrease or disappear with the passage of time. (See Describing the Characteristics; Physical Changes)

10. A student with brain injury may comprehend less of what you say with increases in (a) the rate of your speech, (b) _____, (c) abstract language, and (d) _____ (See Describing the Characteristics; Linguistic Changes)

11. In the 1970s, _____% of people with traumatic brain injury died. Currently, at least _____% survive. Lifetime effects are present for _____% of those with mild injuries, _____ to _____% of those with moderate injuries, and _____% of those with severe injuries. (See Describing the Characteristics; Prognosis)

12. Identify the four major causes of traumatic head injuries and their percentages. (See Identifying the Causes of Traumatic Brain Injury)

    a. _____ (_____%)

    b. _____ (_____%)

    c. _____ (_____%)

    d. _____ (_____%)

13. _____ accounts for the majority of infant head injuries, and more than 80% of deaths from head trauma in children under age two are the result of _____. (See Identifying the Causes of Traumatic Brain Injury)

14. _____ occurs when a caretaker shakes the child violently to try to make the child stop crying. In _____% to _____% of these cases, the child dies. (See Identifying the Causes of Traumatic Brain Injury)

15. Traumatic brain injury is called the _____ because it is the most common cause of death and disability in children and adults. Each year _____ out of every _____ children and adolescents will survive a head injury that requires hospitalization. (See Identifying the Prevalence of Traumatic Brain Injury)

16. What percentage of adolescents may have sustained a brain injury serious enough to cause school problems? _____% (See Identifying the Prevalence of Traumatic Brain Injury)

What Are Evaluation Procedures?

17. Name and briefly describe uses and cautions for three assessment tools that might be used to determine the presence of a traumatic brain injury. (See Determining the Presence of Traumatic Brain Injury)

Name of Assessment	Uses	Cautions

18. Deficits in achievement (are, are not) always present immediately after recovery. (See Determining the Presence of Traumatic Brain Injury)

19. What is the primary goal of programming for students with traumatic brain injury? (See Determining the Nature and Extent of Special Education and Related Services)

He Never Moved

Although we have presented you with a very hopeful picture of recovery for students with traumatic brain injury, there are cases in which the hoped-for recovery does not come. Jamie Butcher was in a car accident in 1977 when he was 17 years old. For 17 years, his parents watched over him tenderly, even though doctors said he "had no brain left." During that time, Jamie never moved, never heard anything, and felt nothing. Finally, in 1994, Jamie's family decided to withdraw his feeding tube. Suddenly, this grieving family became the center of controversy and media attention. You may encounter a similar situation one day that will affect one of your students. What kind of support would you offer the family?

See *U.S. News and World Report*, November 7, 1994, pp. 69-70.

20. What five decisions should the IEP team make for students with brain injuries? (See Determining the Nature and Extent of Special Education and Related Services)
   a. _____
   b. _____
   c. _____
   d. _____
   e. _____

What and How Do Professionals Teach?

21. Name three primary curricular goals for students with traumatic brain injury. (See Curriculum)

    a. _____

    b. _____

    c. _____

22. Describe three forms of cognitive retraining that help students use residual cognitive and perceptual skills more efficiently. (See Curriculum)

Form of Cognitive Retraining	Specific Areas of Retraining
Component Training	
Compensatory Strategy Training	
Functional Retraining	

23. For students with limited attention spans and memory problems, teachers should keep instructional times _____ and use frequent _____. (See Methods; Instructional Methods)

24. List four prevention strategies that can help students with brain injury avoid challenging behaviors. (See Methods; Methods to Improve Behavior)

    a. _____

    b. _____

    c. _____

    d. _____

> We've talked a lot about the value of computers for students with traumatic brain injuries, as well as other disabilities. Do you feel that people are speaking a foreign language when they are talking about computers? Would you not know what a mouse is if it jumped up and bit you? Then you might find the article "Getting Started with Computers" in *Exceptional Parent* (November/December 1993, pp. 27-32) contains the basic information you need to get started. By the way, *Exceptional Parent* prints one technology issue each year. *PC Novice* magazine also prints helpful guides for using computers at reasonable costs.

25. What are the five steps involved in a Personal Intervention Plan? (See Methods; Methods to Improve Behavior)

    a. _____

    b. _____

    c. _____

    d. _____

    e. _____

26. When using a positive reinforcement called _____, you reinforce a positive behavior that is incompatible with the undesired behavior. (See Methods; Methods to Improve Behavior)

How Is Participation Encouraged?

27. Match percentages with placements for students who are leaving rehabilitation facilities. (See Inclusion)

1. 10%	a. _____ Postsecondary education
2. 38%	b. _____ Institution
3. 11%	c. _____ Adult education
4. 14%	d. _____ Full-time special education
5. 8%	e. _____ General education
6. 3%	f. _____ Part-time special education

Besides the student's classroom, the planning committee will need to consider the physical layout of the entire school when planning for reentry. The student may have difficulty getting around the building without getting fatigued or confused. Open classrooms may create frustration for students who have concentration and attention problems. Also, recess, lunch, and unstructured time between classes may cause self-monitoring problems.

(Savage & Allen, 1987)

28. Name two priorities for inclusion for students with brain injury. (See Inclusion)
    a. _____
    b. _____

29. Discuss the significant contributions that can be made by each of the following collaborators. (See Collaboration)

Collaborator	Contributions
Professional Educators	
Professional Rehabilitation Personnel	
Family	
Community	
Peers	

30. List six career options available for working with students who have received head injuries. (See Careers)
    a. _____   d. _____
    b. _____   e. _____
    c. _____   f. _____

Defining Beauty

New vistas are opening up for people with disabilities. Paula Jean Nichols-Klimin was a model before she fell 10 stories in a broken elevator. The accident left her with traumatic brain injury and physical disabilities. Yet, Paula was determined to return to the career she loved. Today she wears a size 14 and is distinguished as the first woman in a wheelchair to work for a major modeling company—Ford Models, Inc. One of her fellow models noted as Paula struck a pose from her wheelchair, "She's amazing, isn't she? And she's no token."

See *Mobile Press Register,* December 12, 1994, p. 7-D.

What Are Program Options?

31. What are two purposes that most rehabilitation centers have for students' programs? (See What Are Program Options?)

     a. _____

     b. _____

32. List characteristics leading to the success of students with traumatic brain injury at each of the four program levels. (See What Are Program Options?)

Program	*Characteristics*
Early Intervention and Preschool Years	
Elementary Years	
Middle and Secondary Years	
Transitional and Postsecondary Year	

Thumbs Up!

Jim Brady's life changed dramatically after he received an open head injury from a gunshot that was meant for President Reagan. Although his rehabilitation has been challenging, he is currently active again in public service as an influential advocate for people with disabilities. As Vice Chairman of the National Organization on Disability, he comments about his perspective on the rights of people with disabilities today: "Sure, we have a long way to go before we reach our goal of full participation for people with disabilities; but, we've come a long way. We need to keep the momentum going."

See *National Community Awards Program of the National Organization on Disability*

APPLICATION EXERCISES FOR CHAPTER 13

Application Exercise 13a. Identifying Areas of Change

You have read about how students with brain injuries vary widely in their characteristics. As you read about the following students, decide which area of change is in focus during their rehabilitation period.

1. Quimby has difficulty staying awake during rehabilitation. He finds his left arm doesn't move like it used to and he can no longer play baseball as he did before.

   Area of Change: _____

2. Chin-wei only talks about himself when he's with others. When others don't listen, he becomes restless and irritable. Then he becomes sad and depressed and won't talk to anyone.

   Area of Change: _____

3. Amal tends to act without thinking and he has fallen behind in his school work because he doesn't think through the instructions.

   Area of Change: _____

4. Samantha's headaches interfere with her ability to pay attention during class. She also now needs both glasses and a hearing aid to see and communicate with friends.

   Area of Change: _____

5. Erin can't seem to think of the appropriate words when talking with her friends. When she does have the words, she finds she is slow to express them.

   Area of Change: _____

6. Rosalba works hard to complete her work, but when finished will loudly announce her great accomplishment to anyone around. Consequently, most of her old friends are finding it difficult to be around her.

   Area of Change: _____

Application Exercise 13b. Curriculum Applications

Reread the section on "Curriculum." Using descriptions of curricular options found there, identify which type of curriculum would most benefit each of the following student needs.

a. Compensatory strategy training	_____ 1. Michaela has difficulty with her memory. She can't seem to remember new information from one day to the next.
b. Component training	_____ 2. Lev needs to develop his reading skills through activities requiring his active involvement and commitment, such as animal training.
c. Functional retraining	_____ 3. Chloe needs help to clarify and express important information.
	_____ 4. Kevin has difficulty with organizing his activities and often feels confused remembering which one he needs to do.
	_____ 5. Matthew has trouble paying attention and is unable to organize what needs to be done.

Application Exercise 13c. Improving Instruction and Retention of Content

For each of the five major questions* addressed in this chapter, try out a different one of the suggestions in Box 13-4, "Improving Instruction," to review chapter contents. For instance, in answering question one, "What is traumatic brain injury?" you may want to use number 7 and redefine all words and terms to help you learn the content. Or you may choose to use number 11 and develop a new system for organizing the material in a memorable way.

*Five Major Questions: What is traumatic brain injury? What are evaluation procedures? What and how do professionals teach? How is participation encouraged? What are program options?

ANSWERS TO MARGIN QUESTIONS

Page 550   Retention is generally not a good idea because students generally regain many of their pre-injury skills and have holding skills in certain areas. The extent of regained pre-injury skills may not be known for a year or two. They also tend to regain appropriate social skills more quickly when they remain with their peers.

Page 570   An important step for providing support for Jimmie's family is to learn as much as you can about his culture. Talking to members of his tribe about their customs and values would be helpful, as well as researching tribal customs. It might be helpful to mention to Agnes that you want to respect her culture and ask her to tell you if you do anything that is offensive. Telling Agnes that you need her help and suggestions because she knows Jimmie better than anyone might encourage her to share more openly.

SAMPLE QUIZ FOR CHAPTER 13

Circle the correct answer.

TRUE OR FALSE

T or F   1.   An acquired brain injury excludes injuries caused by internal forces.

T or F   2.   A postconcussional syndrome does not show damage on medical tests but invariably results in similar effects to a severe brain injury.

T or F   3.   Anosoqnosia, the inability to use language appropriately, is a common side effect of a moderate or severe brain injury.

T or F   4.   Neuropsychological testing can be used for planning cognitive retraining for students with brain injuries.

T or F   5.   Adults are often told not to return to work after they have been in rehabilitation for a head injury.

MULTIPLE CHOICE

6.   Which of the following procedures examines the chemical activity in the brain?

    a.   MRI (magnetic resonance imaging)

    b.   CT (computerized tomography) scan

    c.   PET (positron emission therapy)

    d.   EEG (electroencephalogram)

7.   Which of the following is <u>not</u> a symptom of a mild head injury?

    a.   Brief absence seizure or automaton

    b.   Restlessness

    c.   Temper loss

    d.   Need for extra sleep

8.   What part of the brain controls balance and coordination?

    a.   Parietal lobe

    b.   Frontal lobe

    c.   Occipital lobe

    d.   Cerebellum

9.   What percentage of students with head injuries report headaches during the first year after the injury?

    a.   30%

    b.   45%

    c.   60%

    d.   90%

10.   Malcolm had a severe brain injury. What is most likely true about him?

    a.   He was in a coma for 12 hours.

    b.   He has a 50-50 chance of lifetime effects

    c.   He is at risk for chronic intellectual, psychological, and academic deficits.

    d.   He did not receive medical care within the first three hours after the injury.

11.   Emily, age eight months, died from the leading cause of infant head injuries. What is it?

    a.   Motor vehicle crashes

    b.   Firearms

    c.   Falls

    d.   Child abuse

12. What possible negative effect of a "circle of friends" is mentioned?
    a. One-sided friendships can develop.
    b. The student with the injury can depend on the circle and be reluctant to make friends with other peers.
    c. The circle can receive special treatment from the teacher.
    d. The circle can become a clique.

13. In New Mexico, what is the most common educational placement for students with brain injuries who are leaving rehabilitation centers?
    a. Institution
    b. General education
    c. Full-time special education
    d. Resource room

14. What happens in self-modeling?
    a. The teacher videotapes the student exhibiting appropriate behaviors, with any inappropriate behaviors edited out.
    b. The student chooses an exemplary hero on which to model behavior and researches the person's life and character.
    c. When the student exhibits inappropriate behavior, an aide takes him or her aside and mimics the behavior. The student corrects the aide and role plays the proper behavior in the situation.
    d. The student selects a behavior to work on and with a group of peers, acts out appropriate behavior in various scenarios.

15. What is true about the brain during the elementary years?
    a. It is "supercharged."
    b. If damaged, it results in lack of bonding.
    c. Connections between and within the hemispheres become more efficient.
    d. Logical thought emerges.

SHORT ANSWER

16. List two types of brain injury not served under the IDEA definition for traumatic brain injury.
    a. _____   b. _____

17. List the three major causes of the traumatic brain injuries that are currently included under the definition used in IDEA.
    a. _____
    b. _____
    c. _____

18. Briefly describe the three forms of cognitive retraining.
    a. _____
    b. _____
    c. _____

ESSAY

19. Explain the differences between open and closed head injuries. Include a discussion of the controversy over injuries that are not presently included.

20. Compare and contrast methods to improve behavior, explaining specific details of effective strategies.

CHAPTER 14: COMMUNICATION DISORDERS

CHAPTER OVERVIEW

Communication disorders can be frustrating and uncomfortable to both the speaker and the listener. This chapter examines the diverse characteristics of speech and language disorders along with recognized causes and current prevalence rates. To understand how to help students with communication disorders, several tools for determining the presence of speech and language disorders are discussed. For determining special education and related service, an analysis of how to conduct language samples is explained. The best curriculum and methods are brought into a focused discussion, followed by an evaluation of the speech-language pathologist's role in inclusion and collaboration. Exemplary program options are summarized to understand the potential for students with communication disorders.

The life of four-year-old Martin Krecker highlights the importance of early identification and services for students with language disorders. Martin did not talk until he was two and one half and for several months after beginning to speak, used only one- or two-word sentences. In addition, his early words were difficult for others to understand because he was unable to produce many sounds appropriately. Now four, Martin is speaking in full sentences, using appropriate speech.

CHAPTER AT-A-GLANCE

Chapter Outline	Instructional Goals	Key Concepts
WHAT ARE COMMUNICATION DISORDERS?		
Defining Communication Disorders • The Distinction Between Communication Disorders: Speech and Language • Cultural Differences in Communication	• Distinguish between speech and language communication disorders • Recognize how communication differences may be related to the culture	• A speech disorder is an impairment of one's articulation of speech sounds, fluency, or voice. • A language disorder reflects a problem in receiving information, understanding it, and formulating a spoken, written or symbolic response. • Communication differences that are related to the culture of the individual are not considered impairments
Describing the Characteristics • Typical Speech Development • Characteristics of Speech Impairments • Typical Language Development • Characteristics of Language Impairments • Effects of Communication Disorders	• Explain the typical course of the development of speech and characteristics and effects of speech impairments • Explain the typical course of the development of language and characteristics and effects of language impairments	• Most speech disorders are articulation disorders. • Voice impairments may be noted in pitch, intensity, resonance, and vocal quality. • Language is a shared system of rules and symbols for the exchange of information and includes rules of phonology, morphology, syntax, semantics, and pragmatics. • Communication disorders can impact a student's academic, social, and emotional development.
Identifying the Causes of Communication Disorders	• Identify and evaluate the causes of communication disorders	• Causes may be functional or organic and may be further classified according to when the problem began.
Identifying the Prevalence of Communication Disorders	• Apply prevalence figures to today's population	• It is estimated that 5% to 10% of the population has a communication disorder.

WHAT ARE EVALUATION PROCEDURES?		
Determining the Presence of Communication Disorders • Assessment of Students who are Bilingual or Multilingual • Assessment of Infants and Toddlers • Assessment of Communication Skills During School Years	• Examine the various ways used to determine the presence of communication disorders	• The speech-language pathologist is the professional most likely to determine the presence and extent of a speech and/or language impairment. • Assessments include both formal and informal measures.
Determining the Nature and Extent of Special Education and Related Services	• Analyze the nature and extent of the need for special education and related services	• Analysis of an individual's conversation can provide information to assess language development and use.
WHAT AND HOW DO PROFESSIONALS TEACH?		
Curriculum	• Explain the curricular decisions and means for implementing the curricular with students who have communication disorders	• The speech-language pathologist uses many curricular approaches to remediate or to compensate for communication impairments.
Methods	• Explain how different methods are effective for students who have communication disorders	• The speech-language pathologist may use a variety of service delivery models, from one-on-one, small group, or large group intervention both within and without the general education classroom.
HOW IS PARTICIPATION ENCOURAGED?		
Inclusion	• Summarize benefits and problems associated with inclusion of students who have communication disorders	• Many students receive their speech/language therapy while included in their general education classrooms.
Collaboration • Professional Collaboration • Family Collaboration • Community Collaboration	• Explore ways parents, teachers, and speech and language pathologists may collaborate to ensure the communicative student success	• The collaborative participation of students, teachers, speech-language pathologists, and parents to enhance communicative development results in students' language objectives being targeted with a variety of people in many settings.
Careers	• Examine careers available for professionals who work with students who have communication disorders	• Careers include the field of speech-language pathology, audiology, and/or education of students who are deaf or hard of hearing.
WHAT ARE PROGRAM OPTIONS?		
Early Intervention and Preschool Years	• Describe characteristics of effective preschool programs	• Early emphasis is on the development of language and its use. Therapy can occur in the home, day-care setting, school, or other natural environment.

Elementary Years	• Describe characteristics of effective elementary school programs	• Programs for elementary students focus on helping the students develop social, interactive language and comprehensible speech.
Middle and Secondary Years	• Describe characteristics of effective programs for middle and secondary students	• During the middle and secondary years, some students either no longer require therapy or choose to discontinue.
Transitional and Postsecondary Years	• Describe characteristics of effective programs for adults with communication disorders	• Postsecondary job-training programs for individuals with communication disorders sometimes include therapy. Some universities may offer these services to full-time students at low cost.

PROJECT OPTIONS

1. In a local school, work with a speech-language pathologist and evaluate how he or she differentiates instruction for students with speech disorders and those with language disorders. Construct a chart based on your observations and what you learned in this chapter that clearly identifies differences between these two groups.

2. Create a peer tutoring game that students with and without speech disorders can play to help overcome speech difficulties.

3. Research alternative or augmentative communication approaches and prepare three creative and artistic advertisements for your favorite three approaches based upon the six values guiding special education.

4. Prepare and present two dramatic presentations to demonstrate inappropriate vs. appropriate ways to respond to individuals with speech and/or language impairments. Do one presentation within the classroom and one at a local school.

KEY TERMS

Aphasia

Articulation

Bidialectal

Central auditory processing disorders

Cleft palate/lip

Dialect

Early expressive language delay

Ebonics

Echolalia

Expressive language

Fluency problems

Functional language problems

Hypernasality

Hyponasality

Language disorders

Milieu teaching

Morphology

Multilingualism

Organic language problems

Phonology

Pragmatics

Receptive language disorders

Resonance

Semantics

Social interaction theories

Specific language impairment

Speech disorders

Stuttering

Syntax

Syntax errors

Vocal nodules

CHAPTER 14 GUIDED REVIEW

The Book Report

Fifth grade was one of those years when everything seemed to be changing. Even though I was a good student, I was becoming self-conscious about the impression I made on others. So when our teacher told us that next week we would have special book report presentations in the school auditorium, I was very apprehensive.

I prepared for days, memorizing what I would say and how I would say it. The day arrived too soon. When it was my turn, I floated onto the stage and somehow made it to the conclusion of my report. I had thought that the book *The Secret Garden* by Frances Hodgson Burnett was the best I ever read and planned to recommend it highly. But when I came to my concluding remarks, what I said was, "This is the best book I have ever written."

My valued peers immediately burst into laughter, and I didn't have any idea why. I thought about it and concluded that I must have used the wrong part of speech. I then corrected myself with "I mean it's the best book I ever wrote." More squeals of laughter. By then I was so red in the face that I must have looked like a beet. Then, in one brief moment, I realized what I had said and felt totally humiliated. I corrected myself one final time with "This is the best book I have ever read," and sat down.

The presentations went on, but I was oblivious to them all. How could the wrong words have come out of my mouth like that? I had practiced so carefully and didn't understand how my mouth could say something I didn't mean to say. I was convinced the world was ending and that no one would ever speak to me again. Though that didn't happen, I can still feel the pain of my language failure that day.

—Dorothy Leal

What Are Communication Disorders?

1. Effective communication requires knowledge of _____ and _____. When an individual does not understand and follow these rules, _____ may occur. (See Defining Communication Disorders)

2. Identify the main characteristics of the two types of communication impairments. (See Defining Communication Disorders; The Distinction Between Communication Disorders: Speech and Language)

    Speech disorder: _____

    Language disorder: _____

3. Explain cultural influences on speech and language that are reflected in the ebonics controversy. (See Defining Communication Disorders; Cultural Differences in Communication)

    _____

    _____

    _____

4. Children learn to produce nearly all the consonants and vowels of their native language by the age of _____. However, a _____ year variance between the time that some children learn a sound and the time when others learn that same sound is common. (See Describing the Characteristics; Typical Speech Development)

5. List the major characteristics along with examples of the following speech impairments. (See Describing the Characteristics; Characteristics of Speech Impairments.

Type of Speech Impairment	Characteristics	Examples
Articulation Disorders		
Voice Disorders		
Fluency Disorders		

"Doggie" to "Mutt"

Children typically start out with a small number of words which represent a large number of objects in their environment. For example, toddlers often label all animals as "doggie." Through the development of more precise semantic rules, they differentiate dogs from cows and elephants, and eventually refine dogs to poodles, beagles, or mutts.

---

6. Name the four types of articulation disorders and circle the two that are very common. (See Describing the Characteristics; Characteristics of Speech Impairments; Articulation Disorders)

   a. _____   c. _____

   b. _____   d. _____

7. What type of speech disorder is stuttering? _____. Approximately what percent of the population stutter? _____% (See Describing the Characteristics; Characteristics of Speech Impairments; Fluency Disorders).

8. Match the developmental language characteristic with the age at which it is typically observed (See Describing the Characteristics; Typical Language Development)

1. Five- to fifty-word vocabulary	a. _____ Birth to 6 months
2. 200-300 word vocabulary	b. _____ 6 to 12 months
3. Laughs	c. _____ 12 to 18 months
4. Asks why questions	d. _____ 18 to 24 months
5. Uses past tense	e. _____ 24 to 36 months
6. Shares personal feelings and thoughts verbally	f. _____ 36 to 48 months
7. Recognizes the names of familiar people and objects	g. _____ 4 to 5 years
8. Follows two-step directions	h. _____ 5 to 6 years

Keeping It Short and Simple

Young children, prior to the age of about four years, typically use a phonology rule system that allows them to reduce words so they are more easily pronounced. They may omit final sounds and say <u>ca</u> for <u>cat</u> and may also reduce the number of syllables in a word such as <u>amal</u> for <u>animal</u>. When children become older, these errors may indicate problems with the child's phonological language system. Sound substitutions can also be articulation errors. Differentiating between these errors as articulation or language impairments is sometimes difficult for speech-language pathologists.

---

9. Name each dimension of language that is described below. (See Describing the Characteristics; Typical Language Development)

   a. _____governs the structure of words and the construction of word forms.

   b. _____ encompasses the wide repertoire of individual phonemes and how they are produced, depending on their placement in a syllable or word.

   c. _____ refers to the use of communication in social contexts.

   d. _____ provides rules for putting together a series of words to form sentences and defines relationships among the elements within the sentences.

   e. _____ refers to the content and meaning of what is expressed.

10. _____ _____ theories hold that language development is the outcome of a child's drive for attachment with his or her world. (See Describing the Characteristics; Typical Language Development)

11. Name the language dimension in focus for each type of language impairment described below. (See Describing the Characteristics; Characteristics of Language Impairments)

Language Dimension	Language Impairment
a.	Difficulty using social cues of communication within a shared social environment
b.	Difficulty in ordering words to convey intended meaning
c.	Difficulty in using words together in sentences to show meaning
d.	Difficulty using the structure of words to get or give information
e.	Difficulty discriminating differences in sounds or sound segments that signify differences in words

12. Describe the two types of speech and language disorders according to their cause. (See Identifying the Causes of Communication Disorders)

   Functional disorders: _____

   Organic disorders: _____

Dr. William Magee, a plastic surgeon, is helping to prevent serious speech and language impairments in children with cleft palates. Dr. Magee operates on patients as young as 15 days old. He says that the baby "can immediately begin life with nearly normal functions . . . (and) can coo like any normal child."

Michael, one of his little patients, had three surgeries for bilateral cleft palate before he was 14 months old. The surgeries have been successful. His mother says, "He is able to say a lot of different words: *Papa, Mama, more, yes, no*."

See *People Weekly*, June 13, 1994, pp. 39-43.

---

13. Give causes and examples of problems associated with each of the following disorders. (See Identifying the Causes of Communication Disorders)

	Cause	*Examples of Problem*
Organic language problem		
Functional language problem		
Functional and organic problem		

14. Explain the difference between a congenital impairment and an acquired impairment. (See Identifying the Causes of Communication Disorders)

    _____

    _____

15. Identify the percentages of all children and youth that have the following communication disorders. (See Identifying the Prevalence of Communication Disorders)

    Articulation disorders: _____%

    Fluency disorders: _____%

    Voice disorders: _____%

    Language disorders serious enough to affect academic performance: _____%

16. What education placement is used for nearly 90% of students with communication disorders? (See Identifying the Prevalence of Communication Disorders) _____

Helping Students Who Stutter

1. Allow the student as much time as needed to complete a thought. Be relaxed and unhurried, and avoid the impulse to finish the student's words. Remember that the student needs to feel that you value his or her participation, especially after volunteering.

2. When does the student speak most fluently? Seek to increase those circumstances. Most children who stutter are fluent under some circumstances such as singing or reading and reciting poetry. Even lines learned for plays and skits are often given fluently, as James Earl Jones, who had a stuttering problem as he was growing up, so aptly demonstrates.

3. Remind peers that everyone has areas of strengths and other areas that are challenging. Point out that some are good runners, while others are less able to run quickly. Some get assignments done faster than others. Some can talk more easily than others.

What Are Evaluation Procedures?

17. How are articulation problems assessed both formally and informally? (See Determining the Presence of Communication Disorders)

    Formally: _____

    Informally: _____

18. Fair, unbiased evaluation to determine the presence of communication disorders is difficult for a student who is _____, _____, or

    _____. (See Determining the Presence of Communication Disorders; Assessment of Students who are Bilingual or Multilingual)

19. Arena assessment for young children is recommended because _____

    _____.

    (See Determining the Presence of Communication Disorders; Assessment of Infants and Toddlers)

20. Under IDEA, speech-language therapy is a(n) _____ service rather than a(n)

    _____ service. (See Determining the Nature and Extent of Special Education and Related Services)

What and How Do Professionals Teach?

21. Describe two types of curriculum used with students who have communication disorders. (See Curriculum)

Remediation: _____

Compensation: _____

22. Match the strategy for arranging the environment to stimulate language use with its characteristics. (See Methods)

1. Interesting materials	a. ____ Create an absurd situation to prompt a response.
2. Out of reach	b. ____ Set up a situation that prevents students from completing a task.
3. Inadequate portions	c. ____ Create a situation where student wants help.
4. Choice making	d. ____ Provide an insufficient amount of needed materials.
5. Assistance	e. ____ Present many options available to complete a task.
6. Sabotage	f. ____ Provide an inviting environment with things student enjoys.
7. Silly situations	g. ____ Place materials within view, but difficult to obtain.

Camp Chatterbox

How can kids learn to use augmentative communication devices (AAC) in a nonthreatening atmosphere? Send them to camp. Camp Chatterbox, located at Camp Merry Heart, the Easter Seals Camp of New Jersey, provides children ages 5 to 16 the opportunity to learn and have fun at the same time. For example, one night the counselors dressed up as leprechauns for a scavenger hunt. The campers, using their AAC, had to answer questions posed by the counselors to win.

The children are not the only ones to learn from the experience. One mother comments about her tendency to translate for her son. "The camp helps kids…learn how to effectively communicate for themselves without our interference."

See Joan Bruno, "Mom went to speech…instead of the beach" (1998) in *Exceptional Parent, 28*(4), 48, 51.

How Is Participation Encouraged?

23. What is the name of the model of service provision that allows students to remain in their general education classes with peers who serve as communication models? (See Inclusion) _____

24. Describe things collaborators can do together to facilitate students' language development and interaction. (See Collaboration)

Professional collaborators: _____

_____

Family collaborators: _____

_____

Community collaborators: _____

_____

25. List three changes benefiting individuals with communication disorders that resulted from ADA and IDEA. (See Collaboration; Community Collaboration)

a. _____

b. _____

c. _____

26. Professional careers working with students who have communication disorders include the field of _____, _____, and/or _____. (See Careers)

27. To qualify for a certificate of clinical competence to work as a professional in communication disorders, individuals must complete what four things? (See Careers)

    a. _____

    b. _____

    c. _____

    d. _____

What Are Program Options?

28. Name and describe the largest national program that integrates preschoolers with disabilities into preschool classes. (See Early Intervention and Preschool Years)

_____

_____

29. For therapy to be most effective for elementary age students, it is recommended that _____ and _____ approaches be combined. (See Elementary Years)

30. What is the focus of therapy for students who continue to receive services into the middle and secondary years? (See Middle and Secondary Years)

_____

_____

Does Polly Want a Cracker?

Julia Smith, of Somerset, England, discovered an innovative way to help her students with speech and language impairments. Julie brings her pet cockatiel to work with her. She videotapes the students' attempts to elicit speech from the bird and then plays the tapes back to the students for analysis and discussion. The strategy is proving more effective than typical speech therapies.

See *Times Educational Supplement*, March 26, 1993, p. 4.

APPLICATION EXERCISES FOR CHAPTER 14

Application Exercise 14a. Identifying Characteristics of Typical Language Development

See if you can rank these students by language development according to age, from youngest to oldest. After you have put them in order, see if you can identify the age range for each child from birth to six years.

1. Cedric knows that when mom says "no" she means it, even when he doesn't obey. He responds to simple commands such as "give me a kiss" and uses many sound patterns in response to others' speech.

2. Muhammad uses his vocabulary of 2600 words in complex sentences, though may sometimes be confused. He loves to tell stories and tell you what he thought about the story. He also likes to tell simple jokes.

3. Jana's vocabulary includes over 200 words and she uses possessives, plurals, verbs with some expertise. She listens and imitates everything and makes two to three word sentences.

4. Yu-chen loves to listen to stories and will often discuss them with others, recounting the events of the story. She not only follows two-step directions, but uses simple questions and pronouns.

5. Fidel has a vocabulary of about forty words when talking with people. He recognizes many words and can point to them in books as well as in the environment.

6. Thalalia's questions include who, what, when, where, why, and how. She explains and describes events with verb contractions. She has begun to identify differences and make analogies.

7. Josi laughs and coos in response to familiar situations. Her parents spend a lot of time talking to her and enjoy watching and listening to her responses to them.

8. Julienne uses past tense, but still makes some grammatical errors. She knows her first and last name and uses prepositions and conjunctions in her sentences.

Name	Age Range
1.	
2.	
3.	
4.	
5.	
6.	
7.	
8.	

Application Exercise 14b. Identifying Language Impairments by the Dimension of Language in Focus

Match the language dimension affected with each student's language difficulty.

1. Phonology	a.____ Anish asks questions and doesn't wait for answers or ignores them.
2. Morphology	b.____ Elissa told her six-year-old classmate "me sick" before she went home.
3. Syntax	c.____ Amelia always says, "Give me the thing, please" instead of naming it.
4. Semantics	d.____ Ku tells long stories but won't listen to anyone else's story.
5. Pragmatics	e.____ Jim cannot auditorally differentiate between the words "fire" and "far."
	f.____ Shih Wei told his mom "The boys gone" when his brothers left him behind.
	g.____ Lettie has difficult in spelling and wrote "pin" for pen on the test.

Application Exercise 14c. Expanding Your Understanding of Communication Disorders

Based upon the five major questions* addressed in this chapter, organize your ideas similar to the "expansion" method discussed in this chapter. Start with a simple summary statement for each of the key concepts and then expand these into more detailed summaries. Think of different ways to word your summaries to make the concepts clearer.

*Five Major Questions: What are communication disorders? What are evaluation procedures? What and how do professionals teach? How is participation encouraged? What are program options?

ANSWERS TO MARGIN QUESTIONS

Margin notes in Chapter 14 are reflective only.

Circle the correct answer.

TRUE OR FALSE

T or F   1.   Language disorders are sometimes the primary feature by which mental retardation is identified.

T or F   2.   The larynx is sometimes referred to as the voice box.

T or F   3.   Pragmatics refers to the use of communication in social contexts.

T or F   4.   Nondiscriminatory testing for bilingual students is ensured by translating test items into the child's primary language.

T or F   5.   Remediation is the most common intervention option for students with communication disorders.

MULTIPLE CHOICE

6.   Which of the following is <u>not</u> a skill required for auditory processing?
   a. Blending sounds that are heard
   b. Discriminating between important and unimportant input
   c. Remembering input
   d. Articulating intelligible speech

7.   Celeste is eight years old and speaks English. If she is typical, which sounds should she have mastered?
   a. All the consonants
   b. All the consonants with the possible exception of /r/
   c. All the consonants with the possible exception of /zh/
   d. All the consonants and vowels

8.   Which of the following is <u>not</u> an articulation error?
   a. Substitution
   b. Omission
   c. Addition
   d. Tension

9.   What determines pitch?
   a. The air pressure coming from the lungs through the vocal folds
   b. The rate of vibration in the vocal folds
   c. The way in which the tone coming from the vocal folds is modified by the cavities of the throat, mouth, and nose
   d. The length of time needed for the sound to emerge from the larynx

10.   At what age does a child usually have a vocabulary of at least 2,500 words?
   a. Eight
   b. Six
   c. Four
   d. Three

11.   Victoria has a semantic disorder. Which of the following errors is she most likely to make?
   a. Says "bill" instead of "pill"
   b. Says "her nice"
   c. Does not understand words like "justice" and "freedom"
   d. Misuses negatives

12. What percentage of children in the United States have a speech or language impairment serious enough to warrant special services?
   a. 1%
   b. 3%
   c. 5%
   d. 8%

13. Werner has a functional language problem. How does it most likely manifest itself?
   a. Articulation disorder due to cerebral palsy
   b. Acquired aphasia from meningitis
   c. Cleft palate
   d. Stuttering

14. What is the most common cause for speech and language disorders?
   a. Organic
   b. Neurological
   c. Congenital
   d. Unknown

15. When is prereferral most often used with students who might have a communication disorder?
   a. When they are bilingual
   b. When they are preschoolers
   c. When they are also mildly mentally retarded
   d. Prereferral is typically not used.

SHORT ANSWER

16. List the five dimensions of language that work together to produce language.
   a. _____ d. _____
   b. _____ e. _____
   c. _____

17. Describe the difference between remediation and compensation.

   _____
   _____
   _____

18. List four treatments for stuttering.
   a. _____
   b. _____
   c. _____
   d. _____

ESSAY

19. Explain how communication disorders differ in each of the five dimensions of language.

20. Discuss the different roles of the speech-language pathologist in terms of inclusion and collaboration.

CHAPTER OVERVIEW

In this chapter you will be studying a different culture—the Deaf culture. By your awareness and sensitivity to the unique Deaf culture, you can help build a bridge between the hearing and deaf worlds. We suggest that you see at least one film that portrays the Deaf culture. You are also provided with a case study about Heather Whitestone that asks you to consider the conflict among people with hearing loss about the use of lipreading for communication. This chapter explores many dimensions of hearing loss, including an overview of assessment possibilities and explanation of methods and curriculum that are used by people with hearing loss. Additional program options at each level are described to provide an overview of effective practices for serving these students.

The life of 7th grader Amala Brown provides an illustration of a student with hearing loss who overcame a rough start in life. She has attended a public school in general education classes for much of her education and now has strong language skills in English and ASL. Amala's mother, a teacher of children who are deaf and a sign language interpreter, has provided a home environment that has been ideal for Amala to develop linguistically and socially.

CHAPTER AT-A-GLANCE

Chapter Outline	Instructional Goals	Key Concepts
WHAT IS HEARING LOSS?		
Defining Hearing Loss	• Evaluate the issues surrounding the controversy over how to refer to people who are deaf and hard of hearing • Distinguish between definitions of deafness, hearing impairment, and hard of hearing	• Hearing loss is difficult to define because the point at which hearing stops being normal and starts being a disability cannot be stated. • Degrees of hearing loss are identified as slight, mild, moderate, severe, and profound.
Describing the Characteristics • Language and Communication • Psycho-Social Dimensions • Education	• Describe key characteristics of children who are deaf or hard of hearing	• Communication with parents, peers, and teachers plays a major role in the psychological, social, and emotional development of children with hearing loss. • Achievement levels continue to be a primary concern, particularly among children from diverse racial, ethnic, and linguistic backgrounds.
Identifying the Causes of Hearing Loss • Prelingual Causes • Postlingual Causes	• Identify the major causes of hearing loss	• A conductive loss is caused by a problem in the outer or middle ear. • A sensorineural loss is caused by a problem in the inner ear or along the nerve pathway to the brain stem.
Identifying the Prevalence of Hearing Loss	• Recognize prevalence rates for individuals who are deaf or hard of hearing	• Prevalence is estimated at 1.6% of all students. • Prelingual hearing loss accounts for 95% of students who are deaf and hard of hearing, while postlingual hearing loss accounts for 5%.

WHAT ARE EVALUATION PROCEDURES?		
Determining the Presence of Hearing Loss	• Summarize ways to determine the presence of hearing loss • Explain how an audiogram is used for assessment purposes	• Infants who fail screenings have their hearing tested using an auditory brain stem response (ABR) test. • Older students have a behavioral audiological evaluation to measure hearing levels.
Determining the Nature and Extent of Special Education and Related Services	• List the factors that are critical in determining an appropriate educational setting	• Regular reassessments of language, hearing, speech and/or sign, speech-reading, academic achievement, and socialization are essential to provide an appropriate education.
WHAT AND HOW DO PROFESSIONALS TEACH?		
Curriculum • Language, Reading, Writing • Deaf Culture • Speech • Aural Habilitation	• Describe fundamental components of the curriculum	• Language, reading, and writing form the central curriculum focus, with specialized curriculum in Deaf culture, speech, and aural habilitation.
Methods • Communication —Oral/Aural —Bilingual-Bicultural —Total Communication • Instructional Strategies —Experiential Learning —Scaffolding —Collaborative Learning and Peer Tutoring —Visual Aids —Classroom Design Modifications	• Identify the communication modes used in classrooms • Explain helpful instructional strategies	• Communication methods include oral/aural, bilingual-bicultural and total communication. • Instructional strategies are particularly effective when they emphasize experiential learning, build on the students' current knowledge and skills, require them to interact with peers, capitalize on the visual medium, and reduce environmental distraction.
HOW IS PARTICIPATION ENCOURAGED?		
Inclusion • Educational Placements —Public Schools —Day Schools —Residential Schools	• Provide arguments for both sides of the controversy over the least restrictive environment for students who are deaf or hard of hearing	• Most educators favor appropriateness while members of the Deaf community advocate for placement in schools for the deaf. • More than 80% of students with hearing loss are being served in the public schools.
Collaboration • Professional Collaboration • Family Collaboration • Community Collaboration	• Identify the professionals who should collaborate to meet the educational needs of a child with hearing loss	• The needs of individuals with hearing loss are accommodated through family members as well as through sign language interpreters, special text telephones, telephone relay services, captioned television and real time graphic display, and the Internet.
Careers • Teachers of the Deaf • Interpreters	• Examine the role and responsibilities of teachers of the deaf and sign language interpreters	• While many professionals contribute to the welfare of students who are deaf and hard of hearing, teaching the deaf and interpreting are two important careers in deaf education.

WHAT ARE PROGRAM OPTIONS?		
Early Intervention and Preschool Years	• Distinguish characteristics of effective preschool programs for students who are deaf or hard of hearing	• It is important for early identification programs to have a direct connection to early intervention programs.
Elementary Years	• Distinguish characteristics of effective elementary programs for students with hearing loss	• A top priority in elementary programs is English language acquisition.
Middle and Secondary Years	• Distinguish characteristics of effective programs for middle and secondary students	• During the secondary years, the priority is to maintain high academic standards and expectations.
Transitional and Postsecondary Years	• Distinguish characteristics of effective program options for adults with hearing loss	• The U.S. Congress funds six postsecondary programs for students who are deaf and hard of hearing. • Transition programs recognize that difficulties with English-based communication is the most significant obstacle to successful transition.

PROJECT OPTIONS

1. Interview a person who is deaf or hard of hearing that you meet through a deaf club or the organization Self-Help for the Hard of Hearing. Ask this person questions about LRE, cochlear implants, and the role of ASL in the education of children with hearing loss. Present your findings in chart form.

2. Record and watch a television comedy or drama with the sound off and the captions activated on your TV. Write about your response to the experience. Then watch the same show with the sound on. Summarize the differences and identify what would have made the first experience more comfortable for you.

3. Teach yourself American Sign Language well enough to carry on a brief conversation with someone who is deaf or hard of hearing. Prepare what you will say and questions you will ask. Then enjoy the conversation and have the one you converse with evaluate the strengths and weaknesses of your ASL.

4. Investigate program options and typical placements in your community. Ask the person in charge at each place how the six values guiding special education are operative in their programs. Using their responses, prioritize where you would place Amala and other students you know who have hearing loss.

5. Research available technology for those who are deaf, such as captioned TV and TDDs. Evaluate the benefits and drawbacks for each one. Then interview two or three people who have hearing loss to find out what needs are not yet being met that could be met by technology. Summarize your findings and submit them to a national technology corporation.

KEY TERMS

American Sign Language (ASL)	Fingerspelling
Audiogram	Hearing aid
Audiologist	Interpreters
Cochlear implant	Prelingual hearing loss
Conductive hearing loss	Postlingual hearing loss
Deaf culture	Sensorineural hearing loss
Deafness	TT (Text telephone)

CHAPTER 15 GUIDED REVIEW

A New Voice for America

When Heather Whitestone, who is deaf, was crowned Miss America, she only heard a faint noise when the song announced, "There she is, Miss America." For her talent competition, Heather gracefully performed ballet to *Via Dolorosa* by counting rhythm beats to herself as the music played. This was only one of many remarkable achievements Heather has accomplished.

Heather, who has no hearing in one ear and only 5% in the other ear, commented about her reign, "When children see me speaking and see me dance, they will realize that they have no excuse for not making their dreams come true." Daphne Gray shares her daughter Heather's story in the book *Yes, You Can, Heather* (Zondervan, 1995).

See *People*, October 3, 1994, p. 48 and *Time*, October 3, 1994, pp. 66-67.

What Is Hearing Loss?

1. Why is hearing loss difficult to define? (See Defining Hearing Loss)
   _____

2. Give three problems with categorizing hearing. (See Defining Hearing Loss)
   a. _____
   b. _____
   c. _____

3. Audiologists evaluate hearing in terms of _____ and _____.
   The results are then charted on a(n) _____. (See Defining Hearing Loss)

4. List the five terms used to identify degree of hearing loss. (See Defining Hearing Loss)
   a. _____
   b. _____
   c. _____
   d. _____
   e. _____

Deafness as Culture

Some deaf activists argue that inclusion into the hearing world is not desirable. They emphasize their belief that deafness is a separate culture and not a handicap. If you want to read more about deafness as a culture, we suggest that you read an article in the September 1993 issue of *The Atlantic* (pp. 37-49).

5. In this chapter you read about the diversity of terms used in identifying students with hearing loss. List and explain at least three terms used with a people-first approach. (See Defining Hearing Loss)

People-first Term	*What Does This Term Communicate?*
a.	
b.	
c.	

6. The single greatest challenge for children who are deaf or hard of hearing is _____ _____. (See Describing the Characteristics; Language and Communication)

7. Contrast earlier and recent perceptions about the social and emotional development of children and adolescents who are deaf and hard of hearing. (See Describing the Characteristics; Psycho-Social Dimensions)

   Earlier beliefs: _____

   Recent beliefs: _____

8. Describe the educational issues surrounding the academic achievement of students with hearing loss. (See Describing the Characteristics; Education)

   _____

   _____

9. How is the ear like a radio? (See Identifying the Causes of Hearing Loss)
   a. Inner ear: _____
   b. Middle ear: _____
   c. Outer ear: _____

10. Describe the types of hearing loss and identify in which part of the ear they occur. (See Identifying the Causes of Hearing Loss)

    Conductive hearing loss: _____

    _____

    Sensorineural hearing loss: _____

    _____

11. Match the cause of hearing loss to the percentage and time of onset associated with it.

1. Prelingual cause (95% of all students)	a. _____ Meningitis
2. Postlingual cause (5% of all students)	b. _____ Infants born prematurely
	c. _____ Recurring otitis media
	d. _____ Side effects from medications.
	e. _____ Genetic deafness
	f. _____ Maternal rubella
	g. _____ The virus known as congenital cytomegalovirus

12. What percentage of all students experience hearing loss? (See Identifying the Prevalence of Hearing Loss)
    _____%

What Are Evaluation Procedures?

13. Determining the presence of hearing loss requires various assessments, depending on the age of the individual. Describe the evaluation for an infant and for an older child. (See What Are Evaluation Procedures?; Determining the Presence of Hearing Loss)

    Infants: _____

    Older Children: _____

14. What does an audiogram record? (See What Are Evaluation Procedures?; Determining the Presence of Hearing Loss)

    a. _____ or pitch; the number of vibrations in one second;
    b. _____ or loudness;
    c. pressure of sound rather than its movement, as measured by _____.

15. An audiogram, found in a student's file, provides much useful information. You can tell many things by where the Xs and Os were on the audiogram. Identify two useful things you can learn from the audiogram. (See What Are Evaluation Procedures?; Determining the Presence of Hearing Loss)

    a. _____

    b. _____

16. In determining the appropriate education setting and related services and supplementary aids for a child with hearing loss, six areas are considered. Identify those six areas and explain who is involved and what information they may provide in determining the needs in this area. (See What Are Evaluation Procedures?; Determining the Nature and Extent of Special Education and Related Services)

Area Assessed to Determine Appropriate Education	Contributing Participants and Their Input
a.	
b.	
c.	
d.	
e.	
f.	

Babbling in Sign Language

Deaf children often go through a babbling stage as they learn sign language, similar to the vocal babbling of hearing children. The hand movements of deaf children of deaf parents who use sign language meet the criteria of babbling 71% of the time. The hand movements of children with hearing parents meet the criteria only 15% of the time. The criteria for babbling is the incorporation of sounds (movements) of the parents' language, repetition of those sounds or movements, and the use of those in the first meaningful words used by the infant.

See *Kansas City Star*, April 14, 1991.

What and How Do Professionals Teach?

17. What are the two schools of thought about curriculum for students who are deaf and hard of hearing? (See What and How Do Professionals Teach?; Curriculum)

    a. _____

    b. _____

18. Explain the purpose and characteristics of curriculum for the four identified areas for students who are deaf and hard of hearing. (See What and How Do Professionals Teach?; Curriculum)

Curricular Area	Purpose	Characteristics or Components
a. Language, Reading, and Writing		
b. Deaf Culture		

c. Speech		
d. Aural Habilitation		

19. Match the methods of communication in educational programs used by individuals who are deaf and hard of hearing with the characteristics of the methods. (See What and How Do Professionals Teach?; Methods)

1. Oral/Aural	a. _____ Instruction in ASL
2. Bilingual-Bicultural	b. _____ The expectation that the students use ASL for communication and teaching of English through written form
3. Total Communication	c. _____ Instruction in spoken English, curriculum in speech and aural habilitation, and the expectation that students use speech, speechreading, and auditory skills
	d. _____ Instruction with speech and a manually coded English
	e. _____ Incorporates curriculum in speech and aural habilitation

20. With children who are deaf and hard of hearing, English is sometimes introduced as the second language. What is typically taught as the child's first language? (See What and How Do Professionals Teach?; Methods)

_____

21. Describe key characteristics and examples of five effective instructional strategies for students with hearing loss. (See What and How Do Professionals Teach?; Methods)

Instructional Strategy	Characteristics and Examples
a.	
b.	
c.	
d.	
e.	

How Is Participation Encouraged?

> Would you know what to do if a student's hearing aid stopped working? If you have a student who is deaf or hard-of-hearing in your class, you will want to talk to an audiologist or teacher of the deaf to find out how to do minor repairs. Generally, a battery replacement will be all that's needed. It will be a good idea to have a battery tester on hand as well as a supply of extra batteries. The batteries need to be disposed of properly.

22. What is the stand of virtually all professional and parent organizations involved in the field of deafness regarding educational options for children who are deaf and hard of hearing? (See How Is Participation Encouraged?; Inclusion)

_____

23. Why is appropriateness over the least restrictive environment desirable for students who have hearing loss? (See How Is Participation Encouraged?; Inclusion)

_____

24. What percentage of students who have hearing loss are being served in the public schools? _____%
What percentage of these students are fully included in regular classrooms? _____% (See How Is Participation Encouraged?; Inclusion)

25. Compare and contrast characteristics for how different school placements serve students with different needs. (See How Is Participation Encouraged?; Inclusion)

School Placement	Characteristics
a. Public Schools	
b. Day Schools	
c. Residential Schools	

> **The Power of Community Influence**
>
> King Jordan is the first deaf president of Gallaudet University. Referring to the student/faculty strike in March 1988 that helped him become elected, Jordan stated that it required a revolution for him to become president of Gallaudet. Making sure that Gallaudet had a deaf president was only one important outcome of the Deaf President Now movement, however. President Jordan emphasized that the movement said to the world, "You can no longer pretend we are not as capable as you. You must allow us to shape our own lives."
>
> See *Perspectives on Deafness*, Vol. 41, No. 1-2, pp. 75-78.

26. Using information and boxes from the chapter, identify ways different collaborators can contribute to the success of students with hearing loss. (See How Is Participation Encouraged?; Collaboration)
    Professional: _____
    Family: _____
    Community: _____

27. "TT" stands for _____ _____ and can be used for some of the following purposes:

    _____
    _____
    _____

    (See How Is Participation Encouraged?; Collaboration; Special Telephones)

28. Who certifies teachers of the deaf? (See How Is Participation Encouraged?; Careers)

_____

29. An interpreter's purpose is to _____
_____ , not to
_____. (See How Is Participation Encouraged?; Careers)

What Are Program Options?

23. List key features for each of the following programs. (See Program Options)

Program	Key Features
Tucker-Maxon Oral School, Portland, Oregon	
David Lubin Elementary School, Sacramento, California	
Utah School for the Deaf, Extension Consultant Division	
College support services are offered to all students who request them	

Giving Pride

Curtis John Pride is the first deaf baseball player in the major leagues for 53 years. Curtis's disability became apparent to his parents at an early age. He yelled instead of babbled when he was six-months old and did not flinch or startle when a door slammed. Curtis was diagnosed with sensorineural deafness at 10 months. His father says he felt very negative about his son's future at that time. Then he realized, "As parents it was our responsibility to give him a chance." They enrolled him in a preschool program that used oral communication, and increased their efforts to teach him orally and through pictures at home. Although Curtis knows sign language, he relies on lip reading and speaking. His parents also helped him become as independent as possible by teaching functional skills, like going to the restaurant counter alone and ordering pizza for his family. Curtis attended a school for the deaf in elementary school, but once he reached seventh grade, he pleaded with his parents to return to his neighborhood school. They agreed. "Attending the neighborhood school was a big turning point in Curtis's life," his mother says. "From then on, he just blossomed."

See "Brave Hearts: Giving Curtis Pride" by Bridget Lyne in *Exceptional Parent* (1998), *28*(5), pp. 26-34, 50.

APPLICATION EXERCISES FOR CHAPTER 15

Application Exercise 15a. Identifying Levels of Hearing Loss

Place in order the following students according to their level of hearing loss, listing the student with the greatest hearing difficulty first. You may want to use Figure 15-2 in your textbook, "Frequency Spectrum of Familiar Sounds," to help you.

1. Jaime has difficulty hearing things like waterfalls.
2. Summea is not able to hear the lawn mower outside her bedroom window.
3. Pedro cannot hear the sounds "j" and "n" "ng" and "d" and "b."
4. Najee is able to identify the "f' and "s" sounds, but he struggles to hear the "ch" and "sh" sounds.
5. Juliana can hear the phone ring and can even hear occasional trucks, but is not able to hear rock bands playing.
6. Sammie loves to watch the jets at the airport, but cannot hear the sounds they make.

greatest amount of hearing loss	1.
	2.
	3.
	4.
	5.
least amount of hearing loss	6.

Application Exercise 15b. Differentiating Different Means of Communication

Read the different ways students communicate and identify the communication mode being used.

1. Sully relies on her minimal hearing abilities and speechreading abilities. What communication mode will she use?

   _____

2. NamPrik tells his friends "I have too much homework" by speaking these words at the same time as using a sign for each word and inflection. What communication mode will she use?

   _____

3. Griffin wants to tell a friend that he is going to a movie. He first signs the location ("movie theater"), then signs who is gong ("me") and then finally the signs the verb ("going"). What communication mode will she use?

   _____

4. Sharon receives instruction in spoken English, though her curriculum is in speech and aural habilitation. What communication mode will she use?

   _____

5. Memo receives instruction in ASL. What communication mode will he use?

   _____

6. Kunti receives instruction through the use of speech and manually coded English. What communication mode will she use?

   _____

Application Exercise 15c. Interpreting Key Components of Hearing Loss

Based upon the five major questions* addressed in this chapter, summarize the major concepts concerning hearing loss. For each major chapter question, use what you know about Amala or another individual highlighted in this chapter to explain the key concepts involved in answering each question.

*Five Major Questions: What is hearing loss? What are evaluation procedures? What and how do professionals teach? How is participation encouraged? What are program options?

ANSWERS TO MARGIN QUESTIONS

Page 627   Possible answers:
- School facilities that have good lighting and are carpeted to provide sound absorption.
- School organization that is inclusive and encourages best practices in curriculum and instruction.
- Administrators who support teachers and students who want to try new ideas.
- Teachers who believe that all children can be successful.
- Students who are open to new experiences and to making new friends.

Page 640   Possible answers:
- Bring a deaf person to class to talk about Deaf culture.
- Visit a school for the deaf.
- Ask a sign language interpreter to talk to the class about Deaf culture.
- Read books about Deaf culture, or include books about Deaf culture in a unit on multiculturalism, and have presentations to the class.
- Show videos with deaf characters and ask the students to discuss the story and characters.
- Go to a performance of the National Theater of the Deaf.

Page 644   This question can be answered with any strategy that shows understanding of the deaf or hard of hearing child's communication needs and that incorporates the visual medium.

Page 655   Possible answers:
- It was difficult because parents didn't know how to communicate with their child.
- Parents would have been frustrated because they would have been on their own in figuring out the best ways to communicate, whether to use speech only or sign language, and how to learn sign language.

SAMPLE QUIZ FOR CHAPTER 15

Circle the correct answer.

TRUE OR FALSE

T or F   1.   A hearing loss of 15 decibels is not sufficiently significant to affect learning to read.

T or F   2.   Children who are deaf differ from children who are hearing in their cognitive abilities to process written language and thus fall behind in reading.

T or F   3.   A conductive hearing loss leaves the inner ear unaffected.

T or F   4.   A postlingual hearing loss cannot occur due to maternal rubella.

T or F   5.   Most infants who are born deaf are identified at birth.

MULTIPLE CHOICE

6.   Why is hearing loss difficult to define?
   a.   It is impossible to know the point at which hearing stops being normal.
   b.   Everyone has partial hearing loss to some degree or other.
   c.   There is a difference between hearing loss in a child and in an elderly person.
   d.   Most hearing loss fluctuates to a certain extent.

7.   What does an audiogram measure?
   a.   Frequency and pitch
   b.   Frequency and intensity
   c.   Intensity and loudness
   d.   Intensity and movement

8.   Karl's hearing is at the 80 decibel level. What can he hear?
   a.   A baby crying
   b.   The phone ringing
   c.   A cat purring
   d.   A dishwasher in operation

9.   What percentage of children who are deaf have hearing parents?
   a.   Under 50%
   b.   About 60%
   c.   About 75%
   d.   Over 90%

10.   In intensive care nurseries, how many infants become deaf or hard of hearing?
   a.   1 in 100
   b.   1 in 50
   c.   1 in 25
   d.   1 in 10

11.   Which of the following is <u>not</u> true about hearing aids?
   a.   They can correct hearing loss only up to 40 decibels.
   b.   There is always some distortion with hearing aids.
   c.   The amplifier is worn inside the ear but the microphone and receiver can be worn on the body.
   d.   They are electroacoustic devices that make sounds louder.

12. What is the most common cause of hearing loss in children?
    a. Heredity
    b. Meningitis
    c. Premature birth
    d. Unknown

13. To what does intensity refer?
    a. The number of vibrations in a second
    b. The pitch of a sound
    c. The pressure of a sound
    d. The cycles of frequency

14. Under IDEA, what is the most important criterion for determining program placement?
    a. Meeting students' needs
    b. Least restrictive environment
    c. Student choice
    d. Parental collaboration

15. Why do many educators and members of the Deaf community oppose the use of manually coded English systems?
    a. They take longer to sign than ASL.
    b. They are not true languages, but distortions of ASL.
    c. They are being introduced by the younger generation and older deaf people cannot understand them.
    d. They are not understood overseas, which presents problems at international conferences of the Deaf.

SHORT ANSWER

16. What are four factors that play a significant role in a child's psycho-social development?
    a. _____
    b. _____
    c. _____
    d. _____

17. Name three ways in which deaf people typically communicate and three methods of communication used in educational programs.
    a. _____   d. _____
    b. _____   e. _____
    c. _____   f. _____

18. Name three ways instructional strategies for students with hearing loss can be made particularly effective.
    a. _____
    b. _____
    c. _____

ESSAY

19. You are a teacher and will have a deaf student in your class this year. Describe the classroom design and visual aid modifications you can make to enhance learning for this student.

20. Present a rationale for both sides of the controversy of the least restrictive environment and appropriate placements for students with hearing loss in schools today. Explain the role of Deaf culture in the controversy.

CHAPTER OVERVIEW

This chapter provides an understanding of both the legal definition and IDEA's definition of visual impairment. It describes the characteristics, causes, and prevalence rates associated with this disability and explains how to determine the presence of a visual impairment, how a student uses vision, and how to determine the nature of special education for students who are blind or visually impaired. Three areas of curricula are described along with five methods used to help students learn. A history of inclusion and collaboration gives the background for understanding placement options available today. This chapter concludes with characteristics of program options that demonstrate the best practices for different age students with visual impairments.

The life of high school sophomore Tracy Kiel is a good example of a student with a significant visual impairment for whom the system worked. Her parents were given appropriate interventions early in Tracy's life and they consequently developed a positive attitude, with great expectations about her future. The school system responded to meet Tracy's needs by providing her with qualified and knowledgeable teachers and orientation and mobility specialists. She has been encouraged to do for herself and to be an equal participant in her home and her school. "Special" considerations were provided only to equalize her knowledge of the world and accessibility to it, not make life at home or school "easier" for her.

CHAPTER AT-A-GLANCE

Chapter Outline	Instructional Goals	Key Concepts
WHAT IS VISUAL IMPAIRMENT?		
Defining Visual Impairment • Describing Use and Terminology	• Explain how blindness and visual impairment are defined	• Legal blindness is defined as a central visual acuity of 20/200 or less in the better eye (with corrective lenses) or central visual acuity of greater than 20/200 if the field of vision is less than 20 degrees. • Within education, visual impairment is an impairment in vision that adversely affects a student's educational performance.
Describing the Characteristics • Limitations in the Range and Variety of Experiences • Limitations in the Ability to Get Around • Limitations in Interactions with the Environment	• Describe key characteristics of visual impairment	• Students with visual impairments and blindness have a limited ability to model visually and learn incidentally from the environment. • Students with visual impairments are at risk of being experientially deprived because they are not able to learn about the world from a distance.
Identifying the Causes of Visual Impairment • Transmission of Light Energy • Conversion of Light to Electrical Impulse • Brain Connection • Timing	• Inventory causes and influences on visual impairments	• There are many factors that influence the process of what we refer to as seeing. Damage to or malfunction of any part of the visual system can lead to a significant loss of visual functioning. • Types of visual impairment can be classified as being related to transmission of light energy, conversion of light to electrical impulse, brain connection, and timing.

Identifying the Prevalence of Visual Impairment	• Identify prevalence estimates for individuals with visual impairments	• The best estimates for prevalence state that approximately one student in 1000 has a visual disorder that interferes with learning. • Visual impairment accounts for less than 1% of the total special education population.
WHAT ARE EVALUATION PROCEDURES?		
Determining the Presence of a Visual Impairment	• Identify how visual impairment is determined	• Medical specialists determine the presence of a visual disorder. • Optometrists and low vision specialists determine if the visual disorder can be corrected through lenses or other optical devices.
Determining How a Student Uses Vision	• Differentiate between a clinical examination and a functional vision evaluation	• While a medical exam reports findings in clinical terms (such as 20/120), a functional vision exam reports findings in concrete observable ways.
Determining the Appropriate Reading Medium	• Identify appropriate reading media for students with visual impairments	• A Learning Media Assessment helps determine the most efficient mode of reading and learning: braille, using optical aids, large print, etc.
Determining the Nature and Extent of Special Education and Related Services	• Recognize areas that need to be considered in determining the nature and extent of special education and related services	• Educators determine the effects of the visual impairment on the student's development of academic, communication, social/emotional, sensorimotor, orientation and mobility, daily living, and career/vocational skills.
WHAT AND HOW DO PROFESSIONALS TEACH?		
Curriculum • Accessing the Academic Curriculum • Teaching Skills Learned Incidentally by Students with Vision • Teaching Skills Specific to Students with Visual Impairments	• Differentiate among different curricula in order to evaluate the essentials of facilitating a comprehensive education for students who are blind or visually impaired	• In addition to the general academic curriculum, students must develop skills in two additional areas: those learned incidentally by students with vision and skills specific to students with visual impairments.
Methods • Commonsense Approach • Keeping Expectations High • Adapted Materials • Tactual/Kinesthetic Approach • Additional Experiences	• Evaluate different methods effective for varied student needs	• Professionals meet the academic and functional needs of students through direct instruction, modification of methodology, and adaptation of materials.

HOW IS PARTICIPATION ENCOURAGED?		
Inclusion	• Summarize benefits and problems associated with inclusion for students with visual impairments	• Inclusion means support for individualized services designed to meet individualized needs, taking place in the environment that best facilitates learning for each student.
Collaboration • Professional Collaboration • Family Collaboration • Peer Collaboration • Community Collaboration	• Explore ways to collaborate on behalf of students with visual impairments	• Professional, family, and peer collaboration each contribute much toward successful student learning.
Careers	• Examine unique careers available to work with students with visual impairments	• Three unique careers include teachers with a specialization in visual impairments, orientation and mobility specialists, and braille transcribers.
WHAT ARE PROGRAM OPTIONS?		
Early Intervention and Preschool Years	• Describe characteristics of effective preschool programs	• The focus of early intervention and preschool education is to help parents understand the effects of visual impairment on learning and to present effective methods that reduce the impact of these effects on development.
Elementary Years	• Describe characteristics of effective elementary programs	• Effective programs help students learn to read and write with appropriate media, participate in orientation and mobility training, do physical education, and develop friendships with sighted and blind peers.
Middle and Secondary Years	• Describe characteristics of effective programs for middle and secondary students	• In middle and secondary programs, students' self-confidence, self-esteem, and social skills are especially important in addition to all their sighted peers learn.
Transitional and Postsecondary Years	• Describe characteristics of effective program options for adults with visual impairments	• In postsecondary education, students continue to receive orientation and mobility training along with skills that prepare them for work or college and independent living.

PROJECT OPTIONS

1. Research and find at least five children's books with students who are blind or visually impaired as primary characters. Provide complete biographical information for these five books. Then read at least three of these books and compare and contrast the character's visual characteristics, their curriculum and methods in school, and the collaborative nature of their relationship to their peers and families.

2. Obtain a copy of the *New Programmed Instruction in Braille*, by Ashcroft, Henderson, Sanford, and Koenig, available from Scalars Publishing, P.O. Box 148123, Nashville, TN 37215. Read and study the roles for writing braille and then write about how the complexity of the braille code impacts the need for collaboration between teachers of children with visual impairments and general education teachers.

3. Investigate what curriculum and methods are most common in your local school district for students with low vision. Interview two teachers who work with these students. Evaluate the strengths and weaknesses of the curriculum and methods in use and tell how you would change or adapt them based on what you have learned in this chapter.

4. Research available technology for those who are visually impaired, such as TV and movies which describe the action on the screen, or issues involving computer use. Evaluate the benefits and drawbacks for each one. Then interview two or three people who are visually impaired to find out what needs are not yet being met that could be met by technology breakthroughs. Summarize your findings and submit them to a technology corporation.

KEY TERMS

Albinism

Anterior visual pathway

Cataracts

Cortical visual impairment

Field of vision

Fovea

Functionally blind

Legal blindness

Low vision

Macula

Macular degeneration

Myopia

Optic nerve atrophy

Optic nerve hypoplasia

Reading medium

Retina

Retinopathy of prematurity

Retrolental fibroplasia

Totally blind

Tunnel vision

Visual disability

CHAPTER 16 GUIDED REVIEW

That's Not Right!

Becca Caroline and her family have learned to accept her blindness with a sense of humor. Becca's mom Sally also has a disability—dyslexia—which makes for some interesting interactions between mother and daughter. Once when Becca was looking for a hole punch, she asked her mom to tell her where to find it. Her mother told her that it was on the floor about five steps to her left.

The problem was that Sally and Becca were facing each other so their left wasn't on the same side. Sally realized her mistake but forgot the term for the opposite of left. She told Becca, "I mean your . . .uh . . .uh . . . your other left."

Becca grinned and replied patiently, "Would that be the 'left' that the rest of us call 'right', Mom?"

See *Exceptional Parent* (July 1994, pp. 20-22) for more anecdotes about Becca.

What Is Visual Impairment?

1. What criteria are used for the two different definitions for visual impairment? (See Defining Visual Impairment)

   a. _____

   b. _____

2. What constitutes tunnel vision? (See Defining Visual Impairment)

   _____

3. How does IDEA define visual disability, including blindness? (See Defining Visual Impairment)

   _____

4. Describe the three classifications educators use to classify students with visual impairments. (See Defining Visual Impairment)

Classification	Identifying Characteristics
Low vision	
Functionally blind	
Totally blind	

Did you realize that people who are blind or have visual impairments are perfectly comfortable when others use words like "look" and "see"? As a teacher, you will want to teach your students, by your own comfort level, that it's fine to respond to people with disabilities as they do to others.

See *When You Have a Visually Handicapped Child in Your Classroom: Suggestions for Teachers* (I. Torres & A. Corn) for other suggestions for accommodating students with visual impairments.

5. List terms to use and terms to avoid, identified by the National Federation of the Blind, that refer to individuals with visual impairment. (See Defining Visual Impairment; Describing Use and Terminology)

Terms to Use	Terms to Avoid

6. What is the one characteristic shared by all individuals with visual impairment? (See Describing the Characteristics)

_____

_____

7. Describe areas affected by limitations in the range and variety of experiences for students with visual impairments. (See Describing the Characteristics; Limitations in the Range and Variety of Experiences)

    a. _____

    b. _____

    c. _____

8. Explain how limitations in the ability to get around affect every day life for students with visual impairments. (See Describing the Characteristics; Limitations in the Ability to Get Around)

_____

_____

9. Identify some consequences of not being able to monitor the environment. (See Describing the Characteristics; Limitations in Interactions with the Environment)

    a. _____

    b. _____

    c. _____

10. Thus, students with visual impairments face _____ and _____ deprivation. (See Describing the Characteristics; Limitations in Interactions with the Environment)

11. List the four leading causes of visual impairment. (See Identifying the Causes of Visual Impairment)

    a. _____

    b. _____

    c. _____

    d. _____

Two high school students have invented a vest that contains infrared light sensors to signal the location of obstacles. The battery-operated vest uses a device fitted to the back of the hand to alert the wearer.

See *Design News*, June 7, 1993, pp. 87-90.

12. There are many factors that influence the process of what we refer to as seeing. Identify the area of the eye in focus and resulting conditions when there are problems in this area. (See Identifying the Causes of Visual Impairment)

Category	Area of Eye Affected	Resulting Conditions
Transmission of Light Energy		
Conversion of Light to Electrical Impulse		
Brain Connection		
Timing		

13. The best estimates for prevalence state that approximately one student in _____ has a visual disorder that interferes with learning. (See Identifying the Prevalence of Visual Impairment)
14. Visual impairment accounts for less than _____% of the total special education population. (See Identifying the Prevalence of Visual Impairment)

What Are Evaluation Procedures?

15. The results of a medical examination may be reported in _____ terms, while the results of a functional vision examination are reported in language that _____. Functional vision evaluations describe a student's use of vision in a variety of _____ environments. (See Determining the Presence of a Visual Impairment)
16. Why is it important for the student to be evaluated in these types of environment?
    _____
    _____
    (See Determining How a Student Uses Vision)
17. Ideally, when should a functional vision evaluation occur? _____
    _____
    Why? _____
    (See Determining How a Student Uses Vision)
18. Identify some common reading media for students with visual impairments. (See Determining the Appropriate Reading Medium)
    a. _____   c. _____
    b. _____   d. _____

A Garden For Peter

Gardening is Roger Bossley's favorite leisure activity. His older son Benjamin readily participated in this activity with his father, but Roger hesitated to let his younger son Peter, who is blind, become involved in this activity. However, he decided one day that he would try to find ways to include his son, who was becoming increasingly more curious about the activity. That was the beginning of Peter's 12-square-foot garden. Roger involved Peter in planning, planting, and maintaining the garden.

The result? "His gardening experiences have led to an increased enjoyment of the outdoors and greater knowledge of plants and plant growth." Roger says the most valuable part of the experience, though, is that it is "an activity we can enjoy together."

See *Exceptional Parent*, May 1994, pp. 22-26, to learn more about Peter's garden.

19. What are the seven areas to be evaluated when determining the nature and extent of special education and related services? (See Determining the Nature and Extent of Special Education and Related Services)

    a. _____

    b. _____

    c. _____

    d. _____

    e. _____

    f. _____

    g. _____

20. Based on the model assessment program developed by the California School for the Blind, discuss characteristics of the program that contribute to its success. (See Determining the Nature and Extent of Special Education and Related Services)

    _____

    _____

    _____

    _____

Closed captioning has made television accessible to people with hearing impairments, but how can a blind person *watch* TV? Audetel—an audio description of TV—provides a running commentary of a television program along with the soundtrack. Similar audiodescription devices are being made available in some theaters. The person uses a headset so they can listen without disturbing others.

What and How Do Professionals Teach?

21. Braille is a(n) _____ method of reading. Describe some of the primary characteristics of this reading code. (See Curriculum: Accessing the Academic Curriculum)

    _____

    _____

    _____

22. Two skills learned incidentally by students with vision include _____ and _____. (See Curriculum; Teaching Skills Learned Incidentally by Students with Vision)

23. List and suggest ways to teach skills specific to students with visual impairments. (See Curriculum; Teaching Skills Specific to Students with Visual Impairments and Fig. 16-8)

Skill to Be Learned	Ways to Teach This Skill

The National Federation of the Blind has introduced skill development centers in Colorado, Louisiana, and Minnesota. The centers use blind instructors who have already reduced the impact of blindness in their lives to the level of nuisance. Besides learning blindness skills like Braille reading and writing, participants learn a sense of personal worth and pride in accomplishment through activities like rock climbing and river rafting.

24. What are four important methods for helping students achieve classroom success? (See Methods)

a. _____ c. _____

b. _____ d. _____

25. Name three materials adaptations for students with visual impairments. (See Methods; Adapted Materials)

a. _____

b. _____

c. _____

How Is Participation Encouraged?

26. Identify different placement options that have been used for students with visual impairments since 1900. Each of these may be appropriate, depending on the student's needs. Give the percentage of students in these placements today. (See Inclusion)

a. _____ _____%

b. _____ _____%

c. _____ _____%

d. _____ _____%

e. _____ _____%

f. _____ _____%

27. What are some major roles of collaborators for students with visual impairments? (See Collaboration)

Collaborator	Roles

28. What are two unique careers for working with students with blindness and visual impairments? (See Careers)

a. _____

b. _____

Can Residential Placements Be Least Restrictive?

Placement at a school for the blind with a residential option sometimes is considered the least restrictive environment for a student with a severe visual impairment. Such a placement gives these youngsters the opportunity to learn the skills necessary to eventually access the general curriculum environment.

Michael, who has low vision, became unmotivated and found it easy to get by using his impairment as an excuse in his local school. His mother also realized the challenge she faced of breaking her habit of doing too much for Michael. She thought Michael would learn skills of independence more readily at the residential school. Now, after two years, when Michael comes home on weekends, he demonstrates his pride in doing the laundry and some of the cooking for both of them. His confidence in his academic work also has improved. She believes that after another year, Michael's needs will have changed enough so that his local school will once again be able to serve him appropriately.

What Are Program Options?

29. The focus of early intervention and preschool education is to help parents understand
_____ and to
_____. (See What Are Program Options?; Early Intervention and Preschool Years)
30. At what level is an orientation and mobility specialist especially important? (See What Are Program Options?; Elementary Years) _____
31. In middle and secondary programs, students continue to receive _____ and
_____ training. They also focus on gaining self-confidence, self-esteem, and
_____ _____. (See What Are Program Options?; Middle and Secondary Years; Transitional and Postsecondary Years)

Guiding Future Generations

Blake Lindsay, who became blind when he was 9 months old as a result of a cancerous tumor that destroyed his retinas, is a radio disk jockey with a booming voice. As if one job weren't enough, he is also a customer service representative at a bank in Dallas, Texas.

Despite his 50-hour-per-week schedule, he still finds time to speak to students at local public schools. He answers their questions about his blindness honestly. Blake views these students as future employers. He hopes that by letting them get to know him, they will be more open to contacts with people with disabilities once they are out of school. "I want society to know, in fact, how normal we are. We desire opportunities as much as anyone else."

See *The Mobile Press*, November 12, 1994, pp. 1D and 4D.

APPLICATION EXERCISES FOR CHAPTER 16

Application Exercise 16a. Identifying Causes of Visual Impairment

Match the category of the cause of visual impairment with the type of resulting disorder.

1. Transmission of light energy through the cornea, iris, pupil, lens, aqueous, vitreous	a. _____ Johann has cataracts.
2. Conversion of light to electrical impulse in the fovea, retina, macula	b. _____ Bill has an adventitious visual impairment.
3. Connection to the brain through the optic nerve, visual cortex	c. _____ Habb has tunnel vision and cannot see at night.
4. Timing of the impairment to any part of the eye	d. _____ Christina has severe myopia.
	e. _____ Josephina has cortical visual impairment.
	f. _____ Singh has macular degeneration and cannot distinguish colors.

Application Exercise 16b. Matching Educational Needs with Appropriate Teaching

Match the educational need with the appropriate curriculum or method. Some descriptions have more than one answer. List all appropriate answers for each one.

1. Orientation and mobility training	a. _____ Anita is functionally blind and needs access to the academic curriculum.
2. Learn to use a cane	b. _____ TsangYao, who has low vision, was assigned homework with average size print which he will do using his hand-held magnifier.
3. Instruction in self-advocacy	c. _____ Jenawik has just moved into a new home and is unfamiliar with the layout.
4. Use of braille	d. _____ Susie needs to convince a prospective employer that she has the abilities to do the job with adaptations.
5. Direct instruction in difficult or highly visual academic areas	e. _____ Kunti is learning new math skills for which she does not have the background experience.
6. Additional time to complete or more opportunities to practice	f. _____ Otis wants to cross the street but cannot clearly see the traffic.
7. Adapted materials or techniques	g. _____ Mina has a medical problem but doesn't know who to talk to about it

Application Exercise 16c. Seeing Beyond the Content

Consider the types of limitations discussed in this chapter that must be overcome and apply specific methods that will make the learning effective. For each of the five major questions addressed in this chapter,* summarize the concepts by telling how you would teach a student with low vision to learn this specific information.

*Five Major Questions: What is visual impairment? What are evaluation procedures? What and how do professionals teach? How is participation encouraged? What are program options?

ANSWERS TO MARGIN QUESTIONS

Page 698	People with low vision or some types of functional vision often use visual cues, such as the body shapes or hair styles of people they expect to be attending the party to help them locate people they know. Others might ask friends ahead of time the color of the clothes they intend to wear. People who are totally blind need to rely on auditory cues, though these cues are more difficult to interpret when the noise level is high. Party-goers who are blind sometimes position themselves near a door or the food or drink table, where they are more likely to hear people who they know or can initiate conversations with strangers. "Mingling" at parties is difficult for people who don't see well and on these occasions thoughtful peers will introduce themselves and/or invite the person with visual impairment to join the group.
Page 698	Driving on dates is the biggest problem for teens and adults who are visually impaired. Some ideas are to "double date," use a taxi or limousine service, or to create the illusion of the "specialness" of the event by suggesting a romantic walk or adventuresome bus ride. While not particularly recommended, one student with low vision convinced his prospective date to do the driving because he said he had had his license suspended for reckless driving!

Circle the correct answer.

TRUE OR FALSE

T or F   1.   Most individuals with legal blindness have some usable vision.

T or F   2.   Tunnel vision is considered a visual impairment but alone does not qualify as legal blindness.

T or F   3.   Incidental learning is at risk in all visually impaired children.

T or F   4.   According to IDEA, functional vision evaluations should be performed on all students with visual impairments.

T or F   5.   The learning rate of students with visual impairments tends to be slower than that of sighted children.

MULTIPLE CHOICE

6.   What is the vision requirement for legal blindness when wearing glasses and using both eyes?

    a. 20/100

    b. 20/150

    c. 20/200

    d. 20/250

7.   Which of the following is <u>not</u> a limitation imposed on an individual by a significant visual impairment?

    a. Limitation in the ability to get around

    b. Limitation in the range and variety of experiences

    c. Limitation in interactions with the environment

    d. Limitation in academic ability

8.   Amanda is two years old and has significant visual impairment. What is a likely result of her limitation in movement?

    a. Psychosis

    b. Passivity

    c. Inability to speak

    d. Increased risk of mental retardation

9.   Approximately how many students in the U.S. have a visual disorder that interferes with learning?

    a. 1 in 100

    b. 1 in 500

    c. 1 in 1000

    d. 1 in 5000

10.   What is the leading cause of visual impairment among young children?

    a. Cortical visual impairment

    b. Retinopathy of prematurity

    c. Glaucoma

    d. Myopia and cataracts

11.   What is affected with visual disorders such as optic nerve hypoplasia and optic nerve atrophy?

    a. The interpretation of what is viewed by the brain

    b. The transmission of light energy

    c. The conversion of light energy to electrical nerve impulses

    d. Color blindess

12. At the model assessment program developed by the California School for the Blind, why do the parents tend to consider the test results valid?

    a. The team is composed of individuals with at least some visual impairment, which contributes to a deeper understanding of the problems faced by the blind.

    b. The program is the oldest and most distinguished in the country.

    c. The parents have been a part of the testing.

    d. All of the specialists have M.D.'s or Ph.D.'s and special certification in visual assessment.

13. Why do braille readers have difficulty with some tests?

    a. Feeling the raised dots becomes painful to the touch after about 30 minutes of use.

    b. They tend to get mixed up in their numbering order, although their answers are correct.

    c. The tests are usually composed with a slate writer, which is more difficult to read than commercially prepared braille products.

    d. Scanning is difficult with braille.

14. Why was educational inclusion for blind students a particular challenge until the 1950s?

    a. There was no model of inclusion.

    b. There was no fast and easy method of writing braille.

    c. Blind students were considered stupid until Helen Keller went to college.

    d. The American Foundation for the Blind had not yet been established to lobby for the rights of blind people.

15. Orientation and mobility training is an example of which type of training that students with visual impairments must master?

    a. Regular academic curriculum in physical education

    b. Skills learned incidentally by sighted students

    c. Specialized study skills

    d. Skills to access the academic curriculum

SHORT ANSWER

16. How does IDEA define visual disability?

    _____

    _____

17. List the four components of the process referred to as seeing.

    a. _____

    b. _____

    c. _____

    d. _____

18. What is the position of the National Federation for the Blind on labeling?

    _____

    _____

ESSAY

19. Summarize the differences among these terms: low vision, functionally blind, and totally blind. Explain how you will assess the nature of special education and related services for students in each of these classifications.

20. Discuss how limitations with the environment influence both the curriculum and methods that must be used to help students who are visually impaired learn. Apply what you learned from the various program options in this chapter to add additional insights.

ANSWERS TO APPLICATION EXERCISES FOR CHAPTER 1

Application Exercise 1a. Dignifying Labels: Possible Alternatives:

Words to Avoid	Words with Greater Dignity
Cripple/ Invalid	Person with a disability Disabled
Handicapped	Person with a disability Disabled
Birth defect	Disabled since birth/born with
Victim	Person who experienced or who has
Normal (referring to persons without disabilities as "normal" infers that those with disabilities are abnormal)	Non-disabled
Deaf mute/ Deaf and dumb	Person who is deaf Person without speech, nonverbal
Crazy/ Insane	Person with an emotional disorder Person with mental retardation
Slow	Person with a developmental delay Person with a learning disability
Confined to a wheelchair	Uses a wheelchair

Some Potential Guidelines to Consider in Labeling: Taken from "Portrayal Issues" *in Guidelines for Reporting and Writing About People With Disabilities*, Fifth Edition. (1996). Lawrence, KS: Research and Training Center on Independent Living.

- Do not focus on disability.
- Do not portray successful people with disabilities as superhuman.
- Do not sensationalize a disability.
- Do not use generic labels.
- Put people first, not their disability.
- Emphasize abilities, not limitations.
- Do not imply disease when discussing disabilities.
- Show people with disabilities as active participants of society.

Application Exercise 1b. IDEA's Six Principles

1. e	4. f	7. e	10. c	13. f
2. b	5. d	8. b	11. e	14. b
3. c	6. c	9. a	12. d	15. d

Application Exercise 1c. Assessing What You've Learned

Representations will vary according to the student applications.

ANSWERS TO APPLICATION EXERCISES FOR CHAPTER 2

Application Exercise 2a. Identifying Stages of a Nondiscriminatory Evaluation
1. Referral
2. Screening
3. Prereferral
4. Prereferral
5. Referral

Application Exercise 2b. IQ Scores in the Classroom

1. b	4. a	7. e	10. f
2. d	5. b	8. c	11. f
3. c	6. e	9. d	12. a

Application Exercise 2c: Assessing What You've Learned
Tests will vary according to each student's individual applications.

ANSWERS TO APPLICATION EXERCISES FOR CHAPTER 3

Application Exercise 3a. Identifying Placements for Students with Disabilities
1. Placement: Residential facility   Percentage: 0.7%
2. Placement: Resource room   Percentage: 27.5%
3. Placement: Regular class   Percentage: 43.9%
4. Placement: Homebound/ hospital   Percentage: 0.7%
5. Placement: Separate school   Percentage: 3.7%
6. Placement: Separate class   Percentage: 23.5%

Application Exercise 3b. Matching Collaborators with Professional Roles
Definitions:
    a. Supportive Role: Caring and being there for your colleagues to share in times of need and in times of joy.
    b. Facilitative Role: Helping your colleagues develop a capacity to solve problems, engage in tasks, or deal independently with professional challenges.
    c. Information-giving Role: Providing direct assistance to your colleagues so they are better equipped to deal with problems on an ongoing basis.
    d. Prescriptive Role: Prescribing a path of action to your colleagues.

Professional Roles of Listed Collaborators: Answers may vary depending on the collaborator's experience. Some probable suggestions include:
1. c
2. c, d
3. a, b, c, d
4. a, b, c, d
5. b, c
6. a, c
7. a, c, d
8. a, b, c, d

Application Exercise 3c. Collaborating for Success

Representations will vary according to each student's participation and collaboration.

ANSWERS TO APPLICATION EXERCISES FOR CHAPTER 4

Application Exercise 4a. Identifying Characteristics of Learning Disabilities

1. Misinterprets social clues
2. Learned helplessness
3. Memory deficits
4. Metacognitive deficits
5. Attention deficits
6. Poor social skills
7. Specific academic difficulties

Application Exercise 4b. Determining Eligibility Based on Severe Discrepancy

1. Jose: Reading
2. Chanpen: Written language
3. Julie: Reading, math, written language

Application Exercise 4c. Metacognitive Learning Strategies

Representations will vary according to each student's individual strategies employed.

ANSWERS TO APPLICATION EXERCISES FOR CHAPTER 5

Application Exercise 5a. Identifying Emotional Characteristics

a. 3	d. 6	g. 5
b. 1	e. 1	h. 2
c. 4	f. 2	i. 7

Application Exercise 5b. Identifying Types of Observations

1. Latency
2. Frequency
3. Magnitude
4. Duration
5. Topography

Application Exercise 5c. A Collaborator's View of Emotional or Behavioral Disorders

Representations will vary according to the student applications.

ANSWERS TO APPLICATION EXERCISES FOR CHAPTER 6

Application Exercise 6a. Identifying Types of AD/HD
1. Hyperactive-Impulsive
2. Inattentive
3. Hyperactive-Impulsive
4. Inattentive
5. Combined
6. Inattentive

Application Exercise 6b. Accommodations for Students with AD/HD

a. 7   c. 5   e. 3   g. 4
b. 6   d. 1   f. 2

Application Exercise 6c. Coaching the Concepts
Examples will vary according to the student innovations.

ANSWERS TO APPLICATION EXERCISES FOR CHAPTER 7

Application Exercise 7a. Identifying Multiple Intelligences
1. Bodily-Kinesthetic
2. Interpersonal
3. Linguistic
4. Spatial
5. Spatial
6. Logical-Mathematical
7. Naturalist
8. Musical
9. Intrapersonal

Application Exercise 7b. IQ Scores in the Classroom
1. Total in class with similar IQ: 20
2. Total in class with similar IQ: 12
3. Total in class with similar IQ: 6
4. Total in class with similar IQ: 3
5. Total in class with similar IQ: 1

Application Exercise 7c. Mapping Giftedness in Action
Representations will vary according to the student applications.

ANSWERS TO APPLICATION EXERCISES FOR CHAPTER 8

Application Exercise 8a. Identifying Limitations in Intellectual Functioning
1. Attention
2. Generalization
3. Motivation
4. Memory

Application Exercise 8b. Adaptive Behavior Limitations
1. Health and safety
2. Social skills
3. Functional academics
4. Communication
5. Self-care

Application Exercise 8c. Obstacles to Learning Challenge
Representations will vary according to each student's individual strategies employed.

ANSWERS TO APPLICATION EXERCISES FOR CHAPTER 9

Application Exercise 9a. Determining the Likelihood of a Disability in a Newborn
Averages:

       Miguel: 9, 10

       Susannah: 3, 3

       Vishnu: 9, 10

       Felicia: 0, 3

       Chin-Cheng: 8, 8

Ranking for at risk from greatest at risk to least:

       Susannah: Below 4 and no change after five minutes

       Felicia: Below 4, but some improvement after five minutes

       Chin-Cheng: Well above 8, small risk

       Miguel and Vishnu: Well above 8, almost no risk

Application Exercise 9b. Assessment Methods for Student Learning and Performance
1. a: Developmental Model
2. d: Making Action Plans
3. c: Behavior States
4. b: Ecological Model

Application Exercise 9c. Concept Application in Context
Summaries will vary according to each student's focus and applications.

ANSWERS TO APPLICATION EXERCISES FOR CHAPTER 10

Application Exercise 10a. Identifying Characteristics of Autism
1. c
2. e
3. g
4. f
5. a
6. b
7. d

Application Exercise 10b. Functional Assessment: Matching Situation and Intervention
1. c
2. e
3. a
4. b
5. d

Application Exercise 10c. Social Stories to Convey Conceptual Understanding
Representations will vary according to each student's individual stories.

ANSWERS TO APPLICATION EXERCISES FOR CHAPTER 11

Application Exercise 11a. Identifying Conditions and Symptoms of Health Impairments
1. g: Hypoglycemia
2. h: Childhood leukemia
3. a: Stage 2 of HIV
4. b: Prenatal substance exposure
5. e: Temporal lobe or psychomotor seizure
6. d: Asthma
7. c: Hypoglycemia
8. f: Stage 3 of HIV

Application Exercise 11b. Developmental Responses to Death
1. e: Teenagers
2. c: 6-9
3. b: 3-6
4. d: 9-12
5. a: Newborn-3
6. b: 3-6
7. b: 3-6
8. c: 9-12

Application Exercise 11c. Medical Vocabulary Applications
Representations will vary according to the student applications.

ANSWERS TO APPLICATION EXERCISES FOR CHAPTER 12

Application Exercise 12a. Identifying Forms of Cerebral Palsy by Movement Difficulties
1. Ataxic
2. Athetoid
3. Mixed
4. Spastic

Application Exercise 12b. Identifying Characteristics of Spina Bifida
a. Meningocele
b. Spina bifida occulta
c. Myelomeningocele
d. Myelomeningocele
e. Spina bifida occulta
f. Meningocele
g. Myelomeningocele
h. Myelomeningocele

Application Exercise 12c. The Conceptual Impact of Inclusion and Collaboration on Physical Disabilities
Representations will vary according to each student's individual understandings and interpretations.

ANSWERS TO APPLICATION EXERCISES FOR CHAPTER 13

Application Exercise 13a. Identifying Areas of Change
1. Physical
2. Social, Behavioral, and Personality
3. Cognitive
4. Physical
5. Linguistic
6. Social, Behavioral, and Personality

Application Exercise 13b. Curriculum Applications
1. b. Component training
2. c. Functional training
3. a. Compensatory strategy training
4. a. Compensatory strategy training
5. b. Component training

Application Exercise 13c. Improving Instruction and Retention of Content
Representations will vary according to the student applications.

ANSWERS TO APPLICATION EXERCISES FOR CHAPTER 14

Application Exercise 14a. Identifying Characteristics of Typical Language Development

1.	Josi	Birth to 6 months
2.	Cedric	6 to 12 months
3.	Fidel	12 to 18 months
4.	Jana	18 to 24 months
5.	Yu-chen	24 to 36 months
6.	Thalalia	36 to 48 months
7.	Julienne	4 to 5 years
8.	Muhammad	5 to 6 years

Application Exercise 14b. Identifying Language Impairments by the Dimension of Language in Focus

a. Pragmatics

b. Syntax

c. Semantics

d. Pragmatics

e. Phonology

f. Morphology

g. Phonology

Application Exercise 14c. Expanding Your Understanding of Communication Disorders

Representations will vary according to the students' applications.

ANSWERS TO APPLICATION EXERCISES FOR CHAPTER 15

Application Exercise 15a. Identifying Levels of Hearing Loss

In order of severity of hearing loss:

1. Sammie

2. Summea

3. Julianna

4. Pedro

5. Najee

6. Jaime

Application Exercise 15b. Differentiating Different Means of Communication

Read the different ways students communicate and identify the communication mode being used.

1. Sully: Oral/ aural or Speech, speechreading, and auditory skills

2. NamPrik: Total Communication or simultaneous communication

3. Griffin: American Sign Language

4. Sharon: Oral/ aural or Speech, speechreading, and auditory skills

5. Memo: American Sign Language

6. Kunti: Total Communication or simultaneous communication

Application Exercise 15c. Interpreting Key Components of Hearing Loss

Representations will vary according to each student's individual interpretations employed.

ANSWERS TO APPLICATION EXERCISES FOR CHAPTER 16

Application Exercise 16a. Identifying Causes of Visual Impairment

    a. 1

    b. 4

    c. 2

    d. 1

    e. 3

    f. 2

Application Exercise 16b. Matching Educational Needs with Appropriate Teaching

    a. 4 and 5

    b. 7

    c. 1

    d. 3

    e. 6

    f. 1 and 2

    g. 3

Application Exercise 16c. Seeing Beyond the Content

Representations will vary according to the student applications.

SAMPLE QUIZ ANSWERS FOR CHAPTER 1

1-1 T	1-4 F	1-7 a	1-10 a	1-13 b
1-2 T	1-5 T	1-8 b	1-11 d	1-14 c
1-3 T	1-6 d	1-9 c	1-12 c	1-15 a

SHORT ANSWER

1-16 Specially designed instruction, including instruction in physical education, to meet the unique needs of a student with a disability.

1-17 1) The categorical element—the student must have a disability; 2) The functional element—the disability must cause the student to need specially designed instruction.

1-18 Specific learning disabilities and speech or language impairments

SAMPLE QUIZ ANSWERS FOR CHAPTER 2

2-1 F	2-4 T	2-7 a	2-10 d	2-13 c
2-2 T	2-5 F	2-8 a	2-11 c	2-14 d
2-3 T	2-6 d	2-9 a	2-12 b	2-15 d

SHORT ANSWER

2-16 Screening, prereferral, referral, and nondiscriminatory evaluation procedures and standards.

2-17 Norm-referenced tests and criterion-referenced tests

2-18 Reliability refers to how well a test yields similar results across time and among raters. Validity refers to how well the test measures what it purports to measure.

SAMPLE QUIZ ANSWERS FOR CHAPTER 3

3-1 T	3-4 T	3-7 d	3-10 b	3-13 b
3-2 T	3-5 T	3-8 b	3-11 a	3-14 c
3-3 F	3-6 d	3-9 c	3-12 d	3-15 a

SHORT ANSWER

3-16 Ready to learn, school completion, student achievement and citizenship, mathematics and science, adult literacy and lifelong learning, safe, disciplined, and drug-free schools, teacher-education and professional development, parental participation. (See Fig. 3-1, p. 81)

3-17 Inclusion and collaboration

3-18 Supportive role, facilitative role, information-giving role, prescriptive role

SAMPLE QUIZ ANSWERS FOR CHAPTER 4

4-1 F	4-4 T	4-7 b	4-10 a	4-13 a
4-2 F	4-5 T	4-8 c	4-11 d	4-14 c
4-3 T	4-6 a	4-9 d	4-12 c	4-15 c

SHORT ANSWER

4-16 With learning disabilities, students generally manifest a statistically significant discrepancy between ability and achievement. Their IQs range from average to gifted. Students with mental retardation do not have this discrepancy, and their IQs are approximately 70 or lower. Also, students with mental retardation display significant difficulties with adaptive behavior, while those with learning disabilities generally do not.

4-17 *Inclusionary Criterion:* A demonstrated discrepancy between ability and achievement. *Exclusionary Criterion:* Not the result of other factors, such as sensory impairment, mental retardation, or cultural differences. *Need Criterion:* Student needs special education and/or related services.

4-18 Visual perception, memory, motor functions, language, abstract reasoning, metacognition

SAMPLE QUIZ ANSWERS FOR CHAPTER 5

5-1	T	5-4	T	5-7	d	5-10	b	5-13	a
5-2	F	5-5	F	5-8	b	5-11	d	5-14	c
5-3	F	5-6	a	5-9	d	5-12	a	5-15	a

SHORT ANSWER

5-16 Anorexia nervosa, which occurs when the student cannot be persuaded to maintain normal weight because of a fear of gaining weight, and bulimia nervosa, which causes the individual to eat huge amounts of food at one time and then purge it through vomiting, excess use of laxatives, or extreme exercise.

5-17 Child abuse and neglect include acts or failures to act that could result in an imminent risk of serious harm, death, serious physical or emotional harm, sexual abuse, or exploitation by a parent or caretaker who is responsible for the child's welfare. If you suspect that a child is being abused or neglected, it is your responsibility to report it to your state's child protection agency.

5-18 Frequently off task, poor academic work-related skills, splinter skills in basic academics, underachievement, and poor language skills

SAMPLE QUIZ ANSWERS FOR CHAPTER 6

6-1	T	6-4	T	6-7	a	6-10	d	6-13	b
6-2	F	6-5	T	6-8	d	6-11	a	6-14	d
6-3	T	6-6	c	6-9	a	6-12	b	6-15	c

SHORT ANSWER

6-16 (a) Behavioral skill deficit, (b) problem-solving deficit, (c) cognitive distortion, (d) self-control deficit

6-17 Observe the student to determine effective, poor, and absent social behaviors. Focus on one or two behaviors for change. Directly coach, model, and role-play important behaviors. Praise and reward the student for appropriate behaviors.

6-18 Half-day schedule. Small class size. Low teacher-student ratio. Trained teachers who enjoy their work and who emphasize encouragement and "positively-toned discipline." Structured environment, which includes predictable routines; clear, consistently reinforced rules; limited down time; and exposure to some school-type activities that require sitting quietly and listening. Freedom for the child to choose from several activities that involve quiet and active play as well as freedom to use materials creatively. Emphasis on the development of socialization and appropriate behavioral skills.

SAMPLE QUIZ ANSWERS FOR CHAPTER 7

7-1 T	7-4 T	7-7 c	7-10 a	7-13 a
7-2 F	7-5 F	7-8 d	7-11 b	7-14 b
7-3 F	7-6 b	7-9 b	7-12 b	7-15 c

SHORT ANSWER

7-16 High general intellect, specific academic aptitude, creative productive thinking, leadership ability, and visual or performing arts ability

7-17 Integrated curriculum studies in areas of interest, modification of the pace of learning, and modification of the depth of content coverage in specific topics

7-18 From Box 7-3: Written reflective evaluations that monitor learning, evaluations of content areas, reflections on thinking processes; lists of books, magazines, and other materials evaluated by student; lists of topics and authors in subject areas that interest the student; charts, audio and video recordings of the student's learning; records of strategies used; interviews; regular evaluations of the portfolio of the student, and so forth.

SAMPLE QUIZ ANSWERS FOR CHAPTER 8

8-1 T	8-4 F	8-7 d	8-10 c	8-13 b
8-2 F	8-5 T	8-8 a	8-11 d	8-14 a
8-3 T	8-6 d	8-9 c	8-12 d	8-15 b

SHORT ANSWER

8-16 Attention, memory, generalization, and motivation

8-17 Intermittent: Supports on an "as-needed basis"

Limited: Consistent support over time, time-limited but not of an intermittent nature

Extensive: Need for regular involvement and not time-limited

Pervasive: Need for constancy, high intensity with potential life-sustaining nature

8-18 Three years after graduation, only 41% of students were competitively employed and 15% were living independently.

SAMPLE QUIZ ANSWERS FOR CHAPTER 9

9-1 F	9-4 T	9-7 d	9-10 c	9-13 b
9-2 T	9-5 F	9-8 b	9-11 a	9-14 b
9-3 T	9-6 a	9-9 a	9-12 d	9-15 d

SHORT ANSWER

9-16 The extent of the disability is beyond mild or moderate levels, and typically two or more disabilities occur simultaneously.

9-17 Developmental, ecological, behavioral states, and Making Action Plans

9-18 (a) They may not develop in the same sequence as children without disabilities. (b) This approach assumes that the students have to possess certain skills before they can acquire "higher-level" ones. (c) This approach emphasizes the form of the skill rather than its function.

SAMPLE QUIZ ANSWERS FOR CHAPTER 10

10-1 T	10-4 T	10-7 d	10-10 a	10-13 a
10-2 T	10-5 T	10-8 c	10-11 c	10-14 a
10-3 F	10-6 a	10-9 c	10-12 b	10-15 a

SHORT ANSWER:

10-16 Delayed language and echolalia

10-17 A neuromotor impairment means that there is a breakdown in the brain's capacity to direct the body to engage in movement that produces speech, gestures, written formats, or other alternatives.

10-18 CARS is one of the most frequently used diagnostic scales. It requires behavioral observations in fifteen areas of a child's functioning to determine the presence of autism.

SAMPLE QUIZ ANSWERS FOR CHAPTER 11

11-1 T	11-4 F	11-7 c	11-10 d	11-13 c
11-2 T	11-5 T	11-8 b	11-11 d	11-14 a
11-3 T	11-6 d	11-9 b	11-12 d	11-15 b

SHORT ANSWER

11-16 (a) Limitations in strength, (b) limitations in vitality, and (c) limitations alertness.

11-17 The dog is tied or leashed at all times. A specific toilet area is used by the dog. The dog has been thoroughly tested and screened for any aggressive tendency.

11-18 (a) Use precautions to help prevent the accidental contraction of HIV and (b) honestly inform your students about the disease.

SAMPLE QUIZ ANSWERS FOR CHAPTER 12

12-1 F	12-4 T	12-7 b	12-10 a	12-13 c
12-2 T	12-5 F	12-8 a	12-11 b	12-14 d
12-3 F	12-6 b	12-9 b	12-12 a	12-15 b

SHORT ANSWER

12-16 Orthopedic impairment

12-17 Spastic, athetoid, ataxic, mixed

12-18 Physical therapist and occupational therapist

SAMPLE QUIZ ANSWERS FOR CHAPTER 13

13-1 F	13-4 T	13-7 a	13-10 c	13-13 c
13-2 F	13-5 T	13-8 d	13-11 d	13-14 a
13-3 F	13-6 c	13-9 d	13-12 a	13-15 c

SHORT ANSWER

13-16 Anoxia and brain damage from disease

13-17 Accidents, sports and recreational injuries, and violence

13-18 (a) Component training provides intensive and systematic training of specific cognitive skills, (b) Compensatory strategy training helps the student clarify, organize, and express information, (c) Functional retraining makes use of a student's everyday curriculum and activities to teach cognitive skills.

SAMPLE QUIZ ANSWERS FOR CHAPTER 14

14-1 T	14-4 F	14-7 c	14-10 b	14-13 d
14-2 T	14-5 T	14-8 d	14-11 c	14-14 d
14-3 T	14-6 d	14-9 b	14-12 c	14-15 d

SHORT ANSWER

14-16 Phonology, morphology, syntax, semantics, and pragmatics

14-17 Remediation helps students change inappropriate patterns or develop appropriate patterns. Compensation helps students offset deficits that are not possible to remediate.

14-18 Encourage the child who stutters to (a) prolong certain sounds, (b) stop other activities while communicating, (c) speak more slowly, (d) practice speaking to a rhythmic beat, (e) read aloud while listening to audiotaped books.

SAMPLE QUIZ ANSWERS FOR CHAPTER 15

15-1 F	15-4 T	15-7 b	15-10 b	15-13 c
15-2 F	15-5 F	15-8 b	15-11 a	15-14 a
15-3 T	15-6 a	15-9 d	15-12 d	15-15 b

SHORT ANSWER

15-16 Parent-child interaction, peers and tutors, incidental learning, and language competence

15-17 Oral/aural, ASL, simultaneous communication; oral/aural, bilingual-bicultural, and total communication.

15-18 Emphasize experiential learning, build on the students' current knowledge and skills, require them to interact with peers, capitalize on the visual medium, and reduce environmental distraction.

SAMPLE QUIZ ANSWERS FOR CHAPTER 16

16-1 T	16-4 F	16-7 d	16-10 a	16-13 d
16-2 F	16-5 T	16-8 b	16-11 a	16-14 b
16-3 T	16-6 c	16-9 c	16-12 c	16-15 b

SHORT ANSWER

16-16 An impairment in vision that, even with correction, adversely affects a child's educational performance.

16-17 (a) The transmission of light energy through the eye, (b) the conversion of light energy to electrical energy, (c) the transmission of electrical impulses to the brain, and (d) the interpretation of what is viewed by the brain.

16-18 Euphemisms are awkward and unnecessary since the word "blind" accurately and clearly describes the condition of being unable to see.